The Element

HOW FINDING YOUR PASSION

CHANGES EVERYTHING

Ken Robinson, Ph.D.

with Lou Aronica

D0003990

PENGUIN BOOKS

PENGUIN BOOKS

Published by the Penguin Group
Penguin Books Ltd, 80 Strand, London WC2R 0RL, England
Penguin Group (USA), Inc., 375 Hudson Street, New York, New York 10014, USA
Penguin Group (Canada), 90 Eglinton Avenue East, Suite 700, Toronto, Ontario, Canada M4P 2Y3
(a division of Pearson Penguin Canada Inc.)
Penguin Ireland, 25 St Stephen's Green, Dublin 2, Ireland (a division of Penguin Books Ltd)
Penguin Group (Australia), 250 Camberwell Road, Camberwell, Victoria 3124, Australia
(a division of Pearson Australia Group Pty Ltd)
Penguin Books India Pvt Ltd, 11 Community Centre, Panchsheel Park, New Delhi – 110 017, India
Penguin Group (NZ), 67 Apollo Drive, Rosedale, North Shore 0632, New Zealand
(a division of Pearson New Zealand Ltd)
Penguin Books (South Africa) (Pty) Ltd, 24 Sturdee Avenue, Rosebank, Johannesburg 2196, South Africa

Penguin Books Ltd, Registered Offices: 80 Strand, London WC2R 0RL, England

www.penguin.com

First published in the United States of America by Viking Penguin,
a member of Penguin Group (USA) Inc. 2009
First published in Great Britain by Allen Lane 2009
Published in Penguin Books 2010
016

Copyright © Ken Robinson and Lou Aronica, 2009

The moral right of the authors has been asserted

Artwork on page 65: NASA, ESA, and the Hubble Heritage Team (STScI/AURA) – ESA/
Hubble Collaboration. Acknowledgement: D. Gouliermis (Max Planck Institute for Astronomy, Heidelberg).
All other artwork: NASA/JPL-Caltech

Printed in Great Britain by Clays Ltd, St Ives plc

A CIP catalogue record for this book is available from the British Library

978-0-141-04525-2

www.greenpenguin.co.uk

MIX
Paper from
responsible sources
FSC™ C018179

Penguin Books is committed to a sustainable
future for our business, our readers and our planet.
This book is made from Forest Stewardship
Council™ certified paper.

ALWAYS LEARNING   **PEARSON**

PENGUIN BOOKS

THE ELEMENT

'*The Element* is another reminder of why Sir Ken Robinson is one of America's finest imports. With a crackling wit and a deep humanity, he urges us to ignore the naysayers, bypass the crowd, and find the place where our talents and desires intersect . . . A truly inspiring book'
Daniel H. Pink, author of *A Whole New Mind*

'There is a powerful driving force inside every human being that, once unleashed, can make any vision, any dream, a reality. *The Element* captures that force with passion and insight' Tony Robbins, author of *Awaken the Giant Within: How to Take Immediate Control of Your Mental, Emotional, Physical and Financial Destiny!*

'A great and inspiring book . . . After the first page, you have to abandon your ego and look for your own gifts and graces' Warren Bennis, author of *On Becoming a Leader: The Leadership Classic*

'While the world is changing faster than ever, our organizations, our schools, and too often our minds are locked in the habits of the past. The result is a massive waste of human talent. *The Element* is a passionate and persuasive appeal to think differently about ourselves and a guide to facing the future' Alvin Toffler, author of *Future Shock and The Third Wave*

'In a time when accepted scientific principles and facts themselves are being tossed into the fire of controversy by some, it is time again, now more than ever, to educate our educators. In Sir Ken Robinson's rich, deeply entertaining and inspiring new book, he shows us in the most intriguing way and with humour and humility how we can look again at how we learn and how we teach' Brian Ray, musician

'*The Element* provides a real platform for our futures; it is essential reading for anyone with children, unfulfilled dreams or a life still to live'
Richard Gerver, educational consultant

'*The Element* gives you the feeling that all is possible if we dig deeply within ourselves, using our imaginations and curiosity' Vidal Sassoon

'Written with passion, humour and eloquence, *The Element* shows that everyone has the ability to achieve their ambitions and demonstrates the enabling mechanisms to overcome the obstacles that stifle imagination' *Waterstone's Books Quarterly*

'Robinson emphasizes the importance of mentors and reforming and transforming education, making a convincing argument bolstered by solid strategies for honing creativity. Motivating and persuasive, this entertaining and inspiring book will appeal to a wide audience' *Publishers Weekly*

'Ken Robinson is a remarkable man, one of the few who really look at and into you, so he makes you feel at ease and happy. I'm proud to be in his book as one of the people he feels has attained the Element. Reading his book helps you pinpoint the search we must all make to achieve the best in us' Gillian Lynne, choreographer for *Cats* and *Phantom of the Opera*

ABOUT THE AUTHORS

Ken Robinson is an internationally acclaimed leader in creativity, innovation and human capacity. He has worked throughout the world with governments, Fortune 500 companies, education systems, non-profit groups, cultural organizations and thought leaders. He was knighted in 2003 for his contribution to education and the arts, and in 2008 received the Benjamin Franklin Medal for the Royal Society of Arts, awarded to a global 'big thinker' who has energized public discourse about human progress.

His TED lecture on creativity and education has been downloaded over 3 million times in 200 different countries (see www.ted.com).

Lou Aronica is the author of two novels and co-author of several works of non-fiction, including the American bestseller *The Culture Code* (with Clotaire Rapaille).

To my sister and brothers, Ethel Lena, Keith, Derek, Ian, John, and Neil; to our extraordinary Mum and Dad, Ethel and Jim; to my son, James, and my daughter, Kate, and to my soul mate, Terry. This book is for you. For all your many talents and for the endless love and laughter we put into each other's lives. It's when I'm with you and the ones you love that I really am in my Element.

Acknowledgments

They say it takes a village to raise a baby. Rearing a book like this takes a small metropolis. I know I have to say I can't thank everyone, and I really can't. I do have to single out a few people, though, for special service awards.

First and foremost, my wife and partner, Terry. This book simply wouldn't be in your hands but for her. Its origins were in an off-the-cuff remark I made at a conference a few years ago. I had just told the Gillian Lynne story, which now opens chapter 1 of the book. In passing, I said that one of these days I was going to write a book about stories like that. I've since learned not to say these things out loud in front of Terry. She asked me when did I have in mind. "Soon," I said, "definitely soon." After a few months had passed, she started it herself, wrote the proposal, worked on the ideas, did some of the initial interviews, and then found the agent, Peter Miller, who was to help make it happen. With the foundations laid so solidly, and the escape routes closed so firmly, I finally kept my word and got on with the book.

I want to thank Peter Miller, our literary agent, for all his great work, not least in bringing Lou Aronica and me together. I travel a lot—too much, really—and producing a book like this needs time, energy, and collaboration. Lou was the ideal partner. He is seriously professional: sage, judicious, creative, and patient. He was the calm center of the project as I orbited the earth, sending notes, drafts, and second thoughts from airports and hotel rooms.

Between us, we also managed to steer a successful course between the often comic conflicts of British and American English. Thank you, Lou.

My son, James, gave up his precious, final student summer to pore over archives, journals, and Internet sites, checking facts, dates, and ideas. Then he debated virtually every idea in the book with me until I was worn out. Nancy Allen worked for several months on research issues under increasingly tight deadlines. My daughter, Kate, had a wonderfully creative collaboration with Nick Egan to produce a unique Web site that shows all the other work we're now doing. Our assistant, Andrea Hanna, worked tirelessly to orchestrate the myriad moving parts in a project like this. We wouldn't still be standing up without her.

As the book was taking shape, we were extremely fortunate to have the wise and creative counsel of our publisher, Kathryn Court, at Viking Penguin. Her benign form of intimidation also ensured that we got the book finished in decent time.

Finally, I have to thank all of those whose stories illuminate this book. Many of them spent precious hours, amid very busy lives, to talk freely and passionately about the experiences and ideas that lie at the heart of *The Element*. Many others sent me moving letters and e-mails. Their stories show that the issues in this book reach into the core of our lives. I thank all of them.

It's usual to say, of course, that whatever good things other people have contributed, any faults that remain in the book are my responsibility alone. That seems a bit harsh to me, but I suppose it's true.

Contents

Introduction

A FEW YEARS AGO, I heard a wonderful story, which I'm very fond of telling. An elementary school teacher was giving a drawing class to a group of six-year-old children. At the back of the classroom sat a little girl who normally didn't pay much attention in school. In the drawing class she did. For more than twenty minutes, the girl sat with her arms curled around her paper, totally absorbed in what she was doing. The teacher found this fascinating. Eventually, she asked the girl what she was drawing. Without looking up, the girl said, "I'm drawing a picture of God." Surprised, the teacher said, "But nobody knows what God looks like."

The girl said, "They will in a minute."

I love this story because it reminds us that young children are wonderfully confident in their own imaginations. Most of us lose this confidence as we grow up. Ask a class of first graders which of them thinks they're creative and they'll all put their hands up. Ask a group of college seniors this same question and most of them won't. I believe passionately that we are all born with tremendous natural capacities, and that we lose touch with many of them as we spend more time in the world. Ironically, one of the main reasons this happens is education. The result is that too many people never connect with their true talents and therefore don't know what they're really capable of achieving.

In that sense, they don't know who they really are.

I travel a great deal and work with people all around the world. I work with education systems, with corporations, and with not-for-profit organizations. Everywhere, I meet students who are trying to figure out their futures and don't know where to start. I meet concerned parents who are trying to help them but instead often steer them away from their true talents on the assumption that their kids have to follow conventional routes to success. I meet employers who are struggling to understand and make better use of the diverse talents of the people in their companies. Along the way, I've lost track of the numbers of people I've met who have no real sense of what their individual talents and passions are. They don't enjoy what they are doing now but they have no idea what actually would fulfill them.

On the other hand, I also meet people who've been highly successful in all kinds of fields who are passionate about what they do and couldn't imagine doing anything else. I believe that their stories have something important to teach all of us about the nature of human capacity and fulfillment. As I've spoken at events around the world, I've found it's real stories like these, at least as much as statistics and the opinions of experts, that persuade people that we all need to think differently about ourselves and about what we're doing with our lives; about how we're educating our children and how we're running our organizations.

This book contains a wide range of stories about the creative journeys of very different people. Many of them were interviewed specifically for this book. These people tell how they first came to recognize their unique talents and how they make a highly successful living from doing what they love. What strikes me is that often their journeys haven't been conventional. They've been full of twists, turns, and surprises. Often those I interviewed said that our conversations for the book revealed ideas and experiences they hadn't discussed in this way before. The moment of recognition. The evolution of their talents. The encouragement or discouragement of family, friends, and teachers. What made them forge ahead in the face of numerous obstacles.

Their stories are not fairy tales, though. All of these people are leading complicated and challenging lives. Their personal journeys have not been easy and straightforward. They've all had their disasters as well as their triumphs. None of them have "perfect" lives. But all of them regularly experience moments that feel like perfection. Their stories are often fascinating.

But this book isn't really about them. It's about you.

My aim in writing it is to offer a richer vision of human ability and creativity and of the benefits to us all of connecting properly with our individual talents and passions. This book is about issues that are of fundamental importance in our lives and in the lives of our children, our students, and the people we work with. I use the term *the Element* to describe the place where the things we love to do and the things we are good at come together. I believe it is essential that each of us find his or her Element, not simply because it will make us more fulfilled but because, as the world evolves, the very future of our communities and institutions will depend on it.

The world is changing faster than ever in our history. Our best hope for the future is to develop a new paradigm of human capacity to meet a new era of human existence. We need to evolve a new appreciation of the importance of nurturing human talent along with an understanding of how talent expresses itself differently in every individual. We need to create environments—in our schools, in our workplaces, and in our public offices—where every person is inspired to grow creatively. We need to make sure that all people have the chance to do what they should be doing, to discover the Element in themselves and in their own way.

This book is a hymn to the breathtaking diversity of human talent and passion and to our extraordinary potential for growth and development. It's also about understanding the conditions under which human talents will flourish or fade. It's about how we can all engage more fully in the present, and how we can prepare in the only possible way for a completely unknowable future.

To make the best of ourselves and of each other, we urgently need to embrace a richer conception of human capacity. We need to embrace the Element.

CHAPTER ONE

The Element

GILLIAN WAS ONLY eight years old, but her future was already at risk. Her schoolwork was a disaster, at least as far as her teachers were concerned. She turned in assignments late, her handwriting was terrible, and she tested poorly. Not only that, she was a disruption to the entire class, one minute fidgeting noisily, the next staring out the window, forcing the teacher to stop the class to pull Gillian's attention back, and the next doing something to disturb the other children around her. Gillian wasn't particularly concerned about any of this—she was used to being corrected by authority figures and really didn't see herself as a difficult child—but the school was very concerned. This came to a head when the school wrote to her parents.

The school thought that Gillian had a learning disorder of some sort and that it might be more appropriate for her to be in a school for children with special needs. All of this took place in the 1930s. I think now they'd say she had attention deficit hyperactivity disorder, and they'd put her on Ritalin or something similar. But the ADHD epidemic hadn't been invented at the time. It wasn't an available condition. People didn't know they could have that and had to get by without it.

Gillian's parents received the letter from the school with great concern and sprang to action. Gillian's mother put her daughter in her best dress and shoes, tied her hair in ponytails, and took her to a psychologist for assessment, fearing the worst.

Gillian told me that she remembers being invited into a large oak-paneled room with leather-bound books on the shelves. Standing in the room next to a large desk was an imposing man in a tweed jacket. He took Gillian to the far end of the room and sat her down on a huge leather sofa. Gillian's feet didn't quite touch the floor, and the setting made her wary. Nervous about the impression she would make, she sat on her hands so that she wouldn't fidget.

The psychologist went back to his desk, and for the next twenty minutes, he asked Gillian's mother about the difficulties Gillian was having at school and the problems the school said she was causing. While he didn't direct any of his questions at Gillian, he watched her carefully the entire time. This made Gillian extremely uneasy and confused. Even at this tender age, she knew that this man would have a significant role in her life. She knew what it meant to attend a "special school," and she didn't want anything to do with that. She genuinely didn't feel that she had any real problems, but everyone else seemed to believe she did. Given the way her mother answered the questions, it was possible that even *she* felt this way.

Maybe, Gillian thought, they were right.

Eventually, Gillian's mother and the psychologist stopped talking. The man rose from his desk, walked to the sofa, and sat next to the little girl.

"Gillian, you've been very patient, and I thank you for that," he said. "But I'm afraid you'll have to be patient for a little longer. I need to speak to your mother privately now. We're going to go out of the room for a few minutes. Don't worry; we won't be very long."

Gillian nodded apprehensively, and the two adults left her sitting there on her own. But as he was leaving the room, the psychologist leaned across his desk and turned on the radio.

As soon as they were in the corridor outside the room, the doctor said to Gillian's mother, "Just stand here for a moment, and watch what she does." There was a window into the room, and they stood to one side of it, where Gillian couldn't see them. Nearly immediately, Gillian was on her feet, moving around the room to the music. The two adults stood watching quietly for a few minutes, transfixed by the girl's grace. Anyone would have noticed there was something natural—even primal—about Gillian's movements. Just as they would have surely caught the expression of utter pleasure on her face.

At last, the psychologist turned to Gillian's mother and said, "You know, Mrs. Lynne, Gillian isn't sick. She's a dancer. Take her to a dance school."

I asked Gillian what happened then. She said her mother did exactly what the psychiatrist suggested. "I can't tell you how wonderful it was," she told me. "I walked into this room, and it was full of people like me. People who couldn't sit still. *People who had to move to think*."

She started going to the dance school every week, and she practiced at home every day. Eventually, she auditioned for the Royal Ballet School in London, and they accepted her. She went on to join the Royal Ballet Company itself, becoming a soloist and performing all over the world. When that part of her career ended, she formed her own musical theater company and produced a series of highly successful shows in London and New York. Eventually, she met Andrew Lloyd Webber and created with him some of the most successful musical theater productions in history, including *Cats* and *The Phantom of the Opera*.

Little Gillian, the girl with the high-risk future, became known to the world as Gillian Lynne, one of the most accomplished choreographers of our time, someone who has brought pleasure to millions and earned millions of dollars. This happened because someone looked deep into her eyes—someone who had seen children like her before and knew how to read the signs. Someone else might have put her on medication and told her to calm down. But Gillian wasn't a problem child. She didn't need to go away to a special school.

She just needed to be who she really was.

Unlike Gillian, Matt always did fine in school, getting decent grades and passing all of the important tests. However, he found himself tremendously bored. In order to keep himself amused, he started drawing during classes. "I would draw constantly," he told me. "And I got so good at drawing that I was able to draw without looking, so that the teacher would think that I was paying attention." For him, art class was an opportunity to pursue his passion with abandon. "We were coloring in coloring books, and I thought, I can never color within the lines. Oh, no, I can't be bothered!" This kicked up to another level entirely when he got to high school. "There was an art class and the other kids would just sit there, the art teacher was bored, and the art supplies were just sitting there; nobody was using them. So I did as many paintings as I could—thirty paintings in a single class. I'd look at each painting, what it looked like, and then I'd title it. 'Dolphin in the Seaweed,' okay! Next! I remember doing tons of painting until they finally realized I was using up so much paper that they stopped me.

"There was the thrill of making something that did not exist before. As my technical prowess increased, it was fun to be able to go, 'Oh, that actually looks, vaguely, like what it's supposed to look like.' But then I realized that my drawing was not getting much better so I started concentrating on stories and jokes. I thought that was more entertaining."

Matt Groening, known around the world as the creator of *The Simpsons*, found his true inspiration in the work of other artists whose drawings lacked technical mastery but who combined their distinctive art styles with inventive storytelling. "What I found encouraging was looking at people who couldn't draw who were making their living, like James Thurber. John Lennon was also very important to me. His books, *In His Own Write* and *A Spaniard in the Works*, are full of his own really crummy drawings but funny prose-poems and crazy stories. I went through a stage where I tried to imitate John Lennon. Robert Crumb was also a huge influence."

His teachers and his parents—even his father, who was a cartoonist and filmmaker—tried to encourage him to do something else with his life. They suggested that he go to college and find a more solid profession. In fact, until he got to college (a nontraditional school without grades or required classes), he'd found only one teacher who truly inspired him. "My first-grade teacher saved paintings I did in class. She actually saved them, I mean, for years. I was touched because there's like, you know, hundreds of kids going through here. Her name is Elizabeth Hoover. I named a character on *The Simpsons* after her."

The disapproval of authority figures left him undeterred because, in his heart, Matt knew what truly inspired him.

"I knew as a kid when we were playing and making up stories and using little figurines—dinosaurs and stuff like that—I was going to be doing this for the rest of my life. I saw grown-ups with briefcases going into office buildings and I thought, 'I can't do that. This is all I really wanna do.' I was surrounded by other kids who felt the same way, but gradually they peeled off and they got more serious. For me it was always about playing and storytelling.

"I understood the series of stages I was supposed to go

through—you go to high school, you go to college, you get a credential, and then you go out and get a good job. I knew it wasn't gonna work for me. I knew I was gonna be drawing cartoons forever.

"I found friends who had the same interests at school. We hung out together and we'd draw comics and then bring them to school and show them to each other. As we got older and more ambitious, we started making movies. It was great. It partly compensated for the fact that we felt very self-conscious socially. Instead of staying home on the weekend, we went out and made movies. Instead of going to the football games on Friday night, we would go to the local university and watch underground films.

"I made a decision that I was going to live by my wits. And by the way, I didn't think it was gonna work. I thought I was gonna be working at some lousy job, doing something that I hated. My vision was that I'd be working in a tire warehouse. I have no idea why I thought it was a tire warehouse. I thought I'd be rolling tires around and then on my break, I'd be drawing cartoons."

Things turned out rather differently from that. Matt moved to L.A., eventually placed his comic strip *Life in Hell* with *L.A. Weekly*, and began to make a name for himself. This led to an invitation from the Fox Broadcasting Company to create short animated segments for *The Tracey Ullman Show*. During his pitch to Fox, he invented *The Simpsons* on the spot—he literally had no idea he was going to do this before he went into the meeting. The show evolved into a half-hour program and has been running on Fox every Sunday for nineteen years as of this writing. In addition, it has generated movies, comic books, toys, and countless other merchandise. In other words, it is a pop culture empire.

Yet none of this would have happened if Matt Groening had listened to those who told him he needed to pursue a "real" career.

· · ·

Not all successful people disliked school or did badly there. Paul was still a high school student, one with very good grades, when he walked into a University of Chicago lecture hall for the first time. He didn't realize as he did so that the college was one of the leading institutions in the world for the study of economics. He only knew that it was close to his home. Minutes later, he was "born again," as he wrote in an article. "That day's lecture was on Malthus's theory that human populations would reproduce like rabbits until their density per acre of land reduced their wage to a bare subsistence level where an increased death rate came to equal the birth rate. So easy was it to understand all this simple differential equation stuff that I suspected (wrongly) that I was missing out on some mysterious complexity."

At that point, Dr. Paul Samuelson's life as an economist began. It is a life he describes as "pure fun," one that has seen him serve as a professor at MIT, become president of the International Economic Association, write several books (including the best-selling economics textbook of all time) and hundreds of papers, have a significant impact on public policy, and, in 1970, become the first American to win the Nobel Prize in Economics.

"As a precocious youngster I had always been good at logical manipulations and puzzle-solving IQ tests. So if economics was made for me, it can be said that I too was made for economics. Never underestimate the vital importance of finding early in life the work that for you is play. This turns possible underachievers into happy warriors."

Three Stories, One Message

Gillian Lynne, Matt Groening, and Paul Samuelson are three very different people with three very different stories. What unites them is one undeniably powerful message: that each of them found high levels of achievement and personal satisfaction upon discovering the thing that they naturally do well and that also ignites their passions. I call stories like theirs "epiphany stories" because they tend to involve some level of revelation, a way of dividing the world into before and after. These epiphanies utterly changed their lives, giving them direction and purpose and sweeping them up in a way that nothing else had.

They and the other people you'll meet in this book have identified the sweet spot for themselves. They have discovered their Element—the place where the things you love to do and the things that you are good at come together. The Element is a different way of defining our potential. It manifests itself differently in every person, but the components of the Element are universal.

Lynne, Groening, and Samuelson have accomplished a great deal in their lives. But they are not alone in being capable of that. Why they are special is that they have found what they love to do and they are actually doing it. They have found their Element. In my experience, most people have not.

Finding your Element is essential to your well-being and ultimate success, and, by implication, to the health of our organizations and the effectiveness of our educational systems.

I believe strongly that if we can each find our Element, we all have the potential for much higher achievement and fulfillment. I don't mean to say that there's a dancer, a cartoonist, or a Nobel-winning economist in each of us. I mean that we all have distinctive talents and passions that can inspire us to achieve far more than we may imagine. Understanding this changes everything. It also offers us our best and perhaps our only promise for genuine and sustainable success in a very uncertain future.

Being in our Element depends on finding our own distinctive talents and passions. Why haven't most people found this? One of the most important reasons is that most people have a very limited conception of their own natural capacities. This is true in several ways.

The first limitation is in our understanding of the range of our capacities. We are all born with extraordinary powers of imagination, intelligence, feeling, intuition, spirituality, and of physical and sensory awareness. For the most part, we use only a fraction of these powers, and some not at all. Many people have not found their Element because they don't understand their own powers.

The second limitation is in our understanding of how all of these capacities relate to each other holistically. For the most part, we think that our minds, our bodies, and our feelings and relationships with others operate independent of each other, like separate systems. Many people have not found their Element because they don't understand their true organic nature.

The third limitation is in our understanding of how much potential we have for growth and change. For the most part, people seem to think that life is linear, that our capacities decline as we grow older, and that opportunities we have missed are gone forever. Many people have not found their Element because they don't understand their constant potential for renewal.

This limited view of our own capacities can be compounded by our peer groups, by our culture, and by our own expectations of ourselves. A major factor for everyone, though, is education.

One Size Does Not Fit All

Some of the most brilliant, creative people I know did not do well at school. Many of them didn't really discover what they could do—and who they really were—until they'd left school and recovered from their education.

I was born in Liverpool, England, and in the 1960s I went to a school there, the Liverpool Collegiate. On the other side of the city was the Liverpool Institute. One of the pupils there was Paul McCartney.

Paul spent most of his time at the Liverpool Institute fooling around. Rather than studying intently when he got home, he devoted the majority of his hours out of school to listening to rock music and learning the guitar. This turned out to be a smart choice for him, especially after he met John Lennon at a school fete in another part of the city. They impressed each other and eventually decided to form a band with George Harrison and later Ringo Starr, called the Beatles. That was a very good idea.

By the mid-1980s, both the Liverpool Collegiate and the Liverpool Institute had closed. The buildings stood empty and derelict. Both have since been revived, in very different ways. Developers turned my old school into luxury apartments—a huge change, since the Collegiate was never about luxury when I was there. The Liverpool Institute has now become the Liverpool Institute for Performing Arts (LIPA), one of Europe's leading centers for professional training in the arts. The lead patron is Sir Paul McCartney. The old, dusty classrooms where he spent his teenage years daydreaming now contain students from all over the world doing the very thing he dreamed about—making music—as well as those learning to take the stage in a wide variety of ways.

I had a role in the early development of LIPA, and on its tenth anniversary, the directors rewarded me with a Companionship of the school. I went back to Liverpool to receive the award from Sir Paul at the annual commencement. I gave a speech to graduating students about some of the ideas that are now in this book—the need to find your passion and talents, the fact that education often doesn't help people to do that, and that it often has the opposite effect.

Sir Paul spoke that day as well, and responded directly to what

I'd been saying. He said that he'd always loved music, but that he never enjoyed music lessons at school. His teachers thought they could convey an appreciation for music by making kids listen to crackling records of classical compositions. He found this just as boring as he found everything else at school.

He told me he went through his entire education without anyone noticing that he had any musical talent at all. He even applied to join the choir of Liverpool Cathedral and was turned down. They said he wasn't a good enough singer. Really? How good was that choir? How good can a choir be? Ironically, the very choir that rejected the young McCartney ultimately staged two of his classical pieces.

McCartney is not alone in having his talents overlooked in school. Apparently, organizers kept Elvis Presley from joining his school's glee club. They said his voice would ruin their sound. Like the choir at the Liverpool Cathedral, the glee club had standards to uphold. We all know the tremendous heights the glee club scaled once they'd managed to keep Elvis out.

A few years ago, I spoke at a number of events on creativity with John Cleese from Monty Python. I asked John about his education. Apparently, he did very well at school but not at comedy, the thing that actually shaped his life. He said that he went all the way from kindergarten to Cambridge and none of his teachers noticed that he had any sense of humor at all. Since then, quite a few people have decided he does.

If these were isolated examples, there'd be little point in mentioning them. But they're not. Many of the people you'll meet in this book didn't do well at school or enjoy being there. Of course, at least as many people do well in their schools and love what the education system has to offer. But too many graduate or leave early, unsure of their real talents and equally unsure of what direction to take next. Too many feel that what they're good at isn't valued by schools. Too many think they're not good at anything.

I've worked for most of my life in and around education, and I don't believe that this is the fault of individual teachers. Obviously, some should be doing something else, and as far away from young minds as possible. But there are plenty of good teachers and many brilliant ones.

Most of us can look back to particular teachers who inspired us and changed our lives. These teachers excelled and reached us, but they did this in spite of the basic culture and mindset of public education. There are significant problems with that culture, and I don't see nearly enough improvements. In many systems, the problems are getting worse. This is true just about everywhere.

When my family and I moved from England to America, our two children, James and Kate, started at high school in Los Angeles. In some ways, the system was very different from the one we knew in the UK. For example, the children had to study some subjects they had never taken before—like American history. We don't really teach American history in Britain. We suppress it. Our policy is to draw a veil across the whole sorry episode. We arrived in the United States four days before Independence Day, just in time to watch others revel in having thrown the British out of the country. Now that we've been here a few years and know what to expect, we tend to spend Independence Day indoors with the blinds closed, flicking through old photographs of the Queen.

In many ways, though, the education system in the United States is very similar to that in the United Kingdom, and in most other places in the world. Three features stand out in particular. First, there is the preoccupation with certain sorts of academic ability. I know that academic ability is very important. But school systems tend to be preoccupied with certain sorts of critical analysis and reasoning, particularly with words and numbers. Important as those skills are, there is much more to human intelligence than that. I'll discuss this at length in the next chapter.

The second feature is the hierarchy of subjects. At the top of the hierarchy are mathematics, science, and language skills. In the middle are the humanities. At the bottom are the arts. In the arts, there is another hierarchy: music and visual arts normally have a higher status than theater and dance. In fact, more and more schools are cutting the arts out of the curriculum altogether. A huge high school might have only one fine arts teacher, and even elementary school children get very little time to simply paint and draw.

The third feature is the growing reliance on particular types of assessment. Children everywhere are under intense pressure to perform at higher and higher levels on a narrow range of standardized tests.

Why are school systems like this? The reasons are cultural and historical. Again, we'll discuss this at length in a later chapter, and I'll say what I think we should do to transform education. The point here is that most systems of mass education came into being relatively recently—in the eighteenth and nineteenth centuries. These systems were designed to meet the economic interests of those times—times that were dominated by the Industrial Revolution in Europe and America. Math, science, and language skills were essential for jobs in the industrial economies. The other big influence on education has been the academic culture of universities, which has tended to push aside any sort of activity that involves the heart, the body, the senses, and a good portion of our actual brains.

The result is that school systems everywhere inculcate us with a very narrow view of intelligence and capacity and overvalue particular sorts of talent and ability. In doing so, they neglect

others that are just as important, and they disregard the relationships between them in sustaining the vitality of our lives and communities. This stratified, one-size-fits-all approach to education
marginalizes all of those who do not take naturally to learning
this way.

Very few schools and even fewer school systems in the world
teach dance every day as a formal part of their curricula, as they
do with math. Yet we know that many students only become engaged when they're using their bodies. For instance, Gillian Lynne
told me that she did better at *all* of her subjects once she discovered
dance. She was one of those people who had to "move to think."
Unfortunately, most kids don't find someone to play the role the
psychologist played in Gillian's life—especially now. When they
fidget too much, they're medicated and told to calm down.

The current systems also put severe limits on how teachers
teach and students learn. Academic ability is very important, but
so are other ways of thinking. People who think visually might
love a particular topic or subject, but won't realize it if their teachers only present it in one, nonvisual way. Yet our education systems
increasingly encourage teachers to teach students in a uniform
fashion. To appreciate the implications of the epiphany stories
told here, and indeed to seek out our own, we need to rethink
radically our view of intelligence.

These approaches to education are also stifling some of the
most important capacities that young people now need to make
their way in the increasingly demanding world of the twenty-first
century—the powers of creative thinking. Our systems of education put a high premium on knowing the single right answer to a
question. In fact, with programs like No Child Left Behind (a
federal program that seeks to improve the performance of American public schools by making schools more accountable for meeting mandated performance levels) and its insistence that all

children from every part of the country hew to the same standards, we're putting a greater emphasis than ever before on conformity and finding the "right" answers.

All children start their school careers with sparkling imaginations, fertile minds, and a willingness to take risks with what they think. When my son was four, his preschool put on a production of the Nativity story. During the show, there was a wonderful moment when three little boys came onstage as the Three Wise Men, carrying their gifts of gold, frankincense, and myrrh. I think the second boy lost his nerve a little and went out of sequence. The third boy had to improvise a line he hadn't learned, or paid much attention to during rehearsals, given that he was only four. The first boy said, "I bring you gold." The second boy said, "I bring you myrrh."

The third boy said, "Frank sent this."

Who's Frank, you think? The thirteenth apostle? The lost Book of Frank?

What I loved about this was that it illustrated that, when they are very young, kids aren't particularly worried about being wrong. If they aren't sure what to do in a particular situation, they'll just have a go at it and see how things turn out. This is not to suggest that being wrong is the same thing as being creative. Sometimes being wrong is just being wrong. What is true is that if you're not prepared to be wrong, you'll never come up with anything original.

There is a basic flaw in the way some policymakers have interpreted the idea of going "back to basics" to upgrade educational standards. They look at getting back to basics as a way of reinforcing the old Industrial Revolution–era hierarchy of subjects. They seem to believe that if they feed our children a nationally prescribed menu of reading, writing, and arithmetic, we'll be more competitive with the world and more prepared for the future.

What is catastrophically wrong with this mode of thinking is that it severely underestimates human capacity. We place tremendous significance on standardized tests, we cut funding for what we consider "nonessential" programs, and then we wonder why our children seem unimaginative and uninspired. In these ways, our current education system systematically drains the creativity out of our children.

Most students never get to explore the full range of their abilities and interests. Those students whose minds work differently—and we're talking about many students here; perhaps even the majority of them—can feel alienated from the whole culture of education. This is exactly why some of the most successful people you'll ever meet didn't do well at school. Education is the system that's supposed to develop our natural abilities and enable us to make our way in the world. Instead, it is stifling the individual talents and abilities of too many students and killing their motivation to learn. There's a huge irony in the middle of all of this.

The reason many school systems are going in this direction is that politicians seem to think that it's essential for economic growth and competitiveness and to help students get jobs. But the fact is that in the twenty-first century, jobs and competitiveness depend absolutely on the very qualities that school systems are being forced to tamp down and that this book is celebrating. Businesses everywhere say they need people who are creative and can think independently. But the argument is not just about business. It's about having lives with purpose and meaning in and beyond whatever work we do.

The idea of going back to basics isn't wrong in and of itself. I also believe we need to get our kids back to basics. However, if we're really going to go back to basics, we need to go all the way back. We need to rethink the basic nature of human ability and the basic purposes of education now.

There was a time in our history when the steam engine reigned supreme. It was powerful, it was effective, and it was significantly more efficient than the propulsion system that came before it. Eventually, though, it no longer served the needs of the people, and the internal combustion engine ushered in a new paradigm. In many ways, our current education system is like the steam engine—and it's running out of steam rather quickly.

This problem of old thinking hardly ends when we leave school. These features of education are replicated in public institutions and corporate organizations, and the cycle goes around and around. As anyone in the corporate world knows, it's very easy to be "typed" early in your career. When this happens, it becomes exceedingly difficult to make the most of your other—and perhaps truer—talents. If the corporate world sees you as a financial type, you'll have a difficult time finding employment on the "creative" side of the business. We can fix this by thinking and acting differently ourselves and in our organizations. In fact, it is essential that we do.

The Pace of Change

Children starting school this year will be retiring in 2070. No one has any idea of what the world will look like in ten years' time, let alone in 2070. There are two major drivers of change—technology and demography.

Technology—especially digital technology—is developing at a rate that most people cannot properly grasp. It is also contributing to what some pundits are calling the biggest generation gap since rock and roll. People over the age of thirty were born before the digital revolution really started. We've learned to use digital technology—laptops, cameras, personal digital assistants, the Internet—as adults, and it has been something like learning a foreign language. Most of us are okay, and some are even expert. We do e-mails and PowerPoint, surf the Internet, and feel we're at the cutting edge. But compared to most people under thirty and certainly under twenty, we are fumbling amateurs. People of that age were born after the digital revolution began. They learned to speak digital as a mother tongue.

When my son, James, was doing homework for school, he would have five or six windows open on his computer, Instant Messenger was flashing continuously, his cell phone was constantly ringing, and he was downloading music and watching the TV over his shoulder. I don't know if he was doing any homework, but he was running an empire as far as I could see, so I didn't really care.

But younger children who are growing up with even more sophisticated technologies are already outperforming teenagers of his generation. And this revolution is not over. In fact, it's barely begun.

Some suggest that, in the near future, the power of laptop computers will match the computing power of the human brain. How is it going to feel when you give your computer an instruction, and it asks you if you know what you're doing? Before too long we may see the merging of information systems with human consciousness. If you think about the impact in the last twenty years of relatively simple digital technologies on the work we do and how we do it—and the impact these technologies have had on national economies—think of the changes that lie ahead. Don't worry if you can't predict them: nobody can.

Add to this the impact of population growth. The world population has doubled in the past thirty years, from three to six billion. It may be heading for nine billion by the middle of the century. This great new mass of humanity will be using technologies that have yet to be invented in ways we cannot imagine and in jobs that don't yet exist.

These driving cultural and technological forces are producing profound shifts in the world economies and increasing diversity and complexity in our daily lives, and especially in those of young people. The simple fact is that these are times of unprecedented global change. We can identify trends for the future, but accurate predictions are almost impossible.

For me, one of the formative books of the 1970s was Alvin Toffler's *Future Shock*. In that book, Toffler discussed the seismic impacts of social and technological change. One of the unexpected pleasures and privileges of living in Los Angeles is that my wife, Terry, and I have become friends with Alvin and his wife, Heidi. At dinner with them, we asked if they shared our view that the changes now sweeping the world have no historical precedents. They agreed that no other period in human history could match the present one in the sheer scale, speed, and global complexity of the changes and challenges we face.

In the late 1990s, who would have accurately guessed what the political climate of the world would be ten years later, what overarching impact the Internet would have, the degree to which commerce would become globalized, and the dramatically different ways in which our children would communicate with one another? Some of us might have guessed one of these or maybe even two. But all? Very few have that kind of vision. Yet these changes have altered the way we conduct our lives.

And the changes are accelerating.

And we can't say how.

What we do know is that certain trends indicate that the world will change in fascinating ways. China, Russia, India, Brazil, and others will play an ever more dominant role in the world economy. We know that the population will continue to grow at unprecedented levels. We know that technology will open new frontiers, and that these technologies will manifest in our homes and our offices with stunning velocity.

This combination of things that we do know—that more countries and more people are in the game than ever before, and that technology is in the process of changing the game itself as we speak—leads us to one inescapable conclusion: we can't know what the future will be like.

The only way to prepare for the future is to make the most out of ourselves on the assumption that doing so will make us as flexible and productive as possible.

Many of the people you'll meet in this book didn't pursue their passions simply because of the promise of a paycheck. They pursued them because they couldn't imagine doing anything else with their lives. They found the things they were made to do, and they have invested considerably in mastering the permutations of these professions. If the world were to turn upside down tomorrow, they'd figure out a way to evolve their talents to accommodate these changes. They would find a way to continue to do the things that put them in their Element, because they would have an organic understanding of how their talents fit a new environment.

Many people set aside their passions to pursue things they don't care about for the sake of financial security. The fact is, though, that the job you took because it "pays the bills" could easily move offshore in the coming decade. If you have never learned to think creatively and to explore your true capacity, what will you do then?

More specifically, what will our children do if we continue to prepare them for life using the old models of education? It's very possible that our children will have multiple careers over the course of their working lives, not simply multiple jobs. Many of them will certainly have jobs we haven't conceived yet. Isn't it therefore our obligation to encourage them to explore as many avenues as possible with an eye toward discovering their true talents and their true passions?

When the only thing we know about the future is that it will be different, we would all be wise to do the same. We need to think very differently about human resources and about how we develop them if we are to face these challenges.

We need to embrace the Element.

What Is the Element?

The Element is the meeting point between natural aptitude and personal passion. What you'll find in common among the people you've met in this chapter and the vast majority of the people you will meet in the coming pages is that they are doing the thing they love, and in doing it they feel like their most authentic selves. They find that time passes differently and that they are more alive, more centered, and more vibrant than at any other times.

Being in their Element takes them beyond the ordinary experiences of enjoyment or happiness. We're not simply talking about laughter, good times, sunsets, and parties. When people are in their Element, they connect with something fundamental to their sense of identity, purpose, and well-being. Being there provides a sense of self-revelation, of defining who they really are and what they're really meant to be doing with their lives. This is why many of the people in the book describe finding their Element as an epiphany.

How do we find the Element in ourselves and in others? There isn't a rigid formula. The Element is different for everyone. In fact, that's the point. We aren't limited to one Element, by the way. Some people may feel a similar passion for one or more activities and may be equally good at them. Others may have a singular passion and aptitude that fulfills them far more than anything else does. There's no rule about this. But there are, so to speak, elements of the Element that provide a framework for thinking about this and knowing what to look for and what to do.

The Element has two main features, and there are two conditions for being in it. The features are *aptitude* and *passion*. The conditions are *attitude* and *opportunity*. The sequence goes something like this: I get it; I love it; I want it; Where is it?

I Get It

An aptitude is a natural facility for something. It is an intuitive feel or a grasp of what that thing is, how it works, and how to use it. Gillian Lynne has a natural feel for dance, Matt Groening for telling stories, and Paul Samuelson for economics and math. Our aptitudes are highly personal. They may be for general types of activity, like math, music, sport, poetry, or political theory. They can also be highly specific—not music in general, but jazz or rap. Not wind instruments in general, but the flute. Not science, but biochemistry. Not track and field, but the long jump.

Throughout this book, you will be meeting people with a profound natural grasp for all sorts of things. They're not good at everything, but at something in particular. Paul Samuelson is naturally good at math. Others are not.

I happen to be one of those others. I was never very good at math at school and was delighted to leave it behind when I finished school. When I had my own children, math reared up again like the monster in the movie that you thought was dead. One of the perils of being a parent is that you have to help your kids with their homework. You can bluff it for a while, but you know deep down that the day of reckoning is approaching.

Until she was twelve, my daughter, Kate, thought I knew everything. This was an impression I was very keen to encourage. When she was little, she'd ask me to help if she was stuck with an English or math problem. I'd look up with a confident smile from whatever I was doing, put my arm around her, and say something like, "Well, let's see here," pretending to share the difficulty so she'd feel better about not getting it. Then she'd gaze at me adoringly as I swept effortlessly, like a math god, through the four-times table and simple subtraction.

One day when she was fourteen, she came home with a page full of quadratic equations, and I felt the familiar cold sweat. At this point, I introduced learning-by-discovery methods. I said, "Kate, there's no point in me telling you the answers. That's not how we learn. You need to work this out for yourself. I'll be outside having a gin and tonic. And by the way, even when you've done it, there's no point showing me the answers. That's what teachers are for."

The next week she brought me home a cartoon strip she'd found in a magazine. She said, "This is for you." The strip showed a dad helping his daughter with her homework. In the first frame, he leaned over her shoulder and said, "What have you got to do?" The girl replied, "I have to find the lowest common denominator." The father said, "Are they still looking for that? They were trying to find that when I was in school." I know how he felt.

For some people, though, math is as beautiful and engaging as poetry and music is for others. Finding and developing our creative strengths is an essential part of becoming who we really are. We don't know who we can be until we know what we can do.

I Love It

Being in your Element is not only a question of natural aptitude. I know many people who are naturally very good at something, but don't feel that it's their life's calling. Being in your Element needs something more—passion. People who are in their Element take a deep delight and pleasure in what they do.

My brother Ian is a musician. He plays drums, piano, and bass guitar. Years ago, he was in a band in Liverpool that included an extremely talented keyboard player named Charles. After one of their gigs, I told Charles how well I thought he'd played that night. Then I said that I'd love to be able to play keyboards that well. "No, you wouldn't," he responded. Taken aback, I insisted that I really would. "No," he said. "You mean you like the idea of playing keyboards. If you'd love to play them, you'd be doing it." He said that to play as well he did, he practiced every day for three or four hours in addition to performing. He'd been doing that since he was seven.

Suddenly playing keyboards as well as Charles did didn't seem as appealing. I asked him how he kept up that level of discipline. He said, "Because I love it." He couldn't imagine doing anything else.

I Want It

Attitude is our personal perspective on our selves and our circumstances—our angle on things, our disposition, and emotional point of view. Many things affect our attitudes, including our basic character, our spirit, our sense of self-worth, the perceptions of those around us, and their expectations of us. An interesting indicator of our basic attitude is how we think of the role of luck in our lives.

People who love what they do often describe themselves as lucky. People who think they're not successful in their lives often say they've been unlucky. Accidents and randomness play some part in everybody's lives. But there's more to luck than pure chance. High achievers often share similar attitudes, such as perseverance, self-belief, optimism, ambition, and frustration. How we perceive our circumstances and how we create and take opportunities depends largely on what we expect of ourselves.

Where Is It?

Without the right opportunities, you may never know what your aptitudes are or how far they might take you. There aren't many bronco riders in the Antarctic, or many pearl divers in the Sahara Desert. Aptitudes don't necessarily become obvious unless there are opportunities to use them. The implication, of course, is that we may never discover our true Element. A lot depends on the opportunities we have, on the opportunities we create, and how and if we take them.

Being in your Element often means being connected with other people who share the same passions and have a common sense of commitment. In practice, this means actively seeking opportunities to explore your aptitude in different fields.

Often we need other people to help us recognize our real talents. Often we can help other people to discover theirs.

In this book, we will explore the primary components of the Element in detail. We will analyze the traits that people who have found the Element share, look at the circumstances and conditions that bring people closer to it, and identify the deterrents that make embracing the Element harder. We'll meet people who have found their way, others who pave the way, organizations that lead the way, and institutions that are going the wrong way.

My goal with this book is to illuminate for you concepts that you might have sensed intuitively and to inspire you to find the Element for yourself and to help others to find it as well. What I hope you will find here is a new way of looking at your own potential and the potential of those around you.

CHAPTER TWO

Think Differently

Mick Fleetwood is one of the most famous and accomplished rock drummers in the world. His band, Fleetwood Mac, has sold tens of millions of copies of their recordings, and rock critics consider their albums *Fleetwood Mac* and *Rumours* to be works of genius. Yet when he was in school, the numbers suggested that Mick Fleetwood lacked intelligence, at least by the definitions many of us have come to take for granted.

"I was a total void in academic work, and no one knew why," he told me. "I had a learning disability at school and still do. I had no understanding of math at all. None. I'd be hard pushed right now to recite the alphabet backward. I'd be lucky if I got it right going forward quickly. If someone were to say, 'What letter is before this one?' I'd break out into a cold sweat."

He attended a boarding school in England and found the experience deeply unsatisfying. "I had great friends, but I just wasn't happy. I was aware of being squeezed out. I was suffering. I had no sense of what I was supposed to be because everything academic was a total failure, and I had no other reference points."

Fortunately for Mick (and for anyone who later bought his albums or attended his concerts), he came from a home where his family saw beyond the limits of what they taught and tested in schools. His father was a fighter pilot in the Royal Air Force, but when he left the service, he followed his true passion for writing. He took his family to live on a barge on the river Thames in Kent for three years so he could follow this dream. Mick's sister Sally went to London to become a sculptor, and his sister Susan pursued a career in the theater. In the Fleetwood household, everyone understood that brilliance came in many forms and that being poor at math, or unable to recite the alphabet backward, hardly doomed one to an inconsequential life.

And Mick could drum. "Playing the piano is probably a more impressive signal that there's something creative going on," he said. "I just wanted to beat the shit out of a drum or some cushions on the chair. It's not exactly the highest form of creative signal. It's almost, 'Well, anyone can do that. That's not clever.' But I started doing this tapping business, and it turned out to be the make or break for me."

Mick's epiphany moment—the point at which the "tapping business" became the driving ambition in his life—came when he visited his sister in London as a boy and went to "some little place in Chelsea with this piano player. There were people playing what I now know was Miles Davis and smoking Gitanes cigarettes. I'd watch them and saw the beginnings of this other world and the atmosphere sucked me in. I felt comfortable. I wasn't fettered. That was my dream.

"Back at school, I held on to these images and I dreamt my way out of that world. I didn't even know if I could play with people, but that vision got me out of the morass of this academic bloody nightmare. I had a lot of commitment internally, but I was also incredibly unhappy because everything at school was showing me that I was useless according to the status quo."

Mick's school performance continued to confound his teachers. They knew he was bright, but his scores suggested otherwise. And if the scores said otherwise, there was little they could do. The experience proved extremely frustrating for the boy who dreamed of being a drummer. Finally, in his teens, he'd had enough.

"One day, I walked out of school and I sat under a large tree in the grounds. I'm not religious, but with tears pouring down my face, I prayed to God that I wouldn't be in this place anymore. I wanted to be in London and play in a jazz club. It was totally naive and ridiculous, but I made a firm commitment to myself that I was going to be a drummer."

Mick's parents understood that school was not a place for someone with Mick's kind of intelligence. At sixteen, he approached them about leaving school, and rather than insisting that he press on until graduation, they put him on a train to London with a drum kit and allowed him to pursue his inspiration.

What came next was a series of "breaks" that might never have occurred if Mick had stayed in school. While he was practicing drums in a garage, Mick's neighbor, a keyboard player named Peter Bardens, knocked on his door. Mick thought Bardens was coming to tell him to be quiet, but instead, the musician invited him to play with him at a gig at a local youth club. This led Mick into the heart of the London music scene in the early 1960s. "As a kid, I had no sense of accomplishment. Now I was starting to get markers that it was okay to be who I was and to do what I was doing."

His friend Peter Green proposed him as the replacement for the drummer in John Mayall's Bluesbreakers, a band that, at various times, included Eric Clapton, Jack Bruce of Cream, and Mick Taylor of the Rolling Stones. Later, he joined with Green and another Bluesbreakers alumnus, John McVie, to form Fleetwood Mac. The rest is a history of multiplatinum recordings and sold-out stadiums. But even as one of the most famous drummers in the world, Mick's analysis of his talent still bears the marks of his experiences in school.

"My style has no structured math to it. I would go into a complete petrified mess on the floor if someone said, 'Do you know what a four/eight is?' Musicians that I work with know that I'm actually like a kid. They might say, 'You know in the chorus, in the second beat . . . ,' and I'll say, 'No,' because I don't know what a chorus is from a verse. I can recognize it if you play the song, because I'll listen to the words."

For Mick Fleetwood, getting away from school and the tests that judged only a narrow range of intelligence was the path to a hugely successful career. "My parents saw that the light in this funny little creature certainly wasn't academics." It happened because he understood innately that he had a great aptitude for something that a score on a test could never indicate. It happened because he chose not to accept that he was "useless according to the status quo."

Taking It All for Granted

One of the key principles of the Element is that we need to challenge what we take for granted about our abilities and the abilities of other people. This isn't as easy as one might imagine. Part of the problem with identifying the things we take for granted is that we don't know what they are because we take them for granted in the first place. They become basic assumptions that we don't question, part of the fabric of our logic. We don't question them because we see them as fundamental, as an integral part of our lives. Like air. Or gravity. Or Oprah.

A good example of something that many people take for granted without knowing it is the number of human senses. When I talk to audiences, I sometimes take them through a simple exercise to illustrate this point. I ask them how many senses they think they have. Most people will answer five—taste, touch, smell, sight, and hearing. Some will say there's a sixth sense and suggest intuition. Rarely will anyone offer anything beyond this.

There's a difference, though, between the first five senses and the sixth. The five all have particular organs associated with them—the nose for smell, the eyes for sight, ears for hearing, and so on. If the organs are injured or compromised in any way, that sense is impaired. It isn't obvious what *does* intuition. It's a kind of spooky sense that girls are supposed to have more of. So, the general assumption among the wide range of people I've spoken with over the years is that we have five "hard" senses and a "spooky" one.

There's a fascinating book by the anthropologist Kathryn Linn Geurts called *Culture and the Senses*. In it, she writes about her work with the Anlo Ewe people of southeastern Ghana. I have to say that I have a certain degree of sympathy for marginalized ethnic groups these days. It seems as though anthropologists are always stalking them—as if their average family unit includes three children and an anthropologist who sits around asking what they have for breakfast. Still, Geurts's study was illuminating.

One of the things she learned about the Anlo Ewe is that they don't think of the senses in the same way that we do. First, they never thought to count them. That entire notion seemed beside the point. In addition, when Geurts listed our taken-for-granted five to them, they asked about the *other* one. The *main* one. They weren't speaking of a "spooky" sense. Nor were they speaking of some residual sense that has survived among the Anlo Ewe but that the rest of us have lost. They were speaking of a sense that we all have, and that is fundamental to our functioning in the world. They were talking about our sense of balance.

The fluids and bones of the inner ear mediate the sense of balance. You only have to think of the impact on your life of damaging your sense of balance—through illness or alcohol—to get some idea of how important it is to our everyday existence. Yet most people never think to include it in their list of senses. This isn't because they don't have a sense of balance. It's because they've become so accustomed to the idea that we have five senses (and maybe a spooky one) that they have stopped thinking about it. It's become a matter of common sense. They just take it for granted.

One of the enemies of creativity and innovation, especially in relation to our own development, is common sense. The playwright Bertolt Brecht said that as soon as something seems the most obvious thing in the world, it means that we have abandoned all attempts at understanding it.

If you didn't guess right away that the *other* sense was balance, don't take it too hard. The fact is that most of the people I speak with don't guess it either. And yet this sense is at least as important as the five we take for granted. And it isn't alone among those we fail to consider.

Physiologists largely agree that in addition to the five we all know about, there are four more. The first is our sense of temperature (thermoception). This is different from our sense of touch. We don't need to be touching anything to feel hot or cold. This is a crucial sense, given that we can only survive as human beings within a relatively narrow band of temperatures. This is one of the reasons we wear clothes. One of them.

Another is the sense of pain (nociception). Scientists now generally agree that this is a different sensory system from either touch or temperature. There also seem to be separate systems for registering pains that originate from the inside or the outside of our bodies. Next is the vestibular sense (equilibrioception), which includes our sense of balance and acceleration. And then there is the kinesthetic sense (proprioception), which gives us our understanding of where our limbs and the rest of our body are in space and in relationship to each other. This is essential for getting up, getting around, and getting back again. The sense of intuition doesn't seem to make the cut with most physiologists. I'll come back to it later.

All of these senses contribute to our feelings of being in the world and to our ability to function in it. There are also some unusual variations in the senses of particular people. Some experience a phenomenon known as synesthesia, in which their senses seem to mingle or overlap: they may see sounds and hear colors. These are abnormalities, and seem to challenge even further our commonsense ideas about our common senses. But they illustrate how profoundly our senses, however many we have and however they work, actually affect our understanding of the world and of ourselves. Yet many of us don't know or have never thought about some of them.

Not all of us take our sense of balance or other senses for granted. Take Bart, for example. When he was a baby in Morton Grove, Illinois, Bart wasn't particularly active. But when he was around six years old, he started to do something very unusual. It turned out that he could walk on his hands nearly as well as he could walk on his feet. This wasn't an elegant sight, but it did get him lots of smiles, laughter, and approval from his family. Whenever visitors came to the house, and at family parties, people prompted Bart to perform his signature move. With no further cajoling—after all, he quite enjoyed both his trick and the attention it generated—he dropped onto his hands, flipped up, and proudly teetered around upside down. As he got older, he even trained himself to go up and down the stairs on his hands.

None of this was of much practical use, of course. After all, it wasn't as though the ability to walk on his hands was a skill that led to higher test scores or was marketable in any way. However, it did do wonders for his popularity—a person who can climb stairs upside down is fun to be around.

Then one day, when he was ten, with his mother's approval, his grade-school physical education teacher took him to a local gymnastics center. As he walked in, Bart's eyes bulged in amazement. He'd never seen anything so wondrous in his life. There were ropes, parallel bars, trapezes, ladders, trampolines, hurdles—all kinds of things upon which he could climb, cavort, and swing. It was like visiting Santa's workshop and Disneyland at the same time. It was also the ideal place for him. His life turned in that moment. Suddenly his innate skills were good for something more than amusing himself and others.

Eight years later, after countless hours of jumping, stretching, vaulting, and lifting, Bart Conner stepped onto the mat in the gymnastics hall at the Montreal Olympics to represent the United States of America. He went on to become America's most decorated male gymnast ever and the first American to win medals at every level of national and international competition. He has been a USA champion, an NCAA champion, a Pan-American Games champion, a World champion, a World Cup champion, and an Olympic champion. He was a member of three Olympic teams, in 1976, 1980, and 1984. In a legendary performance in the 1984 Los Angeles Olympics, Bart made a dramatic comeback from a torn biceps injury to win two gold medals. In 1991, he was inducted into the U.S. Olympic Hall of Fame, and in 1996 into the International Gymnastics Hall of Fame.

Conner now facilitates the passion for gymnastics in others. He owns a flourishing gymnastics school with his wife, Olympic champion Nadia Comaneci. They also own *International Gymnast* magazine and a television production company.

Athletes like Bart Conner and Nadia Comaneci have a profound sense of the capacities of their physical bodies, and their achievements show how limited our everyday ideas about human ability really are. If you watch athletes, dancers, musicians, and other performers of their class at work, you can see that they are thinking, as well as performing, in extraordinary ways. As they practice, they engage their whole bodies in developing and memorizing the routines they are shaping up. In the process, they are relying on what some call "muscle memory." In performance, they are usually moving too quickly and in ways that are simply too complex to rely on the ordinary conscious processes of thinking and decision-making. They draw from the deep reserves of feeling and intuition and of physical reflex and coordination that use the whole brain and not only the parts at the front that we associate with rational thinking. If they did that, their careers would never get off the ground, and neither would they.

In these ways, athletes and all sorts of other performers help to challenge something else about human capacity that too many people take for granted and also get wrong—our ideas about intelligence.

How Intelligent Are You?

Another thing I do when I speak to groups is to ask people to rate their intelligence on a 1-to-10 scale, with 10 being the top. Typically, one or two people will rate themselves a 10. When these people raise their hands, I suggest that they go home; they have more important things to do than listen to me.

Beyond this, I'll get a sprinkling of 9s and a heavier concentration of 8s. Invariably, though, the bulk of any audience puts itself at 7 or 6. The responses decline from there, though I admit I never actually complete the survey. I stop at 2, preferring to save anyone who would actually claim an intelligence level of 1 the embarrassment of acknowledging it in public. Why do I always get the bell-shaped curve? I believe it is because we've come to take for granted certain ideas about intelligence.

What's interesting is that most people do put their hands up and rate themselves on this question. They don't seem to see any problem with the question itself and are happy to put themselves somewhere on the scale. Only a few have challenged the form of the question and asked what I mean by intelligence. I think that's what everyone should do. I'm convinced that taking the definition of intelligence for granted is one of the main reasons why so many people underestimate their true intellectual abilities and fail to find their Element.

This commonsense view goes something like this: We are all born with a fixed amount of intelligence. It's a trait, like blue or green eyes, or long or short limbs. Intelligence shows itself in certain types of activity, especially in math and our use of words. It's possible to measure how much intelligence we have through pencil-and-paper tests, and to express this as a numerical grade. That's it.

Put as bluntly as this, I trust this definition of intelligence sounds as questionable as it is. But essentially this definition runs through much of Western culture, and a good bit of Eastern culture as well. It is at the heart of our education systems and underpins a good deal of the multibillion-dollar testing industries that feed off public education throughout the world. It's at the heart of the idea of academic ability, dominates college entrance examinations, underpins the hierarchy of subjects in education, and stands as the foundation for the whole idea of IQ.

This way of thinking about intelligence has a long history in Western culture and dates back at least to the days of the great Greek philosophers, Aristotle and Plato. Its most recent flowering was in the great period of intellectual advances of the seventeenth and eighteenth centuries that we know as the Enlightenment. Philosophers and scholars aimed to establish a firm basis for human knowledge and to end the superstitions and mythologies about human existence that they believed had clouded the minds of previous generations.

One of the pillars of this new movement was a firm belief in the importance of logic and critical reasoning. Philosophers argued that we should not accept as knowledge anything that could not be proved through logical reasoning, especially in words and mathematical proofs. The problem was where to begin this process without taking anything for granted that might be logically questionable. The famous conclusion of the philosopher René Descartes was that the only thing that he could take for granted was his own existence; otherwise, he couldn't have these thoughts in the first place. His thesis was, "I think, therefore I am."

The other pillar of the Enlightenment was a growing belief in the importance of evidence in support of scientific ideas— evidence that one could observe through the human senses— rather than superstition or hearsay. These two pillars of reason and evidence became the foundations of an intellectual revolution that transformed the outlook and achievements of the Western world. It led to the growth of the scientific method and an avalanche of insights, analysis, and classification of ideas, objects, and phenomena that have extended the reach of human knowledge to the depths of the earth and to the far ends of the known universe. It led too to the spectacular advances in practical technology that gave rise to the Industrial Revolution and to the supreme domination of these forms of thought in scholarship, in politics, in commerce, and in education.

The influence of logic and evidence extended beyond the "hard" sciences. They also shaped the formative theories in the human sciences, including psychology, sociology, anthropology, and medicine. As public education grew in the nineteenth and twentieth centuries, it too was based on these newly dominant ideas about knowledge and intelligence. As mass education grew to meet the growing demands of the Industrial Revolution, there was also a need for quick and easy forms of selection and assessment. The new science of psychology was on hand with new theories about how intelligence could be tested and measured. For the most part, intelligence was defined in terms of verbal and mathematical reasoning. These were also processes that were used to quantify the results. The most significant idea in the middle of all this was IQ.

So it is that we came to think of real intelligence in terms of logical analysis: believing that rationalist forms of thinking were superior to feeling and emotion, and that the ideas that really count can be conveyed in words or through mathematical expressions. In addition, we believed that we could quantify intelligence and rely on IQ tests and standardized tests like the SAT to identify who among us is truly intelligent and deserving of exalted treatment.

Ironically, Alfred Binet, one of the creators of the IQ test, intended the test to serve precisely the opposite function. In fact, he originally designed it (on commission from the French government) exclusively to identify children with special needs so they could get appropriate forms of schooling. He never intended it to identify degrees of intelligence or "mental worth." In fact, Binet noted that the scale he created "does not permit the measure of intelligence, because intellectual qualities are not superposable, and therefore cannot be measured as linear surfaces are measured."

Nor did he ever intend it to suggest that a person could not become more intelligent over time. "Some recent thinkers," he said, "[have affirmed] that an individual's intelligence is a fixed quantity, a quantity that cannot be increased. We must protest and react against this brutal pessimism; we must try to demonstrate that it is founded on nothing."

Still, some educators and psychologists took—and continue to take—IQ numbers to absurd lengths. In 1916, Lewis Terman of Stanford University published a revision of Binet's IQ test. Known as the Stanford-Binet test, now in its fifth version, it is the basis of the modern IQ test. It is interesting to note, though, that Terman had a sadly extreme view of human capacity. These are his words, from the textbook *The Measurement of Intelligence*: "Among laboring men and servant girls there are thousands like them feebleminded. They are the world's 'hewers of wood and drawers of water.' And yet, as far as intelligence is concerned, the tests have told the truth. . . . No amount of school instruction will ever make them intelligent voters or capable voters in the true sense of the word."

Terman was an active player in one of the darker stages of education and public policy, one there is a good chance you are unaware of because most historians choose to leave it unmentioned, the way they might a crazy aunt or an unfortunate drinking incident in college. The eugenics movement sought to weed out entire sectors of the population by arguing that such traits as criminality and pauperism were hereditary, and that it was possible to identify these traits through intelligence testing. Perhaps most appalling among the movement's claims was the notion that entire ethnic groups, including southern Europeans, Jews, Africans, and Latinos fell into such categories. "The fact that one meets this type with such frequency among Indians, Mexicans, and Negroes suggests quite forcibly that the whole question of racial differences in mental traits will have to be taken up anew and by experimental methods," Terman wrote.

"Children of this group should be segregated in special classes and be given instruction which is concrete and practical. They cannot master, but they can often be made efficient workers, able to look out for themselves. There is no possibility at present of convincing society that they should not be allowed to reproduce, although from a eugenic point of view they constitute a grave problem because of their unusually prolific breeding."

The movement actually managed to succeed in lobbying for the passage of involuntary sterilization laws in thirty American states. This meant that the state could neuter people who fell below a particular IQ without their having any say in the matter. That each state eventually repealed the laws is a testament to common sense and compassion. That the laws existed in the first place is a frightening indication of how dangerously limited any standardized test is in calculating intelligence and the capacity to contribute to society.

IQ tests can even be a matter of life and death. A criminal who commits a capital offense is not subject to the death penalty if his IQ is below seventy. However, IQ scores regularly rise over the course of a generation (by as much as twenty-five points), causing the scale to be reset every fifteen to twenty years to maintain a mean score of one hundred. Therefore, someone who commits a capital offense may be more likely to be put to death at the beginning of a cycle than at the end. That's giving a single test an awful lot of responsibility.

People can also improve their scores through study and practice. I read a case recently about a death row inmate who'd at that point spent ten years in jail on a life sentence (he wasn't the trigger man, but he'd been involved in a robbery where someone died). During his incarceration, he took a series of courses. When retested, his IQ had risen more than ten points—suddenly making him eligible for execution.

Of course, most of us won't ever be in a situation where we're sterilized or given a lethal injection because of our IQ scores.

But looking at these extremes allows us to ask some important questions, namely, What are these numbers? and, What do they truly say about our intelligence? The answer is that the numbers largely indicate a person's ability to perform on a test of certain sorts of mathematical and verbal reasoning. In other words, they measure some types of intelligence, not the whole of intelligence. And, as noted above, the baseline keeps shifting to accommodate improvements in the population as a whole over time.

Our fascination with IQ is a corollary to our fascination with—and great dependence on—standardized testing in our schools. Teachers spend large chunks of every school year preparing their students for statewide tests that will determine everything from the child's placement in classes the following year to the amount of funding the school will receive. These tests of course do nothing to take the child's (or the school's) special skills and needs into consideration, yet they have a tremendous say in the child's scholastic fate.

The standardized test that currently has the most impact on a child's academic future in America is the SAT. Interestingly, Carl Brigham, the inventor of the SAT, was also a eugenicist. He conceived the test for the military and, to his credit, disowned it five years later, rejecting eugenics at the same time. However, by this point, Harvard and other Ivy League schools had begun to use it as a measure of applicant acceptability. For nearly seven decades, most American colleges have used it (or the similar ACT) as an essential part of their screening processes, though some colleges are beginning to rely upon it less.

The SAT is in many ways the indicator for what is wrong with standardized tests: it only measures a certain kind of intelligence; it does it in an entirely impersonal way; it attempts to make common assumptions about the college potential of a hugely varied group of teenagers in one-size-fits-all fashion; and it drives high school juniors and seniors to spend hundreds of hours preparing for it at the expense of school study or the pursuit of other passions. John Katzman, founder of the Princeton Review, offers this stinging criticism: "What makes the SAT bad is that it has nothing to do with what kids learn in high school. As a result, it creates a sort of shadow curriculum that furthers the goals of neither educators nor students. . . . The SAT has been sold as snake oil; it measured intelligence, verified high school GPA, and predicted college grades. In fact, it's never done the first two at all, nor a particularly good job at the third."

Yet students who don't test well or who aren't particularly strong at the kind of reasoning the SAT assesses can find themselves making compromises on their collegiate futures—all because we've come to accept that intelligence comes with a number. This notion is pervasive, and it extends well beyond academia. Remember the bell-shaped curve we discussed earlier? It presents itself every time I ask people how intelligent they think they are because we've come to define intelligence far too narrowly. We think we know the answer to the question, "How intelligent are you?" The real answer, though, is that the question itself is the wrong one to ask.

How Are You Intelligent?

The right question to ask is the one above. The difference in these questions is profound. The first suggests that there's a finite way of gauging intelligence and that one can reduce the value of each individual's intelligence to a figure or quotient of some sort. The latter suggests a truth that we somehow don't acknowledge as much as we should—that there are a variety of ways to express intelligence, and that no one scale could ever measure this.

The nature of intelligence has always been a matter of controversy, especially among the many professional specialists who spend their lives thinking about it. They disagree about what it is, about who has it, and about how much of it is out there. In a survey conducted in the United States several years ago, a sample of psychologists attempted to define intelligence, choosing and commenting from a list of twenty-five attributes. Only three were mentioned by 25 percent or more of the respondents. As one commentator put it, "If we were asking experts to describe edible field mushrooms so we could distinguish them from the poisonous kinds and the experts responded like this, we might consider it prudent to avoid the subject altogether."

There have always been criticisms of definitions of intelligence based only on IQ, and in recent years they have been gaining in number and strength. There's a range of alternative, sometimes competing theories that argue that intelligence takes in much more than IQ tests can ever hope to assess.

Harvard psychologist Howard Gardner has argued to wide acclaim that we have not one but multiple intelligences. They include linguistic, musical, mathematical, spatial, kinesthetic, interpersonal (relationships with others), and intra-personal (knowledge and understanding of the self) intelligence. He argues that these types of intelligence are more or less independent of each other, and none is more important, though some might be "dominant" while others are "dormant." He says that we all have different strengths in different intelligences and that education should treat them equally so that all children receive opportunities to develop their individual abilities.

Robert Sternberg is a professor of psychology at Tufts University and a past president of the American Psychological Association. He is a long-term critic of traditional approaches to intelligence testing and IQ. He argues that there are three types of intelligence: analytic intelligence, the ability to solve problems using academic skills and to complete conventional IQ tests; creative intelligence, the ability to deal with novel situations and to come up with original solutions; and practical intelligence, the ability to deal with problems and challenges in everyday life.

Psychologist and best-selling author Daniel Goleman has argued in his books that there is emotional intelligence and social intelligence, both of which are essential to getting along with ourselves and with the world round us.

Robert Cooper, author of *The Other 90%*, says that we shouldn't think of intelligence as happening only in the brain in our skulls. He talks of the "heart" brain and the "gut" brain. Whenever we have a direct experience, he says, it does not go directly to the brain in our heads. The first place it goes is to the neurological networks of the intestinal tract and heart. He describes the first of these, the enteric nervous system, as a "second brain" inside the intestines, which is "independent of but also interconnected with the brain in the cranium." He says that this is why we often experience our first reaction to events as a "gut reaction." Whether or not we acknowledge them, he says, our gut reactions shape everything we do.

Other psychologists and intelligence testers worry about all of these sorts of ideas. They say there is no quantifiable evidence to prove their existence. That may be. But the clear fact of everyday experience is that human intelligence is diverse and multifaceted. For evidence, we need only look at the extraordinary richness and complexity of human culture and achievement. Whether we can ever capture all of this in a single theory of intelligence—with three, four, five, or even eight separate categories—is a problem for the theorists.

Meanwhile the evidence of a basic truth of human ability is everywhere: we "think" about our experiences in all the ways we have them. It's clear too that we all have different strengths and natural aptitudes.

I mentioned that I don't have a particular aptitude for mathematics. Actually, I don't have any aptitude for it. Alexis Lemaire, on the other hand, does. Lemaire is a young French doctoral student specializing in artificial intelligence. In 2007, he claimed the world record for calculating in his head the thirteenth root of a random two-hundred-digit number. He did this in 72.4 seconds. In case, like me, you're not sure what this means, let me explain. Alexis sat in front of a laptop computer that had generated at random a two-hundred-figure number and displayed it on the screen. The number was more than seventeen lines long. This is a big number.

Alexis's task was to calculate in his head the thirteenth root of that number (that is, the number that multiplied by itself thirteen times would produce the exact two-hundred-digit number on the screen). He stared at the screen without speaking and then announced correctly that the answer was, 2,397,207,667,966,701. Remember that he did this in 72.4 seconds. In his head.

Lemaire performed this feat at the New York Hall of Science. He has been working on the thirteenth-root challenge for a number of years. Previously, his best time had been a sluggish 77 seconds. Afterward, he told the press, "The first digit is very easy, the last digit is very easy, but the inside numbers are extremely difficult. I use an artificial intelligence system on my own brain instead of on a computer. I believe most people can do it, but I also have a high-speed mind. My brain works sometimes very, very fast. . . . I use a process to improve my skills to behave like a computer. It's like running a program in my head to control my brain."

"Sometimes," he said, "when I do multiplication my brain works so fast that I need to take medication. I think somebody without a very fast brain can also do this kind of multiplication but this may be easier for me because my brain is faster." He practices math regularly. So that he can think faster, he exercises, doesn't drink caffeine or alcohol, and avoids foods that are high in sugar or fat. His experience of math is so intense that he also has to take regular time off to rest his brain. Otherwise, he thinks there is a danger that too much math could be bad for his health and his heart.

I have always felt that too much math can be bad for my health and my heart as well, but for different reasons. Surprisingly, like me, he did not do particularly well in math at school, though the comparisons between us end right there. He was not top of the class in math, and mainly taught himself through books.

He did have a natural flair for numbers, though, which he discovered when he was about eleven years old and which he has refined and cultivated through constantly challenging himself and by developing sophisticated techniques to exploit it. But the foundation of all of these achievements is a unique, personal aptitude combined with a deep passion and commitment. When he is digging around in huge numbers to unearth their roots, Alexis Lemaire is clearly in his Element.

The Three Features of Human Intelligence

Human intelligence seems to have at least three main features. The first is that it is extraordinarily diverse. It is clearly not limited to the ability to do verbal and mathematical reasoning. These skills are important, but they are simply *one way* in which intelligence expresses itself.

Gordon Parks was a legendary photographer who captured the black American experience in a way that few others ever had. He was the first black producer and director of a major Hollywood film. He helped found *Essence* magazine and served as its editorial director for three years. He was a gifted poet, novelist, and memoirist. He was a talented composer who created his own form of musical notation to write his works.

And he was professionally trained at none of this.

In fact, Gordon Parks barely attended high school. Parks's mother died when he was fifteen, and soon after, he found himself on the streets, unable to graduate. The schooling he did get was discouraging—he often mentioned that one of his teachers told her students that college would be a waste for them since they were destined to become porters and house cleaners.

Still, he used his intelligence in ways few could match. He taught himself to play the piano and this helped him make some money to get by in his late teens. A few years later, he bought a camera from a pawnshop and taught himself to take pictures. What he learned about film and writing came largely from observation, an intense level of intellectual curiosity, and an off-the-charts ability to feel for and see into the lives of other people.

"I just kept on and on," he said in an interview at the Smithsonian Institute, "and I had an indomitable courage as far as getting started in photography was concerned. I realized I liked it and I went all out for it. My wife at this time was sort of against it and my mother-in-law, as all mothers-in-law are, was against it. I spent this dough and decided to get myself some cameras. That's just about what happened. I had a tremendous interest and I just kept plugging away and knocking at doors, seeking out encouragement where I could get it."

"My life to me is like sort of a disjointed dream," he said in a PBS interview. "Things have happened to me—incredible. It's so disjointed. But all I know, it was a constant effort, a constant feeling that I must not fail."

Parks's contribution to American culture is considerable: his searing photography, most notably *American Gothic*, which juxtaposed a black woman holding a mop and broom against the American flag; his inspired film work, including the breakout hit *Shaft*, which introduced Hollywood to the black action hero; his unconventional prose work; and his unique musical work.

I don't know if Gordon Parks ever took a standardized academic test or a college entrance exam. Given his lack of traditional education, there's a good chance he wouldn't have scored particularly high on one if he had. Interestingly, while he never completed high school, he amassed forty honorary doctorates—dedicating one of them to the teacher who had been so dismissive when he was in high school. Yet by any reasonable definition of the word, Gordon Parks was remarkably intelligent, a rare human being with an uncanny ability to learn and master complex and nuanced art forms.

I can only guess that Parks considered himself intelligent. However, if he was like so many others I've met in my travels, his lack of formal education might have caused him to rate himself much lower than he should have in spite of his numerous and obvious gifts.

As the stories of Gordon Parks, Mick Fleetwood, and Bart Conner indicate, intelligence can show itself in ways that have little or nothing to do with numbers and words. We think about the world in all the ways that we experience it, including all the different ways we use our senses (however many of those there turn out to be). We think in sound. We think in movement. We think visually. I worked for a long time with the Royal Ballet in Britain and came to see that dance is a powerful way to express ideas and that dancers use multiple forms of intelligence—kinesthetic, rhythmic, musical, and mathematical—to accomplish this. Were mathematical and verbal intelligence the only kinds that existed, ballet never would have been created. Nor would abstract painting, hip-hop, design, architecture, or self-service checkouts at supermarkets.

The diversity of intelligence is one of the fundamental underpinnings of the Element. If you don't embrace the fact that you think about the world in a wide variety of ways, you severely limit your chances of finding the person that you were meant to be.

An individual who represents this wonderful diversity is R. Buckminster Fuller, best known for his design of the geodesic dome and his coining of the term *Spaceship Earth*. Certainly his greatest accomplishments come in the field of engineering (which of course requires the use of mathematical, visual, and interpersonal intelligence), but he was also a clever and unusual writer, a philosopher who challenged the beliefs of a generation, an ardent environmentalist years before the emergence of a true environmental movement, and a challenging and nurturing university professor. He did all of this by eschewing formal education (he was the first in four generations in his family not to graduate from Harvard) and setting out to experience the world to use the fullest range of his intelligence. He joined the navy, started a building supply company, and worked as a mechanic in a textile mill and a laborer in a meatpacking plant. Fuller seemingly saw no limits on his ability to use every form of intelligence available to him.

The second feature of intelligence is that it is tremendously dynamic. The human brain is intensely interactive. You use multiple parts of it in every task you perform. It is in fact in the dynamic use of the brain—finding new connections between things—that true breakthroughs occur.

Albert Einstein, for instance, took great advantage of the dynamics of intelligence. Einstein's prowess as a scientist and mathematician are legend. However, Einstein was a student of all forms of expression, believing that he could put anything that challenged the mind to use in a variety of ways. For instance, he interviewed poets to learn more about the role of intuition and imagination.

In his biography of Einstein, Walter Isaacson says, "As a young student, he never did well with rote learning. And later, as a theorist, his success came not from the brute strength of his mental processing power but from his imagination and creativity. He could construct complex equations, but more important, he knew that math is the language nature uses to describe her wonders."

When confounded by a challenge in his work, Einstein often turned to the violin to help him. A friend of Einstein's told Isaacson, "He would often play his violin in his kitchen late at night, improvising melodies while he pondered complicated problems. Then, suddenly, in the middle of playing he would announce excitedly, 'I've got it!' As if by inspiration, the answer to the problem would have come to him in the midst of the music."

What Einstein seemed to understand is that intellectual growth and creativity come through embracing the dynamic nature of intelligence. Growth comes through analogy, through seeing how things connect rather than only seeing how they might be different. Certainly, the epiphany stories in this book indicate that many of the moments when things suddenly come clear happen from seeing new connections between events, ideas, and circumstances.

The third feature of intelligence is that it is entirely distinctive. Every person's intelligence is as unique as a fingerprint. There might be seven, ten, or a hundred different forms of intelligence, but each of us uses these forms in different ways. My profile of abilities involves a different combination of dominant and dormant intelligences than yours does. The person down the street has another profile entirely. Twins use their intelligences differently from one another, as do people on opposite sides of the globe.

This brings us back to the question I asked earlier: How are you intelligent? Knowing that intelligence is diverse, dynamic, and distinctive allows you to address that question in new ways. This is one of the core components of the Element. For when you explode your preconceived ideas about intelligence, you can begin to see your own intelligence in new ways. No person is a single intellectual score on a linear scale. And no two people with the same scores will do the same things, share all of the same passions, or accomplish the same amount with their lives. Discovering the Element is all about allowing yourself access to all of the ways in which you experience the world, and discovering where your own true strengths lie.

Just don't take them for granted.

CHAPTER THREE

Beyond Imagining

FAITH RINGGOLD is an acclaimed artist, best known for her painted story quilts. She has exhibited in major museums all over the world, and her work is in the permanent collections of the Guggenheim Museum, the Metropolitan Museum of Art, and the Museum of Modern Art. In addition, she is an award-winning writer, having received the Caldecott Honor for her first book, *Tar Beach*. She has also composed and recorded songs.

Faith's life brims with creativity. Interestingly, though, she found herself on this path when illness kept her out of school. She got asthma when she was two, and because of this, had a late start to formal education. During our interview, she told me that she felt that being out of school with asthma made a positive difference in her development "because I was not around for some of the indoctrinations, you know? I was not around to be really formed in the way that I think a lot of kids are formed in a regimented society, which a school is and I guess it has to be in a sense. Because when you have a lot of people in one space, you have to move them around in a certain way to make it work. I just did not ever get hooked into the regimentation. I missed all of kindergarten and the first grade. By the second grade, I was going. But every year, I would be absent for at least, I don't know, maybe two or three weeks with asthma. And I absolutely did not mind missing those classes."

Her mother worked hard with her to help her keep pace with what she was missing in school. And when they weren't studying, they were able to explore the wider world of the arts that existed all around Harlem in the 1930s.

"My mother took me to see all the great acts of that time. Duke Ellington, Billie Holiday, Billy Eckstine—all these old singers and bandleaders and all those people who were so wonderful. And so these people were the ones who I thought of as being highly creative. It was so obvious that they were making this art out of their own bodies. We all lived in the same neighborhood. You just ran into them—here they are, you know? I was deeply inspired by their art and by their willingness to give of themselves to the public and to their audience. It made me understand about the communication aspect of being an artist.

"I was never forced to be like the other kids. I did not dress like them. I did not look like them. And in my family, it was not expected that I should be like that. So, it came quite natural to me to do something that was considered a bit odd. My mother was a fashion designer. She was an artist herself, although she would never have said she was an artist. She helped me a lot, but she was very keen on the fact that she did not know whether art would be a good lifetime endeavor."

When Faith at last began going to school full-time, she found encouragement and excitement in her art classes.

"We had art in elementary school right straight through. An excellent experience. Excellent. I distinctly recall my teachers getting excited about some of the things that I had done and me kind of wondering, Why do they think this is so good?—but I never said anything. In junior high school, the teacher did a project with us in which she wanted us to try to see it without looking. We were supposed to paint these flowers in that way. I said, 'Oh my god, I do not want her to see this, because this is really awful.' And she held it up and said, 'Now, this is really wonderful. Look at this.'

"Now I know why she liked it. It was free and it was the same kind of thing that I like when I see children do art. It is expressive; it is wonderful. This is the kind of magic that children have. Children do not see anything so strange and different about art. They accept it; they understand it; they love it. They walk into a museum and they are looking all around, they do not feel threatened. Whereas adults do. They think there are some messages there they do not get, that they are supposed to have something to say or do in relation to these works of art. The children can just accept it because somehow or other they are born that way. And they stay that way until they begin to start picking themselves apart. Now, maybe it is because we start picking them apart. I try not to do that, but the world is going to pick them apart and, you know, judge them this way and that—this does not look like a tree, or this does not look like a man. When children are little, they are not paying attention to that. They are just—they are just unfolding right before your eyes. 'This is my mommy and this is my daddy and we went to the house and cut down the tree and this and that and the other,' and they tell you a whole story about it, and they accept it and they think it is wonderful. And I do too. Because they are completely unrepressed where these things are concerned."

"I think children have that same natural ability in music. Their little voices are like little bells that they are ringing. I went to a school where I did a forty-minute session with each of the grades, starting with the prekindergarten, going all the way up to the sixth grade. I did this art session with them in which they would read from a book and then I would teach them. I would show them some of my slides and then I would teach them how to sing my song 'Anyone Can Fly.' They just picked that up, whether they were little prekindergarten, kindergarten, first grade, second grade, third grade, fourth grade. By the fifth grade, you are running into trouble. Their little voices are no longer like bells; they are feeling ashamed of themselves, you know, and some of them who can still sing will not."

Fortunately, Faith never felt stifled in this way. She loved exploring her creativity from an early age, and she managed to keep that spark alive into adulthood.

"I think the minute that I started studying art in college in 1948 I knew I wanted to be an artist. I did not know which road I would take, how it would happen, or how I could be that, but I knew that was my goal. My dream was to be an artist, one who makes pictures for a lifetime, as a way of life. Every day of your life you can create something wonderful, so every day is going to be the same kind of wonderful day that every other day is—a day in which you discover something new because as you are painting or creating whatever it is you are creating, you are finding new ways in doing it."

The Promise of Creativity

I mentioned that I like to ask audiences how intelligent they feel they are. I usually ask these same people how they rate their creativity. As with intelligence, I use a 1 to 10 scale, with 10 at the top. And, as with intelligence, most people rate themselves somewhere in the middle. Out of perhaps a thousand people, fewer than twenty give themselves 10 for creativity. A few more will put their hands up for 9 and 8. On the other end, a handful always puts themselves at 2 or 1. I think that people are mostly wrong in these assessments, just as they are about their intelligence.

But the real point of this exercise reveals itself when I ask how many people gave themselves different marks for intelligence and for creativity. Typically, between two-thirds and three-quarters of the audience raise their hands at this point. Why is this? I think it is because most people believe that intelligence and creativity are entirely different things—that we can be very intelligent and not very creative or very creative and not very intelligent.

For me, this identifies a fundamental problem. A lot of my work with organizations is about showing that intelligence and creativity are blood relatives. I firmly believe that you can't be creative without acting intelligently. Similarly, the highest form of intelligence is thinking creatively. In seeking the Element, it is essential to understand the real nature of creativity and to have a clear understanding of how it relates to intelligence.

In my experience, most people have a narrow view of intelligence, tending to think of it mainly in terms of academic ability. This is why so many people who are smart in other ways end up thinking that they're not smart at all. There are myths surrounding creativity as well.

One myth is that only special people are creative. This is not true. Everyone is born with tremendous capacities for creativity. The trick is to develop these capacities. Creativity is very much like literacy. We take it for granted that nearly everybody can learn to read and write. If a person can't read or write, you don't assume that this person is incapable of it, just that he or she hasn't learned how to do it. The same is true of creativity. When people say they're not creative, it's often because they don't know what's involved or how creativity works in practice.

Another myth is that creativity is about special activities. It's about "creative domains" like the arts, design, or advertising. These often do involve a high level of creativity. But so can science, math, engineering, running a business, being an athlete, or getting in or out of a relationship. The fact is you can be creative at anything at all—anything that involves your intelligence.

The third myth is that people are either creative or they're not. This myth suggests that creativity, like IQ, is an allegedly fixed trait, like eye color, and that you can't do much about it. In truth, it's entirely possible to become more creative in your work and in your life. The first critical step is for you to understand the intimate relationship between creativity and intelligence. This is one of the surest paths to finding the Element, and it involves stepping back to examine a fundamental feature of all human intelligence—our unique powers of imagination.

It's All in Your Imagination

As we discussed in the last chapter, we tend to underestimate the range of our senses and our intelligence. We do the same with our imaginations. In fact, while we largely take our senses for granted, we tend to take our imaginations for granted completely. We'll even criticize people's perceptions by telling them that they have "overactive imaginations" or that what they believe is "all in their imagination." People will pride themselves on being "down to earth," "realistic," and "no-nonsense," and deride those who "have their heads in the clouds." And yet, far more than any other power, imagination is what sets human beings apart from every other species on earth.

Imagination underpins every uniquely human achievement. Imagination led us from caves to cities, from bone clubs to golf clubs, from carrion to cuisine, and from superstition to science. The relationship between imagination and "reality" is both complicated and profound. And this relationship serves a very significant role in the search for the Element.

If you focus on your actual, physical surroundings, you generally assume, I'm sure, that there's a good fit between what you perceive and what's actually there. This is why we can drive cars on busy roads, get what we're looking for in shops, and wake up with the right person. We know that in some circumstances— through illness, delirium, or excessive use of controlled substances, for instance—even that assumption can be mistaken, but let's keep moving forward for now.

We know too that we can routinely step outside of our immediate sensory environment and conjure mental images of other places and other times. If I ask you to think of your best friends at school, your favorite food, or your most annoying acquaintance, you can do that without having any of those things directly in front of you. This process of seeing "in our mind's eye" is the essential act of imagination. So my initial definition of imagination is "the power to bring to mind things that are not present to our senses."

Your response to this might very well be, "Duh." That would be an appropriate response, but it helps make a critical point— that perhaps more than any other capacity, imagination is the one we take for granted most. This is unfortunate because imagination is vitally important to our lives. Through imagination, we can visit the past, contemplate the present, and anticipate the future. We can also do something else of profound and unique significance.

We can create.

Through imagination, we not only bring to mind things that we have experienced but things that we have never experienced. We can conjecture, we can hypothesize, we can speculate, and we can suppose. In a word, we can be *imaginative.* As soon as we have the power to release our minds from the immediate here and now, in a sense we are free. We are free to revisit the past, free to reframe the present, and free to anticipate a whole range of possible futures. Imagination is the foundation of everything that is uniquely and distinctively human. It is the basis of language, the arts, the sciences, systems of philosophy, and all the vast intricacies of human culture. I can illustrate this power with an example of cosmic proportions.

Does Size Matter?

What's the purpose of life? This is another good question. It doesn't seem to bother other species much, but it bothers human beings quite a bit. The British philosopher Bertrand Russell presented this question simply and brilliantly. It's in three parts, and it's worth reading twice: "Is man what he seems to the astronomer, a tiny lump of impure carbon and water crawling impotently on a small and unimportant planet? Or is he what he appears to Hamlet? Is he perhaps both at once?"

You'll have to forgive the male language here. Russell wrote this a long time ago, when he didn't know people might frown upon it later. Russell's three questions capture some of the core puzzles of Western—though not necessarily Eastern—philosophy. Is life essentially accidental and meaningless, or is it as profound and mysterious as Shakespeare's great tragic hero believed it to be? I'll come back to Hamlet in a minute. Let's look first at this idea of our inhabiting a small and unimportant planet.

For years now, the Hubble telescope has been beaming back to Earth thousands of dazzling images of distant galaxies, white dwarfs, black holes, nebulas, and pulsars. We've all seen spectacular documentaries about the facts and fantasies of space travel, all framed with ungraspable statistics about billions of light-years and infinite distances. Most of us now get the point that the universe is gigantic. We also get the point that Earth is relatively small.

But how small?

It's very hard to get a clear sense of this because with planets, as with everything else, size is relative. Given the immense distances between us and the other heavenly bodies, it's difficult to have much of a basis for comparison.

I was delighted to come across a great set of images that helped me get a sense of the relative size of the Earth. Someone had the bright idea of taking distance out of the equation altogether by plucking the Earth and some other planets out of the cosmos and laying them side by side on the floor like a team photograph. In this way, we get some sense of the scale of things, and it's frankly surprising. Here's the first image:

This is Earth, sitting down with some of our immediate neighbors. We're looking rather good here, especially in relation to Mars and Mercury. I think too that we're less worried than ever about being invaded by Martian hordes. Bring it on, I'd say! Pluto, by the way, is no longer a planet and we can see why in this picture. What were we thinking of in the first place? It's barely a boulder.

Let's pull back a bit now. Suddenly, the scenario seems a bit less encouraging. Here's Earth with some of our larger partners in the solar system.

Earth's looking a little less impressive now compared with Uranus and Neptune, and certainly in the company of Saturn and Jupiter. Pluto at this point has become a cosmic embarrassment. Still, we're holding our own—I mean, at least we're visible.

We already know there's more to the story, though. For instance, we know that Earth is small when compared with the Sun. But how small? Here's how:

On this scale, Earth is the size of a grape seed, and we should stop talking about Pluto now. But as big as it is, the Sun is far from the cosmic giant it seems here.

If we pull back a little more, the picture changes dramatically, even for sun worshippers.

If we pull back a little more, the picture changes dramatically, even for sun worshippers.

Earth has simply disappeared on this scale, and the Sun itself is barely a garbanzo bean. But even now, we're still comparing ourselves to objects that are comparatively small and close in cosmic terms.

Keep your eye on Arcturus as we pull back just once more to take in Betelgeuse and Antares.

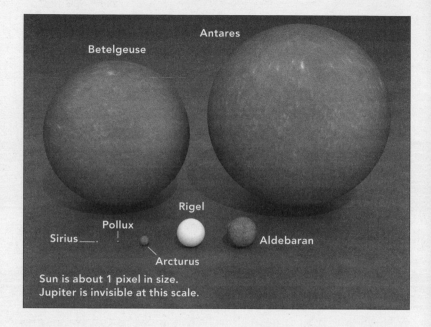

On this scale, the Sun is a grain of sand and Arcturus is a kumquat. Antares, by the way, is the fifteenth-brightest star in the sky. It is more than a thousand light-years away. Astronomers would say it is *only* a thousand light-years away. A light-year, you'll recall, is the distance that a beam of light travels in a year. That's far. So a thousand light-years sounds impressive, especially if you're Pluto. But it's actually not that much in galactic terms. Compare it with this final image, which is from the Hubble telescope.

This is an image of the Magellanic Cloud, one of the closest galaxies to our Milky Way, a near neighbor in the scheme of things. Scientists estimate the Magellanic Cloud to be about 170,000 light-years across. It's almost impossible to picture the size of Earth on this scale. It's pitifully, unimaginably, undetectably small.

And yet . . .

We can take away some encouraging things from this. One is a bit of perspective. I mean, really, whatever you woke up worrying about this morning, get over it. How important in the greater scheme of things can it possibly be? Make your peace and move on.

The second is this. At first glance, these images do indeed suggest that the answer to Russell's first question might be yes. We certainly do seem to be clinging to the face of an extraordinarily small and unimportant planet. But that's not really the end of the story. We may well be small and insignificant. However, uniquely among all known species on Earth—or anywhere else, to our knowledge—we are able to do something remarkable. We can conceive of our insignificance.

Using the power of imagination, someone made the images I just showed you. Using this same power, I'm able to write about them and have them published, and you're able to understand them. The fact, too, is that as a species we produced the Hamlet of which Russell speaks—as well as Mozart's Mass in C, the Blue Mosque, the Sistine Chapel, the Renaissance, Las Vegas, the Silk Road, the poetry of Yeats, the plays of Chekhov, the blues, rock and roll, hip-hop, the theory of relativity, quantum mechanics, industrialism, *The Simpsons*, digital technology, the Hubble telescope, and the whole dazzling cornucopia of human achievements and aspirations.

I don't mean to say that no other species on Earth has any form of imaginative ability. But certainly none comes close to showing the complex abilities that flow from the human imagination. Other species communicate, but they don't have laptops. They sing, but they don't produce musicals. They can be agile, but they didn't come up with Cirque du Soleil. They can look worried, but they don't publish theories on the meaning of life and spend their evenings drinking Jack Daniel's and listening to

Miles Davis. And they don't meet at water holes, poring over images from the Hubble telescope and trying to figure out what those might mean for themselves and all other hyenas.

What accounts for these yawning differences in how humans and other species on our small planet think and behave? My general answer is imagination. But this is really about the much more sophisticated evolution of the human brain and the highly dynamic ways in which it can work. The dynamics of human intelligence account for the phenomenal creativity of the human mind. And our capacity for creativity allows us to rethink our lives and our circumstances—and to find our way to the Element.

The Power of Creativity

Imagination is not the same as creativity. Creativity takes the process of imagination to another level. My definition of creativity is "the process of having original ideas that have value." Imagination can be entirely internal. You could be imaginative all day long without anyone noticing. But you would never say that someone was creative if that person never did anything. To be creative you actually have to do something. It involves putting your imagination to work to make something new, to come up with new solutions to problems, even to think of new problems or questions.

You can think of creativity as applied imagination.

You can be creative at anything at all—anything that involves using your intelligence. It can be in music, in dance, in theater, in math, science, business, in your relationships with other people. It is because human intelligence is so wonderfully diverse that people are creative in so many extraordinary ways. Let me give you two very different examples.

In 1988, former Beatle George Harrison had a solo album

coming out. The album featured a song called "This is Love" that both Harrison and his record company felt could be a big hit. A common practice in those pre-download days was for the artist to accompany a single release with a B-side—a song that didn't appear on the album the single appeared on—as added value for consumers. The only problem in this case was that Harrison didn't have a recording to use as a B-side. However, Bob Dylan, Roy Orbison, Tom Petty, and Jeff Lynne were all spending time with him in the Los Angeles area, where Harrison was living at the time.

As Harrison came up with the bones of the song he wanted to record, he realized that Lynne was already working with Orbison. Harrison soon asked Dylan and Petty to join them and to sing along on the song's chorus. In a casual setting with the minimal pressure associated with recording a B-side, these five rock legends generated "Handle with Care," one of the most memorable songs of Harrison's post-Beatle career.

When Harrison played the song a few days later for Mo Ostin, chairman of Warner Brothers Records, and Lenny Waronker, head of A&R, the two were stunned. Not only was the song much too good to serve as a lowly B-side, but the collaboration generated a sound at once easygoing and brilliant that begged for a grander platform. Ostin and Waronker wondered to Harrison if the team that created "Handle with Care" could generate an entire album. Harrison found the idea intriguing and took it back to his friends.

Some logistical items needed addressing. Dylan was going out on a long tour in two weeks, and getting everyone in one place after that was going to be a problem. The five decided to squeeze whatever they could into the time they had before Dylan's departure. Using a friend's studio, they laid down the tracks for the entire album. They didn't have months to dedicate to polishing the songwriting, doing dozens of alternate takes, or worrying over a guitar part. Instead, they relied on something much more innate—the creative spark generated by five distinctive musical voices joining together.

They all collaborated on songs. Each donated vocal harmonies, guitar lines, and arrangements. They fed off each other, goaded each other, and, most importantly, had a great time. The result was a recording that was both casual—the songs seem invented on the spot—and unmistakably classic. In fitting with the relaxed nature of the project, the five decided to downplay their stardom and to call their makeshift band the Traveling Wilburys. The album they recorded went on to sell five million copies and spawn multiple hit singles, including "Handle with Care." *Rolling Stone* magazine named *The Traveling Wilburys* one of the "100 Best Albums of All Time." I think that this is a great example of the creative process at work.

Here's another one that seems completely different.

In the early 1960s, an unknown student at Cornell University threw a plate into the air in the university restaurant. We don't know what happened after that to the student or to the plate. The student may have caught the plate with a smile, or it may have shattered on the floor. Either way, this would not have been an extraordinary event but for the fact that someone extraordinary happened to be watching it.

Richard Feynman was an American physicist, and one of the undisputed geniuses of the twentieth century. He was famous for his groundbreaking work in several fields including quantum electrodynamics and nanotechnology. He was also one of the most colorful and admired scientists of his generation, a juggler, a painter, a prankster, and an exuberant jazz musician with a particular passion for playing the bongos. In 1965, he won the Nobel Prize in Physics. He says this was partly because of the flying plate.

"That afternoon while I was eating lunch, some kid threw up a plate in the cafeteria," Feynman said. "There was a blue medallion on the plate, the Cornell sign, and as he threw up the plate and it came down, the blue thing went around and it seemed to me that the blue thing went around faster than the wobble, and I wondered what the relation was between the two. I was just playing, no importance at all, but I played around with the equations of motion of rotating things, and I found out that if the wobble is small the blue thing goes around twice as fast as the wobble goes round."

Feynman jotted some thoughts down on his napkin, and after lunch, he got on with his day at the university. Some time later, he looked again at the napkin and carried on playing with the ideas he'd sketched out on it.

"I started to play with this rotation, and the rotation led me to a similar problem of the rotation of the spin of an electron according to Dirac's equation, and that just led me back into quantum electrodynamics, which was the problem I had been working on. I kept continuing now to play with it in the relaxed fashion I had originally done and it was just like taking the cork out of a bottle—everything just poured out, and in very short order I worked the things out for which I later won the Nobel Prize."

Apart from the fact that they both spin around, what do making records and understanding electrons have in common that can help us understand the nature of creativity? As it happens, quite a lot.

Creative Dynamics

Creativity is the strongest example of the dynamic nature of intelligence, and it can call on all areas of our minds and being.

Let me begin with a rough distinction. I said earlier that many people think they're not creative because they don't know what's involved. This is true in two different ways. The first is that there are some general skills and techniques of creative thinking that everyone can learn and can apply to nearly any situation. These techniques can help in generating new ideas, in sorting out the useful ones from the less useful ones, and in removing blocks to new thinking, especially in groups. I think of these as the skills of general creativity, and I'm going to say more about them in the chapter on education. What I want to discuss in this chapter is personal creativity, which in some ways is very different.

Faith Ringgold, the Traveling Wilburys, Richard Feynman, and many of the other people in this book are all highly creative people in their own unique ways. They work in different domains, and individual passions and aptitudes drive them. They have found the work they love to do, and discovered a special talent for doing it. They are in their Element, and this drives their personal creativity. Having some understanding of how creativity works in general can be instructive here.

Creativity is a step beyond imagination because it requires that you actually do something rather than lie around thinking about it. It's a very practical process of trying to make something original. It may be a song, a theory, a dress, a short story, a boat, or a new sauce for your spaghetti. Regardless, some common features pertain.

The first is that it is a process. New ideas do sometimes come to people fully formed and without the need for much further work. Usually, though, the creative process begins with an inkling—like Feynman watching the wobble of the plate or George Harrison's first idea for a song—which requires further development. This is a journey that can have many different phases and unexpected turns; it can draw on different sorts of skills and knowledge and end up somewhere entirely unpredicted at the outset. Richard

Feynman eventually won the Nobel Prize in Physics, but they didn't give it to him for the napkin he'd scribbled on over lunch.

Creativity involves several different processes that wind through each other. The first is generating new ideas, imagining different possibilities, considering alternative options. This might involve playing with some notes on an instrument, making some quick sketches, jotting down some thoughts, or moving objects or yourself around in a space. The creative process also involves developing these ideas by judging which work best or feel right. Both of these processes of generating and evaluating ideas are necessary whether you're writing a song, painting a picture, developing a mathematical theory, taking photographs for a project, writing a book, or designing clothes. These processes don't come in a predictable sequence. Instead, they interact with each other. For example, a creative effort might involve a great deal of idea generation while holding back on the evaluation at the start. But overall, creative work is a delicate balance between generating ideas and sifting and refining them.

Because it's about making things, creative work always involves using media of some sort to develop ideas. The medium can be anything at all. The Wilburys used voices and guitars. Richard Feynman used mathematics. Faith Ringgold's media were paints and fabrics (and sometimes words and music).

Creative work also often involves tapping into various talents at your disposal to make something original. Sir Ridley Scott is an award-winning director with such blockbuster films as *Gladiator*, *Blade Runner*, *Alien*, and *Thelma and Louise* to his credit. His films have a look distinct from other film directors. The source of this look is his training as an artist.

"Because of my background in fine art," he told me, "I have very specific ideas about making films. I've always been told I have this eye. I've never thought about what it is, but I'm usually accused of being too pretty, or too beautiful, or too this, or too that. I've gradually realized that this is an advantage. My first film, *The Duellists*, was criticized for being too beautiful. One critic complained about 'the overuse of filters.' Actually, there were no filters used. The 'filters' were fifty-nine days of pissing rain. I think what he was taken by was how I look at the French landscape. Probably the best photographers of the Napoleonic period would be painters. So I looked at the Russian painters of Napoleon going to the front on that disastrous journey to Russia. A lot of great nineteenth-century views on that are frankly just photographic. I would take everything from those and apply that to the film."

People who work creatively usually have something in common: they love the media they work with.

Musicians love the sounds they make, natural writers love words, dancers love movement, mathematicians love numbers, entrepreneurs love making deals, great teachers love teaching. This is why people who fundamentally love what they do don't think of it as work in the ordinary sense of the word. They do it because they want to and because when they do, they are in their Element.

This is why Feynman talks about working on the equations of motion "just for the fun of it." It's why he talks about "playing" with the ideas in "a relaxed fashion." The Wilburys produced some of their best work when they were just trying things out and having a good time together making music. The fun factor isn't essential to creative work—there are many examples of creative pioneers who were hardly a laugh a minute. But sometimes when we're playing around with ideas and laughing, we're most open to new thoughts. In all creative work, there may be frustrations, problems, and dead ends along the way. I know some wonderfully creative people who find parts of the process difficult and deeply exasperating. But there's always profound pleasure at some point, and a deep sense of satisfaction from "getting it right."

Many of the people I talk about in this book think they were lucky to find what they love to do. For some of them, it was love at first sight. That's why they call the recognition of their Element an epiphany. Finding the medium that excites your imagination, that you love to play with and work in, is an important step to freeing your creative energies. History is full of examples of people who didn't discover their real creative abilities until they discovered the media in which they thought best. In my experience, one of the main reasons that so many other people think they're not creative is that they simply haven't found their medium. There are other reasons, which we'll come to, including the idea of luck. But first let's look more closely at why the actual media we use are so important to the creative work we do.

Different media help us to think in different ways. A great friend of mine, the designer Nick Egan, recently gave my wife Terry and me two paintings he'd done for us. A couple of things I'd said in some public lectures had moved Nick in a significant way. The first was, "If you're not prepared to be wrong, you'll never produce anything original." The second was, "Great education depends on great teaching." I think both of these are true, which is why I go around saying them. Nick found himself thinking about these ideas and about how they'd applied to his own life, growing up and then working as an artist in London. He decided to create some paintings about them, and he worked on them nearly full-time for several weeks.

Each of the paintings he did for us features one of those statements and is a kind of visual improvisation on it. They are both powerful images with an almost primal energy. One of them is primarily black, with the words scrawled and scratched into the paint on half of the canvas like graffiti. The other one is largely white, with the words written in a childlike way in dripping black paint across the background. One features a glaring cartoonlike face that's somewhere between a cave painting and child's drawing.

At first glance, the paintings seem rushed and chaotic. But a careful examination of the canvases reveals layers upon layers of other images beneath, carefully built up and partly painted over. This gives the paintings real depth. He also laced each with intricate textures of colors and brushstrokes that become more vibrant as you look at them. All of the complexity in the paintings generates their sense of simplicity and urgent energy.

Although my words inspired them, I couldn't have created these paintings. Nick is a designer and a visual artist. He has a natural aptitude and passion for visual work—sensitivity to line, color, shapes, and textures and to how they can be formed into new, creative ideas. He develops his ideas through paint, chalks, pastels, printmaking, film, digital imaging, and a whole host of other visual media and materials. The materials he uses on any given project affect the ideas he has and how he works on them. You can think of creativity as a conversation between what we're trying to figure out and the media we are using. The paintings that Nick finally gave us were different from how they started out. Their appearance evolved as he worked on them, and what he wanted to express became clearer as the paintings took shape.

Creativity in different media is a striking illustration of the diversity of intelligence and ways of thinking. Richard Feynman had a great visual imagination. But he wasn't trying to paint a picture of electrons; he was trying to develop a scientific theory about how they actually work. To do that, he had to use mathematics. He was thinking about electrons, but he was thinking about them mathematically. Without mathematics, he simply couldn't have thought about them as he did. The Wilburys were thinking about love and relationships, life and death, and the whole damn thing; but they weren't trying to write a psychology textbook. They were thinking about these things through music. They were having musical ideas, and music is what they made.

Understanding the role of the media we use for creative work is important for another reason. To develop our creative abilities, we also need to develop our practical skills in the media we want to use. It's important that we develop these skills in the right way. I know plenty of people who have been turned off math for life because they were never helped to see its creative possibilities—as you already know, I'm one of those people. Teachers always presented math to me as an interminable series of puzzles to which someone else already knew the answers, and the only options were to get it right or wrong. This is not how Richard Feynman thought of math.

Equally, I know many people who spent endless hours as children practicing scales on the piano or guitar and never want to see an instrument again because the whole process was so dull and repetitive. Many people have decided that they were simply no good at math or music when it's possible that their teachers taught them the wrong way or at the wrong time. Maybe they should look again. Maybe I should. . . .

Opening Your Mind

Creative thinking involves much more than the sorts of logical, linear thinking that dominate the Western view of intelligence and especially education. The frontal lobes of the brain are involved in some higher-order thinking skills. The left hemisphere is the area that's most involved in logical and analytical thinking. But creative thinking usually involves much more of the brain than the bits at the front and to the left.

Being creative is about making fresh connections so that we see things in new ways and from different perspectives. In logical, linear thinking, we move from one idea to another through a series of rules and conventions. We allow some moves while rejecting others because they're illogical. If A + B = C, we can figure out what C + B equals. Conventional IQ exams typically test for this type of thinking. The rules of logic or linear thought don't always guide creative thinking. On the contrary.

Creative insights often come in nonlinear ways, through seeing connections and similarities between things that we hadn't noticed before. Creative thinking depends greatly on what's sometimes called divergent or lateral thinking, and especially on thinking in metaphors or seeing analogies. This is what Richard Feynman was doing when he saw a connection between the wobbling plate and the spin of electrons. The idea for George Harrison's song "Handle with Care" came from a label he saw on a packing crate.

I don't mean that creativity is the opposite of logical thinking. The rules of logic allow enormous room for creativity and improvisation within themselves. So do all activities that are bound by rules. Think of all the creativity in chess and in different types of sport, poetry, dance, and music, where there can be very strict rules and conventions. Logic can be very important at different stages in the creative process, according to what sort of work we're doing, particularly when we're evaluating new ideas and how they fit into or challenge existing theories. Even so, creative thinking goes beyond linear and logical thought to involve all areas of our minds and bodies.

It's now widely accepted that the two halves of the brain have different functions. The left hemisphere is involved in logical, sequential reasoning—with verbal language, mathematical thinking, and so on. The right hemisphere is involved in recognition of patterns, of faces, with visual perception, orientation in space, and with movement. However, these compartments of the brain hardly work in isolation from each other. If you look at images of the brain at work, you'll see that it is highly interactive. Like the rest of our bodies, these functions are all related.

Legs have a major role in running, but a leg on its own is frankly rather poor at it. In the same way, many different parts of the brain are involved when we play or listen to music, from the more recently evolved cerebral cortex to the older, so-called reptilian parts of the brain. These have to work in concert with the rest of our body, including the rest of the brain. Of course, we all have strengths and weaknesses in the different functions and capacities of the brain. But like the muscles in our arms and legs, these capacities can grow weaker or stronger depending on how much we exercise them separately and together.

By the way, there's some suggestion in recent research that women's brains may be more interactive than men's brains. The jury is still out on this, but reading about it reminded me of an old question in Western philosophy that professors often give college freshmen to debate. It's about the relationship between our senses and our knowledge of the world. The essence of the question is whether we can know something is true if we don't have direct evidence of it through our senses, and the usual example is this: "If a tree falls in a forest and no one is around to hear it, does it make a sound?" I used to teach some philosophy courses, and the students and I could debate this sort of thing in an earnest way for weeks on end. The answer, I think, is, "Of course it does, don't be so ridiculous." But, you know, I had tenure, so there was really no need to rush this conversation. A recent trip to San Francisco reminded me of these debates. I was wandering through a street market and saw someone wearing a T-shirt that said, "If a man speaks his mind in a forest and no woman hears him, is he still wrong?" Probably.

Whatever gender differences there may be in everyday thinking, creativity is always a dynamic process that may draw on many different ways of thinking at the same time. Dance is a physical, kinesthetic process. Music is a sound-based art form. But many dancers and musicians use mathematics as an integral part of their performances. Scientists and mathematicians often think in visual ways to picture and test their ideas.

Creativity also uses much more than our brains. Playing instruments, creating images, constructing objects, performing a dance, and making things of every sort are also intensely physical processes that depend on feelings, intuition, and skilled coordination of hands and eyes, body and mind. In many instances—in dance, in song, in performance—we do not use external media at all. We ourselves are the medium of our creative work.

Creative work also reaches deep into our intuitive and unconscious minds and into our hearts and feelings. Have you ever forgotten someone's name, or the name of somewhere you've visited? Try as you may, it's often impossible to bring it to mind, and the more you think about it, the more elusive it becomes. Usually, the best thing you can do is stop trying and "put it to the back of your mind." Sometime later, the name will probably show up in your head when you're least expecting it. The reason is that there is far more to our minds than the deliberate processes of conscious thought. Beneath the noisy surface of our minds, there are deep reserves of memory and association, of feelings and perceptions that process and record our life's experiences beyond our conscious awareness. So at times, creativity is a conscious effort. At others, we need to let our ideas ferment for a while and trust the deeper unconscious ruminations of our minds, over which we have less control. Sometimes when we do, the insights we've been searching for will come to us in a rush, like "letting a cork out of a bottle."

Getting It Together

While you can see the dynamic nature of creative thinking in the work of single individuals, it becomes much more obvious when you look at the work of great creative groups like the Traveling Wilburys. The success of the group came about not because they all thought in the same way, but because they were all so different. They had different talents, different interests, and different sounds. But they found a process of working together where their differences stimulated each other to create something they wouldn't have come up with individually. It's in this sense that creativity draws not just from our own personal resources but also from the wider world of other people's ideas and values. This is where the argument for developing our powers of creativity moves up a gear.

Let's go back to Shakespeare's *Hamlet*. In Shakespeare's play *Hamlet*, the prince of Denmark is torn by raging feelings about the death of his father and the treachery of his mother and uncle. Throughout the play, he wrestles with his feelings about life and death, loyalty and betrayal, and his significance in the wider universe. He struggles to know what he should think and feel about the events that are engulfing his spirit. Early in the play, he greets Rosencrantz and Guildenstern, two visitors to the royal Danish court. He welcomes them with these words:

> My excellent good friends! How dost thou, Guildenstern? Ah,
> Rosencrantz! Good lads, how do you both?
> . . . what have you,
> My good friends, deserved at the hands of fortune,
> That she sends you to prison hither?

The question surprises Guildenstern. He asks Hamlet what he means by "prison." Hamlet says, "Denmark's a prison." Rosencrantz laughs and says that if that's true, then the whole world is a prison. Hamlet says it is, and "a goodly one, in which there are many confines, wards and dungeons, Denmark being one of the worst." Rosencrantz says, "We think not so, my lord." Hamlet's reply is profound. "'Tis none to you for there is nothing either good or bad, but thinking makes it so: to me it is a prison."

The power of human creativity is obvious everywhere, in the technologies we use, in the buildings we inhabit, in the clothes we wear, and in the movies we watch. But the reach of creativity is very much deeper. It affects not only what we put in the world, but also what we make of it—not only what we do, but also how we think and feel about it.

Unlike all other species, so far as we can tell, we don't just get on in the world. We spend much of our time talking and thinking about what happens and trying to work out what it all means. We can do this because of the startling power of imagination, which underpins our capacity to think in words and numbers, in images and gestures, and to use all of these to generate theories and artifacts and all the complex ideas and values that make up the many perspectives on human life. We don't just see the world as it is; we interpret it through the particular ideas and beliefs that have shaped our own cultures and our personal outlook. All of these stand between us and our raw experiences in the world, acting as a filter on what we perceive and how we think.

What we think of ourselves and of the world makes us who we are and what we can be. This is what Hamlet means when he says, "There is nothing good or bad, only thinking makes it so." The good news is that we can always try to think differently. If we create our worldview, we can re-create it too by taking a different perspective and reframing our situation. In the sixteenth century, Hamlet said that he thought of Denmark metaphorically as a prison. In the seventeenth century, Richard Lovelace wrote a poem for his love, Althea. Taking the opposite view, Lovelace says that for him an actual prison would be a place of freedom and liberty so long as he could think of Althea. This is how he closes his poem:

> Stone walls do not a prison make,
> Nor iron bars a cage;
> Minds innocent and quiet take
> That for an hermitage;
> If I have freedom in my love
> And in my soul am free,
> Angels alone, that soar above,
> Enjoy such liberty.

In the nineteenth century, William James became one of the founding thinkers of modern psychology. By then, it was becoming more widely understood that our ideas and ways of thinking could imprison or liberate us. James put it this way: "The greatest discovery of my generation is that human beings can alter their lives by altering their attitude of mind. . . . If you change your mind, you can change your life."

This is the real power of creativity and the true promise of being in your Element.

CHAPTER FOUR

In the Zone

Ewa Laurance is the most famous female billiards player on the planet. Known as "the Striking Viking," she has been ranked number 1 in the world, won both the European and U.S. national championships, has appeared on the cover of the *New York Times Magazine*, been featured in *People*, *Sports Illustrated*, *Forbes*, and many other publications, makes regular television appearances, and serves as a commentator on ESPN.

Growing up in Sweden, Ewa discovered the game while trailing after her older brother.

"Me and my best friend, Nina, we were always hanging around, just as close as friends can be. One day, when I was fourteen, the two of us followed my brother and his friend to this bowling alley to play and decided to check it out. We were there for a while and then got really bored. And then we found out that they had gone to something called a poolroom. I had never heard of pool. We followed them up there and I remember, the minute I walked in, I reacted to it right away. I loved the whole thing—this dark room with lights over each table and the clicking of the balls. I just thought it was mesmerizing right off the bat.

"There was this whole society there where everybody knew this thing about billiards and it grabbed me right away. We were intimidated and curious, but just sat and watched everything. When you sit and watch it, or do it yourself, everything disappears. It's easy for that to happen with billiards because each table is a stage. So, everything around it disappeared for me and that's all I saw. I was watching these players who knew exactly what they were doing. I realized that there's more to this than just banging the balls around and hoping something goes in. There was one guy who ran ball, after ball, after ball, and made sixty, seventy, eighty balls in a row and I realized he was moving the white ball around to shoot his next shot. And somehow, it clicked in. It was their knowledge and skill that really amazed me—that chess part of billiards, of playing three, four moves ahead and then having to execute it on top of it."

From that moment of epiphany, Ewa knew that she wanted to dedicate her life to billiards. Fortunately, her parents supported her, allowing her to spend six to ten hours a day playing at a local poolroom, doing her homework in between shots. "People there knew I was serious about the game, so they left me alone. But we also had a lot of fun there. If you find a place where everybody else likes the same thing that you do, it really becomes fun. So these odd characters—because we all had billiards together—we became like a family."

In 1980, at sixteen, Ewa won the Swedish championship. At seventeen, she won the first-ever European Women's Championship. This led to an invitation to go to New York to represent Europe in the World Championship. "That whole summer I practiced. The poolroom didn't open until five in the afternoon, so I would take the bus in the morning up to the part of town where the owner lived, get the key to the poolroom, and then take the bus into town and let myself in. I did that all summer and then played ten, twelve hours a day. Then I went to the tournament in New York. I didn't win, though; I came in seventh. I was disappointed I didn't do better, but at the same time I thought, 'Wow, that's like seventh in the world!'"

Though her parents didn't like her being so far away, Ewa decided to stay in New York to continue her pursuit of the sport, knowing that in the United States, she would have the opportunity to play regularly against the best in the world. In addition to scoring victories, she also became a leading voice for women in billiards. Her talent, her passion, and her stunning good looks made her a media star and helped bring new levels of popularity to the game she loved.

Fame and financial reward accompanied Ewa Laurance on her rise to the top. But for her, the biggest charge continued to be the game itself.

"You're almost unconscious to what's going on around you. It's literally the most peculiar feeling. It's like being in a tunnel but you don't see anything else. You just see what you're doing. Time changes. Somebody could ask you how long you've been doing it and you could have said twenty minutes but it was actually nine hours. I just don't know. I have never had it with anything before or since, even though I am very passionate about a lot of other things. But the feeling of playing billiards is unique for me.

"Part of the beauty that pool offers you is how much you can learn. It's a never-ending deal. Every layout is different, so there's always something to keep you interested. I just love the physics and the geometry of it—learning and understanding the angles and finding out how far you can push to change the angle to get the cue ball where you want it to go. And learning what the limits and possibilities are. Being able to control the cue ball scooting forward two and a half inches instead of three is a pretty amazing feeling. So instead of fighting the elements, you actually figure out a way to work with them.

"I wasn't at all interested or good at geometry or physics at school. For some reason, when I'm playing I see it a lot. I look at the table and I literally see lines and diagrams all over the place. I see 'I'm going to make the 1 here, the 2 over here, the 3's going to go down here, I'm going to have to go three rails around for the 4, the 6 is down here, no problem, I've got 7, 8, 9, I'm out.' I see them all lined up. And then if you hit one ball a little bit incorrectly, all of a sudden a whole new diagram in your head pops up. You need to resolve the problem because you're not where you wanted to be. You were six inches off, so now you have to reformulate the whole thing.

"Geometry at school did not get my attention. Maybe if I'd had a different teacher it would have been different—somebody that just said, 'Ewa, think of it this way,' or, 'Look at it this way and you will get it.' Or they could have taken our whole class to a poolroom and said, 'Check this out!' But it was so boring at school. I couldn't even keep my eyes open in class, you know? But now, when I give lessons to someone, I try to figure out as quickly as I can if they have hand-eye coordination and also, are they just interested in the game or are they interested in the geometry and the physics of it. Are they math-oriented."

Ewa has been playing billiards professionally for nearly thirty years. Yet she still gets the same charge that the sport has always given her. "Even when I do an exhibition, after all these years, I get nervous. People say, 'Well you've done it so many times.' But it doesn't matter; it's about being in that moment."

Playing billiards puts Ewa Laurance in the zone. And being in the zone puts Ewa Laurance face to face with the Element.

The Zone

To be in the zone is to be in the deep heart of the Element. Doing what we love can involve all sorts of activities that are essential to the Element but are not the essence of it—things like studying, organizing, arranging, limbering up, etc. And even when we're doing the thing we love, there can be frustrations, disappointments, and times when it simply doesn't work or come together. But when it does, it transforms our experience of the Element. We become focused and intent. We live in the moment. We become lost in the experience and perform at our peak. Our breathing changes, our minds merge with our bodies, and we feel ourselves drawn effortlessly into the heart of the Element.

Aaron Sorkin is the writer of two Broadway plays, *A Few Good Men* and *The Farnsworth Invention*; three television series, *Sports Night*, *The West Wing*, and *Studio 60 on the Sunset Strip*; and five feature films, *A Few Good Men*, *Malice*, *The American President*, *Charlie Wilson's War*, and the soon-to-be-released *Trial of the Chicago 7*. He's been nominated for thirteen Emmy Awards, eight Golden Globes, and the Academy Award for Best Picture.

"I never set out to be a writer," he told me. "I always saw myself as an actor. I got an acting degree at college. I was so passionate about this that when I was in high school, I'd take the train into New York City when I was broke and wait until the second half of a play when there would be empty seats to sneak into after the intermission. Writing for fun was not something I was ever introduced to. It always seemed like a chore. I had written one sketch for a college party and my teacher, Gerard Moses, had said to me, 'You could do this for a living, you know, if you wanted.' But I hadn't a clue what he was talking about. *Do what?* I thought, and moved on.

"A few months after I left school, a friend of mine was going out of town. He had his grandfather's antique typewriter and asked me to hang onto it for him. At this time I was paying a friend of mine fifty dollars a week to sleep on his floor in a tiny apartment on the Upper East Side of New York. I'd got a job with a children's theater company for a while and some work on a soap. This was in 1984 and I was doing the rounds of auditions.

"This particular weekend all of my friends were out of town.

It was one of those Friday nights in New York where you feel like everyone but you has been invited to a party. I was broke, the TV wasn't working, and all there was to do was muck around with this piece of paper and the typewriter. I sat down at it and wrote from nine o'clock at night until noon the next day. I fell in love with it all.

"I realized that all those years of acting classes and taking the train to the theater was not about acting but about what the play actually was. I'd been a cocky actor—I wasn't ever a wallflower—but writing had been so far removed from my consciousness until that night.

"The first play I wrote was a one-act play called *Hidden in This Picture*, and that was well received and reviewed. Then my sister, who is a lawyer, told me about a case in Guantánamo Bay involving some marines accused of killing a fellow marine. The story intrigued me and I spent the next year and a half writing the stage play for *A Few Good Men*.

"When it was playing on Broadway, I remembered that conversation with Gerard. I rang him up. 'Is this what you meant?' I asked him."

I asked Aaron how he feels when he's writing. "When it's going well," he said, "I feel completely lost in the process. When it's going poorly, I'm desperately looking for the zone. I have flashlights on and I'm desperately looking for it. I wouldn't speak for other writers, but I'm basically an on-and-off switch. When I feel that something I'm writing is going well, everything in my life is good and the things in my life that aren't good are completely manageable. If it's not going well, Miss America could be standing there in a swimsuit handing me a Nobel Prize and I wouldn't be happy about it."

Doing the thing you love to do is no guarantee that you'll be in the zone every time. Sometimes the mood isn't right, the time is wrong, and the ideas just don't flow. Some people develop their own personal rituals for getting to the zone. They don't always work. I asked Aaron if he had techniques of his own. He said he doesn't and he wished that he had. But he does know when to stop pushing.

"When it's not going well, I put it away and try again tomorrow or the next day. One thing I do is drive around in my car with music on. I try to find someplace where I don't have to think about driving too much, like a freeway, where you don't have to stop at red lights or turn or anything.

"What I don't do is watch other people's movies or television shows or read their plays for fear that they're going to be very good and either make me feel worse or simply make me inclined to imitate what they're doing."

At its best, the process of writing for Aaron is completely absorbing. "Writing for me is a very physical activity. I'm playing all the parts, I'm getting up and down from my desk, I'm walking around. When it's going well, in fact, I'll find that I've been doing laps around my house, way out in front of where I type. In other words, I've been writing without writing. Then I have to go back to where I am on the page and make sure I actually type what I just did."

In all likelihood, you've had instances in your life where you've become "lost" in an experience the way Aaron Sorkin did when he finally connected with writing. You begin to do something you love, and the rest of the world slips away. Hours pass, and it feels like minutes. During this time, you have been "in the zone." Those who have embraced the Element find themselves in this place regularly. This is not to suggest that they find every experience of doing the thing they love blissful, but they regularly have optimal experiences while doing these things, and they know they will again.

Different people find the zone in different ways. For some it comes through intense physical activity, through physically demanding sports, through risk, competition, and maybe a sense of danger. For others it may come through activities that seem physically passive, through writing, painting, math, meditation, and other modes of intense contemplation. As I said earlier, we don't only get one Element apiece, nor is there only one road for each of us to the zone. We may have different experiences of it in our lives. However, there are some common features to being in that magical place.

Are We There Yet?

One of the strongest signs of being in the zone is a sense of freedom and of authenticity. When we are doing something that we love and are naturally good at, we are much more likely to feel centered in our true sense of self—to be who we feel we truly are. When we are in our Element, we feel we are doing what we are meant to be doing and being who we're meant to be.

Time also feels very different in the zone. When you're connecting this way with your deep interests and natural energy, time tends to move more quickly, more fluidly. For Ewa Laurance, nine hours can feel like twenty minutes. We know the opposite is true when you have to do things to which you don't feel a strong connection. We've all had experiences where twenty minutes can feel like nine hours. At those times, we're not in the zone. In fact, we're probably zoning out.

For me, this time shift (the good one, not the bad one) happens most often when I'm working with people, and especially when I'm giving presentations. When I am deep in the throes of exploring and presenting ideas with groups, time tends to move more quickly, more fluidly. I can be in a room with ten or twenty people or several thousand, and it's always the same. For the first five or ten minutes, I'm feeling for the energy of the room and trying things out to catch the right wavelength there. Those first minutes can feel slow. But then, when I do make the connection, I slip into a different gear. When I have the pulse of the room with me, I feel a different energy—and I think they do too—which carries us forward at a different pace and in a different space. When that happens, I can look at the clock and see that almost an hour has gone by.

The other feature common among those familiar with this experience is the movement into a kind of "meta-state" where ideas come more quickly, as if you're tapping a source that makes it significantly easier to achieve your task. You develop a facility for the thing you are doing because you've unified your energy with the process and the efforts you are making. So there's a real sense of ideas flowing through you and out of you; that you're in some way channeling these things. You're being an instrument of them rather than being obstructive to them or struggling to reach them. Rock and Roll Hall of Famer Eric Clapton describes it as being "in harmony with time. It's a great feeling."

You can see and experience this shift in all sorts of performances, in acting, in dance, in musical performances, and in sports. You see that people have suddenly entered a different phase. You see them relaxed, you see them loosen up and become instruments of their own expression.

Grand Prix racer Jochen Rindt said simply that when he's racing, "You ignore everything and just concentrate. You forget about the rest of the world and become part of the car and track. It's a very special feeling. You're completely out of this world and completely into it. There's nothing like it."

Aviator Wilbur Wright described it this way: "When you know, after the first few minutes, that the whole mechanism is working perfectly, the sensation is so keenly delightful as to be almost beyond description. More than anything else the sensation is one of perfect peace mingled with an excitement that strains every nerve to the utmost, if you can conceive of such a combination."

Superstar athlete Monica Seles says, "When I am consistently playing my best tennis, I am also consistently in the zone," but notes, "Once you think about being in the zone, you are immediately out of it."

Dr. Mihaly Csikszentmihalyi (it's pronounced "chicks-sent-me-HIGH-ee," if you'd like to try it at home) performed "decades of research on the positive aspects of human experience—joy, creativity, the process of total involvement with life I call flow." In his landmark work *Flow: The Psychology of Optimal Experience*, Dr. Csikszentmihalyi writes of a "state of mind when consciousness is harmoniously ordered, and [people] want to pursue whatever they are doing for its own sake." What Dr. Csikszentmihalyi calls "flow" (and what many others call "being in the zone") "happens when psychic energy—or attention—is invested in realistic goals, and when skills match the opportunities for action. The pursuit of a goal brings order in awareness because a person must concentrate attention on the task at hand and momentarily forget everything else."

Dr. Csikszentmihalyi speaks of the "elements of enjoyment," the components that comprise an optimal experience. These include facing a challenge that requires a skill one possesses, complete absorption in an activity, clear goals and feedback, concentration on the task at hand that allows one to forget everything else, the loss of self-consciousness, and the sense that time "transforms" during the experience. "The key element of an optimal experience," he says in *Flow*, "is that it is an end in itself. Even if initially undertaken for other reasons, the activity that consumes us becomes intrinsically rewarding."

This is a crucial point to grasp. Being in the Element and especially being in the zone doesn't take energy away from you; it gives it to you. I used to watch politicians fighting elections or trying to stay in office and wonder how they kept going. You see them traveling all over the world, under constant pressure to perform, making critical decisions with every appearance and living irregular hours in a constant spotlight of attention. I wondered how they didn't fall over from sheer exhaustion. The fact is, though, that they love most of it, or they wouldn't do it. The very thing that would wear me out is fueling them up.

Activities we love fill us with energy even when we are physically exhausted. Activities we don't like can drain us in minutes, even if we approach them at our physical peak of fitness. This is one of the keys to the Element, and one of the primary reasons why finding the Element is vital for every person. When people place themselves in situations that lead to their being in the zone, they tap into a primal source of energy. They are literally more alive because of it.

It is as though being in the zone plugs you into a kind of power pack—for the time you are there, you receive more energy than you expend. Energy drives all of our lives. This isn't a simple matter of physical energy we think we have or don't have but of our mental or psychic energy. Mental energy is not a fixed substance. It rises and falls with our passion and commitment to what we are doing at the time. The key difference is in our attitude, and our sense of resonance with an activity. As the song says, "I could have danced all night."

Being in your Element, having that experience of flow, is empowering because it's a way of unifying our energies. It's a way of feeling deeply connected with our own sense of identity and it curiously comes about through a sense of relaxing, of feeling perfectly natural to be doing what you're doing. It's a profound sense of being in your skin, of connecting to your own internal pulse or energy.

These peak experiences are associated with physiological changes in the body—there may be a release of endorphins in the brain and of adrenaline through the body. There may be an increase in alpha wave activity and changes in our metabolic rates and in the patterns of our breathing and heartbeats. The specific nature of these physiological changes depends on the sorts of activities that have brought us to the zone and on what we're doing to keep ourselves there.

However we get there, being in the zone is a powerful and transformative experience. So powerful that it can be addictive, but an addiction that is healthy for you in so many ways.

Reaching Out

When we connect with our own energy, we're more open to the energy of other people. The more alive we feel, the more we can contribute to the lives of others.

Hip-hop poet Black Ice learned at a very young age that his words could bring out emotions in himself and others. "My mom used to make me write about everything," he told an interviewer. "When I got in trouble, when I was happy or even when I was scared. I was a giddy little kid. When I started liking little girls, I used to write letters for my friends. Mine were better than the 'circle yes, no, maybe so.' I came upon spoken word as an adult. I went to a poetry spot, looking to meet women. It was 'open mic' night and when this cat messed up, the audience gave him lots of love and support. I was blown away. Being the aggressive person that I am, it surprised me to see what I would talk about everyday in the barbershop in spoken word form at the club. I was able to release what was on my chest and people would understand what I was saying."

Black Ice, born Lamar Manson, moved from those early performances to increasingly bigger stages. He appeared for five consecutive seasons on HBO's *Def Poetry Jam*, was a lead cast member in the Tony Award–winning *Def Poetry on Broadway*, released his first album on a major label, and appeared in front of millions at the Live 8 concert. His message is life-affirming and motivating, speaking of the importance of family and the power of youth. To back up his words, he started the Hoodwatch Movement Organization to help inner-city kids stay on the right track and understand the extent of their potential. Critics laud his work and audiences respond passionately, and when you see him on-stage, you can sense that he is very much in the zone.

For Black Ice, though, this entry into the zone comes from a sense of mission. "My life has been so meaningful I have to write something that touches folks," he said in another interview. "I have a legacy to uphold. I grew up around great men. My father, my uncles, and my grandfather are my heroes and just in that alone, there are some things I could never say. I could never look my father in his face knowing I have something that's playing on the radio that's absolutely asinine.

"My voice is my gift," Black Ice says. "It's pointless if I'm not going to say anything. It's mad important. I can see in society now, how important it is. Sometimes I'm discouraged, but I definitely know what I can contribute. We are who we are, but I want to get at the kids and stay in the seven- and eight-year-old's ears. Telling them, 'you're going to be something . . . there is no other compromise, there is no if or you might; you are going to be something.'"

This is another secret of being in the zone—that when you are inspired, your work can be inspirational to others. Being in the zone taps into your most natural self. And when you are in that place, you can contribute at a much higher level.

One of the ideas we've already discussed—and which we will come back to again (no point using a good idea only once)—is that intelligence is distinct for every individual. This is an especially important point to recognize when exploring the concept of being in the zone. Being in the zone is about using your particular kind of intelligence in an optimal way. This is what Ewa Laurance touches on when she talks about pool and geometry. It's what Monica Seles connects with when her physical intelligence and her mental acuity become one, what Black Ice conjures when he weaves his words born of both careful observation and a refined ear for rhythm.

Being Yourself

When people are in the zone, they align naturally with a way of thinking that works best for them. I believe this is the reason that time seems to take on a new dimension when you are in the zone. It comes from a level of effortlessness that allows for such full immersion that you simply don't "feel" time the same way. This effortlessness has a direct relationship to thinking styles. When people use a thinking style completely natural to them, everything comes more easily.

It's obvious that different people think about the same things in different ways. I saw a great example of this a few years ago with my daughter. Kate is very visual in her approach to the world. She's extremely bright, articulate, and well read, but she loses interest quickly during lectures (of all types, not simply the ones involving the need for her to clean her room). Not long after we moved to Los Angeles from England, her history teacher began a

section on the Civil War. Not being American, Kate knew little
about this period in American history, and she got little out of her
teacher's recitation of dates and events. This approach—filling
students' heads with bullet points—had little impact on her. With
a test coming up on the subject, though, she couldn't simply ignore the topic.

Knowing that Kate had a very strong visual intelligence, I suggested that she consider creating a mind map. Mind mapping, a
technique created by Tony Buzan, allows a person to create a visual representation of a concept or piece of information. The primary concept sits at the center of the map, and lines, arrows, and
colors connect other ideas to that concept. I had the feeling that,
as someone who tends to think visually, Kate would benefit from
looking at the Civil War from this perspective.

A few days later, Kate and I went out to lunch, and I asked her
if she'd had a chance to try out the mind map. As it turned out,
she'd done much more than try it. Through this technique, she'd
created such a strong visual representation of the Civil War in her
mind that she spent the next forty minutes telling me about the
major events and the consequences of those events. By looking at
it from this new perspective—one that made use of one of the
primary ways in which she thinks—Kate was able to understand
the war in a way that bullet points never would have provided.
Because she'd produced a mind map, she was seeing the images in
her mind clearly, as if she had photographed them.

Getting Out of the Box

There have been various attempts to categorize thinking styles,
and even whole personality types, so that we can understand and
organize people more effectively. These categories can be more or
less helpful, as long as we remember that they are just a way of

thinking about things and not the things themselves. These systems of personality types are often speculative and not very reliable because our personalities often refuse to sit still and tend to flutter restlessly between whatever boxes the testers devise.

Anyone who has ever taken a Myers-Briggs test knows about the various box-placing tools out there. The Myers-Briggs Type Indicator (MBTI) is something that human resource departments seem to enjoy using to "type" people. More than two and a half million people take the MBTI annually, and many of the companies in the Fortune 100 use it. It's essentially a personality quiz, though more sophisticated than what you might find in the pages of a pop magazine. People answer a series of questions in four basic categories (energy attitude, perception, judgment, and orientation to life events), and their answers indicate whether they are more one thing or another in each of these categories (for example, more extroverted or introverted). From the four categories and the two places in which people fall in these categories, the test identifies sixteen personality types. The underlying message of the test is that you and each of the other six billion people on the planet fit into one of these sixteen boxes.

There are several problems with this. One is that neither Ms. Briggs nor her daughter, Ms. Myers, had any qualifications in the field of psychometric testing when they designed the test. Another is that test takers often don't settle neatly into any of the categories when they take the MBTI. They tend to be just a little more to one side of the line or the other (a little more extroverted than introverted, for example), rather than being clearly one thing or the other. Most telling, though, is that many people who repeat the test end up in a different box when they do so. It's true in at least half of the cases, according to some studies. This suggests either that a huge percentage of the population has serious personality disorder problems, or that the test might not be such a reliable indicator of "type" after all.

My guess is that sixteen personality types might be a bit of an underestimate. My personal estimate would be closer to six billion (though I'll need to revise that estimate in future editions of this book, because the population keeps growing).

Another test is the Hermann Brain Dominance Instrument. I feel a bit more relaxed about this one, because it talks about cognitive preferences in terms that I believe most people would find acceptable. Like the MBTI, the Hermann Brain Dominance Instrument (HBDI) is an assessment tool that uses participants' answers to a series of questions. It doesn't seek to put people in a box. Instead, it tries to show people which of four brain quadrants they tend to use more often.

The A quadrant (cerebral left hemisphere) relates to analytic thinking (collecting data, understanding how things work, and so on). The B quadrant (limbic left hemisphere) relates to implementation thinking (organizing and following directions, for example). The C quadrant (limbic right hemisphere) relates to social thinking (expressing ideas, seeking personal meaning). The D quadrant (cerebral right hemisphere) relates to future thinking (looking at the big picture, thinking in metaphors).

The HBDI acknowledges that everyone is capable of using each of these thinking styles, but tries to indicate which of these styles is dominant in any individual. The function of this seems to be that people are more likely to be effective at work, at play, at any pursuit, if they understand how they approach each of these tasks. Though I'm suspicious of typing people categorically, and I still think four modes may be too few, this seems to me to be a more open approach than Myers-Briggs.

The risk in saying that there is a set number of personality types, a set number of dominant ways of thinking, is that it closes doors rather than opening them. To make the Element available to everyone, we need to acknowledge that each person's intelligence is distinct from the intelligence of every other person on the planet, that everyone has a unique way of getting in the zone, and a unique way of finding the Element.

Do the Math

At the age of two, Terence Tao taught himself to read by watching *Sesame Street*, and he tried to teach other kids to count using number blocks. Within the year, he was doing double-digit mathematical equations. Before his ninth birthday, he took the SAT-M (a math-specific version of the SAT given primarily to college candidates) and scored in the ninety-ninth percentile. He received his Ph.D. at age twenty. And when he was thirty, he won a Fields Medal, considered the Nobel Prize of mathematics, and a MacArthur Fellowship.

Dr. Tao is extraordinarily gifted. He's earned the moniker "the Mozart of Math," and his lectures—his *math lectures*—draw standing-room-only crowds. His academic record suggests that he could have been successful in several disciplines, but his real calling, his discovery of the Element, came via math when he was still a toddler.

"I remember as a child being fascinated with the patterns and puzzles of mathematical symbol manipulation," he told an interviewer. "I think the most important thing for developing an interest in mathematics is to have the ability and the freedom to play with mathematics—to set little challenges for oneself, to devise little games, and so on. Having good mentors was very important for me, because it gave me the chance to discuss these sorts of mathematical recreations; the formal classroom environment is of course best for learning theory and applications, and for appreciating the subject as a whole, but it isn't a good place to learn how to experiment. Perhaps one character trait which does help is the ability to focus, and perhaps to be a little stubborn. If I learned something in class that I only partly understood, I wasn't satisfied until I was able to work the whole thing out; it would bother me that the explanation wasn't clicking together like it should. So I'd often spend a lot of time on very simple things until I could understand them backwards and forwards, which really helps when one then moves on to more advanced parts of the subject."

"I don't have any magical ability," Dr. Tao told another interviewer. "I look at a problem, and it looks something like one I've already done; I think maybe the idea that worked before will work here. When nothing's working out then I think of a small trick that makes it a little better, but still is not quite right. I play with the problem, and after a while, I figure out what's going on. If I experiment enough, I get a deeper understanding. It's not about being smart or even fast. It's like climbing a cliff—if you're very strong and quick and have a lot of rope, it helps, but you need to devise a good route to get up there. Doing calculations quickly and knowing a lot of facts are like a rock climber with strength, quickness, and good tools; you still need a plan—that's the hard part—and you have to see the bigger picture."

Terence Tao probably finds himself in the zone regularly. In addition to being born with rare skills, he is also extremely fortunate because he arrived at his version of the Element when he was very, very young. He found the place where his brilliance and his passion met, and he never looked back.

What we can glean from his devotion to math and the magnetic pull it has for him has resonance for all of us. I think it is significant that he discovered his passion at such a young age and could express it before he was out of diapers (I'm not certain about whether Dr. Tao was still in diapers at age two, actually; I suppose he could have been a toilet-training genius as well). He could be what he was naturally inclined to be before the world put any restrictions on him (we'll talk more about these restrictions later in this book). No one was going to tell Terence Tao to stop doing math because he'd make more money if he were a lawyer. In that way, he and others like him have an unencumbered path toward the Element.

But they *provide* a path as well. For they show all of us the value of asking a vitally important question: If left to my own devices—if I didn't have to worry about making a living or what others thought of me—what am I most drawn to doing? Terence Tao probably never had to wonder what he was going to do with his life. He probably never used the Myers-Briggs Type Indicator or the Hermann Brain Dominance Instrument to determine which career options offered a spark for him. What the rest of us need to do is to see our futures and the futures of our children, our colleagues, and our community with the childlike simplicity prodigies have when their talents first emerge.

This is about looking into the eyes of your children or those you care for and, rather than approaching them with a template about who they might be, trying to understand who they really are. This is what the psychologist did with Gillian Lynne, and what Mick Fleetwood's parents and Ewa Laurance's parents did with them. Left to their own devices, what are they drawn to do? What kinds of activities do they tend to engage in voluntarily? What sorts of aptitude do they suggest? What absorbs them most? What sort of questions do they ask, and what type of points do they make?

We need to understand what puts them and us in the zone.

And we need to determine what implications that has for the rest of our lives.

CHAPTER FIVE

Finding Your Tribe

FOR MOST PEOPLE, a primary component of being in their Element is connecting with other people who share their passion and a desire to make the most of themselves through it. Meg Ryan is the popular actor best known for her work in such movies as *When Harry Met Sally . . .* and *Sleepless in Seattle.* Her acting career has been buoyant for more than a quarter of a century, yet she didn't imagine a lifetime in that profession when she was at school. In fact, the whole thought of acting or even speaking in public terrified her. She told me that at school performances, she'd always preferred to be on the bleachers than on the stage. She was a good student, though, and in the eighth grade, she was valedictorian. She was thrilled at her achievement until she realized that she had to give a speech in front of the whole school.

Although she practiced for weeks, when she found herself at the podium she simply froze in terror. She said that her mother had to go up onto the platform and bring her back down to her seat. And yet she went on to become one of the most accomplished comedy actresses of her generation. This was, in part, because she found her tribe.

Following a successful career at school, Meg won a scholarship to New York University to study journalism. She had always loved to write, and her intention was to focus on becoming a writer, something she considered at the time to be her true passion. To help pay for tuition, though, she found work in the occasional commercial. This led to producers choosing her for a regular role in the soap opera *As the World Turns*, and to Meg's discovery that she loved traveling in this circle.

"I found the world of actors fascinating," she told me. "I was around hilarious people. The job was like being in this nutty extended family. It was a kick. I was doing sixteen-hour days and I became more and more comfortable with the 'everyday' of it. I loved the fact that we were always talking about why someone would do something and examining human behavior. I found I had all these opinions about what my character would or wouldn't do. I didn't know where I got them from but I had lots and lots of them. I would say things like, 'OK, that's what the subtext is. So why am I speaking my subtext?' I would find myself rewriting lines and really engaging in the character and their world. Every day we'd get a new script and I had to memorize all these lines. It was absolutely, overwhelmingly engaging. There was no time to think about anything else. It was complete immersion."

Still, after leaving *As the World Turns* and graduating from college, Meg did not set off immediately for Hollywood. Believing she had more to discover about herself, she spent some time in Europe and even considered joining the Peace Corps. But when a movie offer took her to Los Angeles and she returned to the acting milieu, she found once again that she was in a rare place when doing this work.

"I met up with this really great acting teacher. Her name was Peggy Fury. Peggy started talking to me about the art and craft of acting and what being an artist meant to her. Sean Penn was in the class above me, and Anjelica Houston, Michelle Pfeiffer, and Nicolas Cage were there, too. I was surrounded by people who worked from really deep, deep down in themselves and were interested in the human condition and the idea of bringing writing to life. All these things just started to bloom in my mind and in my heart and in my soul. So I stayed in Los Angeles and got an apartment. My agent in New York hooked me up with an L.A. agent, and that's when it all came together for me.

"Various movies have come along and taught me so many things and helped me grow as a human being. When I decide to do a movie, it may be because I think it's funny, or I want to work with a particular actor, but in the end, it always has a profound effect on my life. If it's not the subject matter, it may be a particular group of people. My evolution is served by the different incarnations that are part of every single movie."

Meg Ryan could have been many things. She has genuine skill as a writer. She has considerable academic talents. She has a wide variety of interests and fascinations. However, when she's acting, she finds herself with a group of people who see the world the way she does, who allow her to feel her most natural, who affirm her talents, who inspire her, influence her, and drive her to be her best. She is close to her true self when she is among actors, directors, camera and lighting people, and all of the others who populate the film world.

Being a part of this tribe brings her to the Element.

A Place to Discover Yourself

Tribe members can be collaborators or competitors. They can share the same vision or have utterly different ones. They can be of a similar age or from different generations. What connects a tribe is a common commitment to the thing they feel born to do. This can be extraordinarily liberating, especially if you've been pursuing your passion alone.

Don Lipski, one of America's most acclaimed sculptors and public artists, always knew that he had an artistic bent. There were some early signs that he had unusual creative energy. "When

I was a child," he told me, "I was always making things. I didn't think of myself as a creative person but as someone with nervous energy. I had to be doodling and putting things together. I didn't think of it as an asset. If anything, it was a peculiarity." This "nervous energy" made him feel different from other kids, and sometimes uncomfortable. "As a child," he said, "more than anything else you just want to be like all the other kids. So rather than me seeing my creativity as something special, it seemed to set me apart."

Through elementary school and into junior high, Lipski was pulled in different directions. He was academically bright but bored by academic work. "Academic work came very easily to me. I would finish assignments very quickly and with the least effort rather than the most depth." He was gifted in math, and his school moved him into an accelerated math group, but in other respects teachers thought of him as an underachiever because he did just enough to get by. He spent more time drawing on his books than thinking about what to write in them: "When I should have been doing academic work, I was drawing or folding paper. Rather than being encouraged, I was chided for it."

One teacher strongly encouraged his artistic talents, but Don didn't take art that seriously. The teacher became so upset with Don that "he literally wouldn't speak to me." Shortly afterward, the teacher left, and another art teacher arrived at the school. He brought with him a revelation for Don. "They had a very rudimentary welding setup in the sculpture department, and he taught me how to weld. To me it was like magic that I could actually take pieces of steel and weld them together. It felt like everything I had done before in art was just child's play. Welding steel and making steel sculptures was like real adult art."

Discovering welding was like finding the Holy Grail. Still, he wasn't sure what to make of this fascination. He didn't think of himself as an artist because he wasn't good at drawing. He had friends who drew well. While they were drawing, "I was playing with blocks or building things out of my erector set. None of that felt like real art. It was the kids who could draw a horse that looked like a horse that felt like the real artists."

Even when he began winning school art shows for his sculptures, he never thought about going to an art school. When he graduated from high school, he enrolled at the University of Wisconsin as a business major. He subsequently switched his major to economics and then history, but he stayed away from the art department, even though he found little inspiration in any other classes.

In his final year, he bluffed his way into taking two electives, woodworking and ceramics, for which he wasn't actually qualified. He loved and excelled in both. Most importantly, he felt, almost for the first time, the true exhilaration of working as an artist on his own terms. In the ceramics class, he also found something he'd been missing throughout his college experience: an inspirational teacher. "He was a very romantic and enthusiastic guy. Everything he did was like an artwork. If he was buttering his bread, he was totally into it. He served as a model for me and made me think that I could really make my life by making things."

For the first time, a career as an artist seemed possible and worthwhile to Lipski. He decided to go to graduate school at the Cranbrook Art Institute in Michigan to study ceramics. Then he hit an obstacle. His parents had encouraged his creative work as long as it was a hobby. When he applied to Cranbrook, his father, a businessman, called him in and tried to drum some economic sense into him. Don agreed; studying ceramics made no practical sense. But it was all he wanted to do. His father looked at Don long and hard, saw that his mind was set, and stood aside. And when Don went to Cranbrook, he discovered a new world of people and possibilities." I'd had very little exposure to arts students other than in the few courses I had taken," he said. "Cranbrook is almost completely a graduate school. There were maybe two hundred art students there, and about a hundred and eighty of them were graduate students. So for the first time I was around a big body of people who were very serious, knowledgeable, and committed to making their artwork, and it was fantastic for me. I went to all the critiques, not just in the ceramics department but in the painting department, the sculpture department, the weaving department, and everywhere, just soaking it all up. I spent a lot of time visiting with other students in their studios absorbing what everybody was doing. I started to read the art magazines and go to museums and fully immerse myself in art for the first time."

At Cranbrook Don found his tribe, and it set him on a different path.

Finding the right tribe can be essential to finding your Element. On the other hand, feeling deep down that you're with the wrong one is probably a good sign that you should look somewhere else.

Helen Pilcher did just that. She stopped being a scientist and became one of the world's few science comedians. She fell into it after falling out of science. In fact, falling around has been a theme of her professional life. As she puts it, "I wasn't pushed into science, rather I stumbled." After school, she was offered a university place to study psychology and "to drink cider and watch daytime TV." After university, "a generalized apathy and unwillingness to find a real job" led her to take a one-year master's degree in neuroscience. At this point, science itself started to get interesting for Helen. "There were big experiments, brain dissections, and ridiculously unflattering safety specs."

Bitten by the science bug and little else, she stayed on to

complete her Ph.D. She learned some useful science, as well as "how to play pool like a diva." She also learned something else. She enjoyed science, but scientists were not her tribe. In her experience, science, unlike pool, was not played on a level surface. "I learned that seniority in the scientific community is inversely proportional to communication skills, but directly related to the thickness of trouser corduroy."

She did learn something of her craft too. "I learned how to make forgetful rats remember. I 'made' and grafted genetically modified stem cells into the brains of absent-minded rodents, which, shortly after my meddlings, went on to develop the cognitive capacity of a London cabby. But, at the same time, my own attention began to wander."

Most of all, she found that the world of science as she experienced it was not the utopia of free inquiry that she hoped for. It was a business. "Whilst corporate science pours cash and man-hours into medical research, its downfall is that it's driven by business plans. Experiments are motivated less by curiosity, and more by money. I felt disappointed and confined. I wanted to communicate science. I wanted to write about science. I wanted out."

So she formed "a one-woman escape committee and started digging a tunnel." She enrolled for a diploma in science communication at Birkbeck College in London, and there found "like-minded friends." She was offered a degree in media fellowship "and spent two wonderful months writing and producing funny science films for Einstein TV." She plucked up the courage to sell her freelance science writing to anyone who would have it: "I whored my wares to radio, to print, and to the Internet." Finally, she left the laboratory and went to work for the Royal Society. "My role was to find ways of making science groovy again—not the official job description."

And then, unexpectedly, she received an e-mail message offering her prime-time stage space at the Cheltenham Science Festival to do stand-up comedy about science. No sooner had she said yes than the panic set in. "Science, as we all know, is serious stuff. Einstein's theory of relativity does not a one-liner make. I enlisted the help of friend and fellow comedian and writer Timandra Harkness and several pints later, The Comedy Research Project (CRP) was born."

She went on to join the London comedy circuit, and for the next five years, she "cultured stem cells by day and audiences by night." The CRP became a live stage show where Timandra and Helen counted down the "Five Best Things in Science Ever." Members of the audience "find themselves joining in with the formula for nitrous oxide, volunteering to catch a scientist recreating early experiments in flight, and singing along with Elvis about black holes."

The CRP, she says, aims to prove scientifically the hypothesis that science can be funny. "We are methodologically sound. During each show, a control audience is locked in an identical, adjoining room without comedians. We then assess whether this control audience laughs more or less than the experimental audience who are exposed to jokes about science. Preliminary data gathered from shows around the country looks promising."

For Helen Pilcher, a life in science has given way to a life of writing and communicating about science. Leaving the lab was scary, she says, "but not as scary as the prospect of staying. My advice, should you be contemplating making that leap, is to make like a lemming and jump."

Domains and Fields

When I talk about tribes, I'm really talking about two distinct ideas, both of which are important for anyone who is looking to find their Element. The first is the idea of a "domain" and the second, of a "field." Domain refers to the sorts of activities and disciplines that people are engaged in—acting, rock music, business, ballet, physics, rap, architecture, poetry, psychology, teaching, hairdressing, couture, comedy, athletics, pool, visual arts, and so on. Field refers to the other people who are engaged in it. The domain that Meg Ryan discovered was acting, particularly soaps. The field was the other actors she worked with who loved acting the way she did, and who fed Meg's creativity. Later, she moved to another part of the domain, to film acting and within that from comedy to more serious roles. She extended her field as well, especially when she met Peggy Fury and the other actors in her class.

Understanding Meg's domain and her connection to her field helps explain how the shy girl who couldn't give a valedictorian speech became an accomplished, world-renowned actor. "When I was working, it was just me and a couple of other actors in a black room with a camera team. I wasn't worried about an audience, because there wasn't one. The everyday of it has no audience. The everyday of it is a black sound stage with cameras and one other person you're doing scenes with. And the activity was so absorbing; these people were so great that I just got carried away in the whole process."

The confidence she got from that experience was strong enough to carry her further into her domain and to fresh fields of people. Even now, though, she still dislikes talking in public or television talk show interviews. "I do it if I have to. I'd just rather not. It's just not who I am. I really don't feel comfortable in that spotlight."

Brian Ray is an accomplished guitarist who has worked with Smokey Robinson, Etta James, and Peter Frampton and toured on bills with the Rolling Stones and the Doobie Brothers. He came to his domain early, and it ultimately led him into the inner circle of a hero that as a child he never dreamed he would meet.

Brian was born in 1955, in Glendale, California, the year that Alan Freed coined the term *rock and roll*. He was one of four kids, including a half sister, Jean, who was fifteen years his elder.

"Jean would take me over to her girlfriend's house, and they would be playing Rick Nelson, Elvis Presley, and Jerry Lee Lewis while poring over photos of these guys. It had such a visceral impact on me, the reactions of these girls to this music that was pouring out of the radio and their response to these photos. There was a part of me that just got the whole thing, right then and there at age three. My dad played piano, and we had a little phonograph-making kit. It had a microphone, and you could cut a record and put this other needle on it to play the record. I remember sitting, at two or three, with my dad at the piano and cutting records.

"Right out of high school Jean started getting into music, and she joined a folk band called the New Christy Minstrels. They did a tour throughout the country. She'd tell us stories and would be glowing from this life she had grown into. Jean imparted to me her love and joy of music and sealed that by bringing me to clubs and concerts when I was nine and ten years old. I would see and meet people that I worshipped.

"My brother was given a really nice Gibson guitar plus lessons. He didn't have a big desire to play music, and while he was busy not caring about the lessons, I was busy practicing on his guitar. Then I was given a $5 nylon string guitar by my sister Jean that she bought in Tijuana. I just started crying. My passion for music was so big that it was almost a crusade, without my meaning to or knowing that I wanted to share it and spread it around a little. I started a band with guys before I even knew how to tune a guitar."

"One Sunday night when I was ten or eleven we heard this new band on *The Ed Sullivan Show*, the Beatles. It was such a different kind of music. It was a mixture of that black R&B that I loved so much, but it was mixed with some other X factor or element that I didn't know. It was from Mars. It changed everything.

"I knew I wanted to play music, but now they'd closed the deal for me. It was just the most exciting thing I had ever seen. It made being in a band seem like something that was doable and attractive and something I could do for a living. They took away all the 'maybe I'll be a fireman.' I was driven now to what ended up being my life."

In the next twenty years, Brian played with some of the most outstanding musicians of his generation. Then came the call he never expected—an invitation to audition for Paul McCartney's new band. He has been touring and playing with McCartney ever since.

"Never in my wildest dreams would I have thought that, you know, this little blond kid sitting Indian-style in front of the TV in 1964 would end up playing with that guy singing 'All My Lovin'' and 'I Saw Her Standing There' on *The Ed Sullivan Show*. There is something really gratifying about this story, this, you know, just being a part of this scene."

The people in this book have found their Element in different domains and with different fields of people. No one is limited to one domain, and many people move in several. Often, break-through ideas come about when someone makes a connection between different ways of thinking, sometimes across different domains. As Pablo Picasso explored the limits of his Blue and Rose periods, he became fascinated with the collections of African art at the Musée d'Ethnographie du Trocadéro in Paris. This work was vastly different from his, but it sparked a new level of creativity in him. He incorporated influences from the ceremonial masks of the Dogon tribe into his landmark painting *Les Demoiselles d'Avignon*, and thus launched himself into the Cubist work for which he is most celebrated.

As cultures and technologies evolve, new domains emerge, new fields of practitioners populate them, and old domains fade away. The techniques of computer animation have generated an entire new domain of creative work in cinema, television, and advertising. These days, though, people aren't spending quite as much time as they used to illuminating manuscripts.

Finding your tribe can have transformative effects on your sense of identity and purpose. This is because of three powerful tribal dynamics: validation, inspiration, and what we'll call here the "alchemy of synergy."

It's Not Just Me

Debbie Allen's career in dance, acting, singing, producing, writing, and directing has dazzled and touched millions. Her career soared in 1980 with the hit TV series *Fame*. She holds the distinction of having choreographed the Academy Awards for six consecutive years, and she has won many awards herself, including the Essence Award in 1992 and 1995. She is the founder and director of the Debbie Allen Dance Academy, which offers professional training for young dancers and professionals. It also commissions opportunities for new choreographers and provides an introduction to dance for all ages.

"As a young child," she told me, "very young, four or five years old, I can remember putting on my pink shiny bathing suit and tying a towel around my neck, climbing a tree, and dancing on the roof of my house performing to the birds and the clouds. I was always dancing as a little girl; I was inspired by the beautiful pictures of ballerinas. Because I was black and lived in Texas, I hadn't seen a dance performance but I watched musical films, Shirley Temple, Ruby Keeler, the Nicholas Brothers.

"When the Ringling Brothers Circus came to town, when I saw the spectacle, the people in beautiful costumes and the dancers flying in the air, toes pointed, I just thought it was amazing! I was so inspired by movies. Margot Fonteyn and Rudolf Nureyev were the most incredible things I had ever seen.

"As a young girl, I couldn't go to serious dance schools because everything was segregated. I joined Debato Studios. I got a full grant scholarship and attended ten dance classes a week. I still remember my first dance recital—I wore a white shiny satin skirt, a white jacket and orange blouse, white tap shoes and was playing a triangle. The feeling of performing was like being on top of the world! I was always wearing leotards as a child. In fact, at my fiftieth birthday party one of my aunts brought a picture of me at age five in my leotard. I knew I was a dancer very early on.

"I first saw the Alvin Ailey Company at age seventeen. I knew then that I was going to throw away my point shoes, put on high heels and long white skirts, and dance to that kind of music. I identified myself with them so much onstage. It was glorious.

"One summer I went to the Spoleto Dance Festival in the Carolinas. That was when it all fell into place for me. I had ideas as a child but I was challenged by segregation, and so this opportunity to be taught by Dudley Williams in those classes was amazing. Alvin Ailey was there, the resident dance company taught Revelations Dance Classes, and I just shone. They wanted me in the company but Alvin thought I was too young. I never joined them but I knew I had to do that kind of dancing and teach.

"The Academy is born out of my desire to give back. It offers all styles of dance from flamenco, African, modern, and character to tap and hip-hop. We have incredible teachers from all over the world. Every child has the right to learn to dance. It is an incredible language. These are not the kids that are going to get into trouble, believe me."

Connecting with people who share the same passions affirms that you're not alone; that there are others like you and that, while many might not understand your passion, some do. It doesn't matter whether you like the people as individuals, or even the work they do. It's perfectly possible that you don't. What matters first is having validation for the passion you have in common. Finding your tribe brings the luxury of talking shop, of bouncing ideas around, of sharing and comparing techniques, and of indulging your enthusiasms or hostilities for the same things. Making this connection was a significant spur to many of the people we've met so far in this book—from Matt Groening to Ewa Laurance to Meg Ryan to Black Ice—and to many of those ahead.

Being among other artists at Cranbrook gave Don Lipski a deeper sense that what he was doing mattered and was actually worth doing. He said, "In graduate school I started taking seriously for the first time the little doodles I had made. If I saw a rubber band in the street, I'd pick it up and then start looking for something to wrap it around or combine it with. That's the sort of activity I'd always done, but when I was in graduate school, I realized that that indeed was sculpture. Although modest, it really was art making and not just passing time."

Some people are most in their Element when they are working alone. This is often true of mathematicians, poets, painters, and some athletes. Even with these people, though, there's a tacit awareness of a field—the other writers, other painters, other mathematicians, other players, who enrich the domain and challenge their sense of possibility.

The great philosopher of science Michael Polanyi argues that the free and open exchange of ideas is the vital pulse of scientific inquiry. Scientists like to work on their own ideas and questions, but science is also a collaborative venture. "Scientists, freely making their own choice of problems and pursuing them in the light of their own personal judgment," he said, "are in fact cooperating as members of a closely knit organization."

Polanyi argues passionately against state control of science because it can destroy the free interactions on which genuine science depends. "Any attempt to organize the group . . . under a single authority would eliminate their independent initiatives and thus reduce their joint effectiveness to that of the single person directing them from the centre. It would, in effect, paralyze their cooperation." It was partly this pressure on science that made Helen Pilcher jump ship from stem cells to the comedy stage.

Interaction with the field, in person or through their work, is as vital to our development as time alone with our thoughts. As the physicist John Wheeler said, "If you don't kick things around with people, you are out of it. Nobody, I always say, can be anybody without somebody being around." Even so, the rhythms of community life vary in the Element just as they do in daily life. Sometimes you want company; sometimes you don't. The physicist Freeman Dyson says that when he's writing, he closes the door, but when he's actually doing science, he leaves it open. "Up to a point you welcome being interrupted because it is only by interacting with other people that you get anything interesting done."

How Do They Do That?

Finding your tribe offers more than validation and interaction, important as both of those are. It provides inspiration and provocation to raise the bar on your own achievements. In every domain, members of a passionate community tend to drive each other to explore the real extent of their talents. Sometimes, the boost comes not from close collaboration but from the influence of others in the field, whether contemporaries or predecessors, whether directly associated with one's particular domain or associated only marginally. As Isaac Newton famously said, "If I saw further it was because I stood on the shoulders of giants." This is not just a phenomenon of science.

Bob Dylan was born in Hibbing, Minnesota, in 1942. In his autobiography, *Chronicles*, he tells of his sense of alienation from the people there, from his family, and from the popular culture of the day. He knew he had to get away from there to become whoever he was going to be. His one lifeline was folk music. "Folk music," he said, "was all I needed to exist. . . . I had no other cares or interests besides folk music. I scheduled my life around it. I had little in common with anyone not like-minded."

As soon as he could, he moved on instinct to New York City. There he found the artists, the singers, the writers, and the "scene" that began to unleash his own talents. He had begun to find his people. But among all of those who inspired and shaped his passion, there was one who led him to an artistic place that he had never imagined. When he first heard Woody Guthrie, he said, "It was like a million megaton bomb had dropped."

One afternoon in the early 1960s in New York City, a friend invited Dylan to look through his record collection. It included a few record albums of old 78s. One was *The Spirituals to Swing Concert at Carnegie Hall*, a collection of performances by Count

Basie, Meade Lux Lewis, Joe Turner and Pete Johnson, Sister Rosetta Tharpe, and others. Another was a Woody Guthrie set of about twelve double-sided records. Dylan had listened casually to some of Guthrie's recordings when he was living in Hibbing, but hadn't paid them close attention. This day in New York City was going to be different.

Dylan put one of the old 78s on the turntable, "and when the needle dropped, I was stunned. I didn't know if I was stoned or straight." He listened entranced to Guthrie singing solo a range of his own compositions: "Ludlow Massacre," "1913 Massacre," "Jesus Christ," "Pretty Boy Floyd," "Hard Travelin'," "Jackhammer John," "Grand Coulee Dam," "Pastures of Plenty," "Talkin' Dust Bowl Blues," and "This Land Is Your Land."

"All these songs together, one after another made my head spin," he said. "It made me want to gasp. It was like the land parted. I had heard Guthrie before but mainly just a song here and there—mostly things that he sang with other artists. I hadn't actually heard him, not in this earth shattering kind of way. I couldn't believe it. Guthrie had such a grip on things. He was so poetic and tough and rhythmic. There was so much intensity, and his voice was like a stiletto."

Guthrie sang like no other singer Dylan had listened to, and he wrote songs like no one he'd ever heard. Everything about Guthrie—his style, his content, his mannerisms—came to him as a revelation of what folk music could be and had to be.

"It all just about knocked me down. It was like the record player itself had just picked me up and flung me across the room. I was listening to his diction, too. He had perfected a style of singing that it seemed like no one else had ever thought about. He would throw in the sound of the last letter of a word whenever he felt like it and it would come like a punch. The songs themselves, his repertoire, were really beyond category. They had the infinite sweep of humanity in them. Not one mediocre song in the bunch. Woody Guthrie tore everything in his path to pieces. For me it was an epiphany, like some heavy anchor had just plunged into the waters of the harbor."

Dylan listened to Guthrie for the rest of that day "as if in a trance." It was not only a moment of revelation about Guthrie; it was a moment of truth for Dylan. "I felt like I had discovered some essence of self-command, that I was in the internal pocket of the system feeling more like myself than ever before. A voice in my head said, 'So this is the game.' I could sing all these songs, every single one of them, and they were all that I wanted to sing. It was like I had been in the dark and someone had turned on the main switch of a lightning conductor."

By traveling to New York City to find like-minded people, Dylan was looking for himself. By discovering the journey of Woody Guthrie, he began to imagine his own. Like Newton, he saw further because he stood on the shoulders of giants.

Circles of Influence

Tribes are circles of influence, and they can take many forms. They may be scattered far and wide or huddled closely together. They may be present only in your thoughts or physically present in the room with you. They may be alive or dead and living through their works. They may be confined to a single generation or cross over them.

Nobel laureate Richard Feynman spoke of ultra-miniaturized machines long before anyone had any thought of creating such things. Years later, Marvin Minsky, inspired by Feynman's idea, became the founding father of artificial intelligence and moved the conversation forward. Then K. Eric Drexler approached Minsky at MIT, and asked the esteemed professor to sponsor his thesis on miniature devices. That thesis served as the foundation for Drexler's pioneering work in nanotechnology. Through an extended, multigenerational tribe, a concept that critics dismissed as purely science fiction when Feynman introduced it became a reality.

When tribes gather in the same place, the opportunities for mutual inspiration can become intense. In all domains, there have been powerful groupings of people who have driven innovation through their influence on each other and the impetus they've created as a group.

Sociologist Randall Collins writes about how nearly all great philosophical movements came via the dynamics of tribes. In ancient Greece, the history of philosophy "can be recounted in terms of a series of interlinked groups: the Pythagorean brotherhood and its offshoots; Socrates' circle, which spawned so many others; the acute debaters of the Megara school; Plato's friends, who constituted the Academy; the breakaway faction that became Aristotle's Peripatetic school; the restructuring of the network that crystallized with Epicurus and his friends withdrawing into their Garden community, and their rivals, the Athenian Stoics, with their revisionist circles at Rhodes and Rome; the successive movements at Alexandria."

If it can happen in Ancient Greece, it can happen in Hollywood. The documentary *Easy Riders, Raging Bulls* examines the "raucous, inspired, and occasionally sordid cultural revolution" that led to the reinvention of Hollywood filmmaking in the 1960s. In a few short years, the bobby socks and beach blankets that characterized wholesome 1950s Americana were replaced with sex, drugs, and rock 'n' roll. Inspired by the French New Wave and British New Cinema, a new generation of directors and actors set out to revolutionize American cinema and make films that expressed their personal vision.

The breakthrough successes of landmark films such as *Easy Rider*, *The Godfather*, and *Taxi Driver* gave these filmmakers unprecedented financial and creative independence. The box-office and critical success of their films forced the old guard of the Hollywood studio system to relinquish their power. This became the age of a new breed of iconic filmmakers such as Francis Ford Coppola, Robert Altman, Martin Scorsese, Peter Bogdanovich, and Dennis Hopper.

With each success, the filmmakers gained greater creative control. They created a culture of feverish innovation as each inspired the others to explore new themes and forms for popular movies. This newfound freedom also gave birth to an explosion of excess, ego, soaring budgets, and a seemingly endless supply of drugs. Eventually, the filmmakers' mutual support and encouragement degenerated into intense competition and bitter rivalries. The emergence from this culture of blockbuster movies such as *Jaws* and *Star Wars* changed the landscape of Hollywood films once again, and creative and financial control returned to the hands of the studios.

The power of tribal clustering was clear too in the period of wild invention surrounding the software industry that accompanied the dawn of the personal computer. Silicon Valley has had a huge impact on digital technology. But, as Dorothy Leonard and Walter Swap have noted, it's surprisingly small geographically. "Viewing the valley from the flight approach to San Francisco International, one is struck by how small the region is. As Venture Law Group's Craig Johnson notes, Silicon Valley 'is like any gas that is compressed; it gets hotter.' Its tribes overlap socially and professionally based on work discipline (software engineers, for example), organizational affiliation (Hewlett-Packard), or background (Stanford MBAs or South Asian immigrants). The most skillful players do not have to travel far to make deals, change jobs, or find professional partners. John Doerr of Kleiner Perkins is fond of saying that the Valley is a place where you can change your job without changing your parking spot.

"Shared values also bind longtime Silicon Valley natives. The personal convictions of the Valley's remarkable innovators, who created not just a company but an industry, still echo through the community. Bill Hewlett and David Packard influenced the older generation directly; many of them were early employees. Through this old guard, collegiality and high standards for performance are being carried down to next-generation entrepreneurs."

Other examples of tribes inspiring individuals to greater heights abound: the sports teams—the 1969 New York Knicks, the "No Name Defense" of the undefeated 1972 Miami Dolphins, the 1991 Minnesota Twins—that performed as a collective that was more distinguished than any of the individuals; the Bauhaus movement in architecture in the early decades of the twentieth century. In each case, the physical clustering of a tribe of creative individuals led to explosive innovation and growth.

The Alchemy of Synergy

The most dramatic example of the power of tribes is the work of actual creative teams. In *Organizing Genius: The Secrets of Creative Collaboration*, Warren Bennis and Pat Ward Biederman write of what they call "Great Groups," collections of people with similar interests who create something much greater than any of them could create individually—who become more than the sum of the parts. "A Great Group can be a goad, a check, a sounding board, and a source of inspiration, support, and even love," they say. The combination of creative energies and the need to perform at the highest level to keep up with peers leads to an otherwise unattainable commitment to excellence. This is the alchemy of synergy.

One of the best examples of this is the creation of Miles Davis's landmark album *Kind of Blue*. While music lovers of every sort widely consider the recording a "must have," and legions of jazz fans—and classical and rock fans for that matter—know each note of the album by heart, none of the players on that album knew what they were going to play before they entered the studio.

"Miles conceived these settings only hours before the recording dates and arrived with sketches which indicated to the group what was to be played," pianist Bill Evans says in the original liner notes to the album. "Therefore, you will hear something close to pure spontaneity in these performances. The group had never played these pieces prior to the recordings and I think without exception the first complete performance of each was a 'take.'" In fact, the songs that appear on the album are all the first full takes, with the exception of "Flamenco Sketches," which was the second take.

When trumpeter Davis gathered Evans, along with tenor saxophonist John Coltrane, alto saxophonist Julian "Cannonball" Adderley, pianist Wynton Kelly, bassist Paul Chambers, and drummer Jimmy Cobb in the studio in 1959, he laid out the scales—itself somewhat revolutionary, since jazz at the time was traditionally built around chord changes—and turned on the tape recorder. Each of these players was an active participant in the tribe moving jazz in new directions at that time, and they'd worked together in the past. What happened during the *Kind of Blue* sessions, though, was a perfect storm of affirmation, inspiration, and synergy. These artists set out to break barriers, they had the skill to take their music in new directions, and they had a leader with a bold vision.

Their improvisational work that day was the result of powerful creative forces merging and creating something outsize—the ultimate goal of synergy. When the tape started rolling, magic happened. "Group improvisation is a further challenge," said Evans. "Aside from the weighty technical problem of collective coherent thinking, there is the very human, even social need for sympathy from all members to bend for the common result. This most difficult problem, I think, is beautifully met and solved on this recording." The music they created in those next few hours—working with each other, playing off each other, synchronizing with each other, challenging each other—would last several lifetimes. *Kind of Blue* is the best-selling jazz album of all time and, nearly fifty years later, still sells thousands of copies every week.

Why can creative teams achieve more together than they can separately? I think it's because they bring together the three key features of intelligence that I described earlier. In a way, they model the essential features of the creative mind.

Great creative teams are *diverse*. They are composed of very different sorts of people with different but complementary talents. The team that created *Kind of Blue* was made up of extraordinary musicians who not only played different instruments but brought with them different musical sensibilities and types of personality. This was true too of the Beatles. For all that they had in common, culturally and musically, Lennon and McCartney were very different as people, and so too were George Harrison and Ringo Starr. It was their differences that made their creative work together greater than the sum of their individual parts.

Creative teams are *dynamic*. Diversity of talents is important, but it is not enough. Different ways of thinking can be an obstacle to creativity. Creative teams find ways of using their differences as strengths, not weaknesses. They have a process through which their strengths are complementary and compensate for each other's weaknesses too. They are able to challenge each other as equals, and to take criticism as an incentive to raise their game.

Creative teams are *distinct*. There's a big difference between a great team and a committee. Most committees do routine work and have members who are theoretically interchangeable with other people. Committee members are usually there to represent specific interests. Often a committee can do its work while half the members are checking their BlackBerrys or studying the wallpaper. Committees are often immortal; they seem to persist forever, and so often do their meetings. Creative teams have a distinctive personality and come together to do something specific. They are together only for as long as they want to be or have to be to get the job done.

One of the most famous examples of powerful teamwork is the administration of President Abraham Lincoln. In her book *Team of Rivals*, Doris Kearns Goodwin tells the story of Lincoln and four members of his cabinet, Edwin M. Stanton, secretary of war, Salmon P. Chase, secretary of the treasury, William H. Seward, secretary of state, and Edward Bates, attorney general. These five men were unquestionably part of the same tribe, passionate in their desire to lead and move America forward. However, each of the four others had opposed Lincoln openly and bitterly prior to his presidency. Stanton once even called Lincoln a "long armed ape." Each had strongly held positions that sometimes differed greatly from Lincoln's. In addition, each of them believed they were more deserving of the presidency than the man the people elected.

Still, Lincoln believed that each of these rivals had strengths the administration needed. With an equanimity difficult to imagine in current American politics, he brought this team together. They argued ceaselessly, and often viciously. What they found in working with each other, though, was the ability to forge their differing opinions into sturdy national policy, navigating the country through its most perilous period through the effort of their combined wisdom.

Lost in the Crowd

There's an important difference between being in a tribe as I'm defining it and being part of a crowd, even when the members of a crowd are all there for the same reason and feel the same passions. Sports fans come to mind immediately. There are vociferous and passionate fans all over the sports landscape—football devotees in Green Bay, soccer (or as those of us from the rest of the world know it, *football*) enthusiasts in Manchester, ice hockey zealots in Montreal, and so on. They cover their walls, their cars, and their front lawns with team paraphernalia. They might know the regular lineup for their local teams when they finished in fourth place in 1988. They might have postponed their weddings because the date conflicted with the World Series or the European Cup. They are dedicated to their teams, rhapsodic about their teams, and their moods might be dictated by the performance of their teams. But their fandom does not place them in a tribe with their fellow fans, at least not in the way that I'm describing it here.

Fan behavior is a different form of social affiliation. Some people, including Henri Tajfel and John Turner, refer to this as social identity theory. They argue that people often derive a large sense of who they are through affiliation with specific groups and tend to associate themselves closely with groups likely to boost their self-esteem. Sports teams make fans feel as though they are part of a vast, powerful organization. This is especially true when the teams are winning. Look around at the end of any sports season, and you'll notice team jerseys of that season's champion sprouting all over the street, even in places far distant from the team's home city. Fans boast their affiliation with victorious teams much more loudly because at some level they believe that being associated in a tangential way with such a team makes them look better.

The social psychologist Robert Cialdini has a term for this. He calls it Basking in Reflected Glory, or BIRGing. In the 1970s, Cialdini and others conducted a study about BIRGing and found that students at a number of American universities were much more likely to wear university-related clothing on the Monday after their school won a football game. They also found that students were more likely to use the pronoun *we* regarding the team—as in "We destroyed State on Saturday"—than they were if their team lost. In the latter instance, the pronoun usually switched to *they*—as in, "I can't believe they blew that game."

The point about BIRGing as it relates to our definition of tribes is that the person doing the basking has little or nothing to do with the glory achieved. We'll give a tiny bit of credit to the effect of fan support if the fan attended the actual sports event. Though serious sports fans are a notoriously superstitious lot, only the most irrational among them actually believe that their actions—wearing the same hat to every game, sitting perfectly still during a rally, using a specific brand of charcoal during the tailgate party—have any impact on the results.

Membership of a fan group—whether it's the Cheeseheads or Red Sox Nation—is not the same as being in a tribe. In fact, such membership can create the opposite effect. Tribe membership as I define it here helps people become more themselves, leading them toward a greater sense of personal identity. On the other hand, we can easily lose our identity in a crowd, including a group of fans. Being a fan is about being partisan; cheering or jeering and finding joy in victory and agony in defeat. This might be fulfilling and thrilling in many ways, but it normally doesn't take you to the Element as a means of self-realization.

In fact, fandom is in many ways a form of what psychologists rather awkwardly call "deindividuation." This means losing your sense of identity through becoming part of a group. Extreme forms of deindividuation lead to mob behavior. If you've ever been to a European soccer match, you know how this can apply to the sports world. But even in more benign versions, it results in a sense of anonymity that leads people to lose inhibitions and sometimes perform acts they later regret, and in most cases do things outside their normal personalities. In other words, these actions can take you far from your true self.

My youngest brother Neil used to be a professional soccer player for Everton, one of the major teams in Britain. Whenever I was in Liverpool, I would watch him play. It was an exhilarating and often terrifying experience. Football fans in Liverpool are very enthusiastic, let's say. They are passionate about winning, and when things on the pitch aren't going as they'd like, they willingly offer tactical advice from the terraces. It's a form of mentoring for the players, and often for the referee too. If Neil failed to place a shot exactly where the fans wanted it, they would scream words of encouragement. "Poor shot, Robinson," they might say, or, "Come on, you can do better than that, surely." Or words to that effect.

On one occasion, there was an hysterical outburst from someone immediately behind me, offering a robust criticism of my younger brother's tactics in words that implicated my mother and, by extension, me. On instinct, I whirled around to deal with what was clearly a question of family honor. When I saw the manic fan's size and facial expressions, however, I agreed that he was probably right. Crowd behavior is like that.

Look, Listen, and Learn

Some spectators really are skilled critics, and what they think about an event can genuinely help others to make better sense of it. The domains of literary criticism, music journalism, and sports commentary all have distinguished members whose words speak to us deeply and who belong to tribes passionately dedicated to extending the discourse. This is different from simple fandom. It is a performance in the service of fandom that has definable levels of excellence and the makings of a true calling. Sportscaster Howard Cosell called one of his autobiographies *I Never Played the Game*, yet he served for decades as one of the most important and influential voices in the U.S. sports world.

My guess is that Cosell found his Element in sports, even though he wasn't an athlete. He knew he could enhance the average fan's sports experience, and found a greater sense of who he was in doing so. Cosell once said, "I was infected with my desire, my resolve, to make it in broadcasting. I knew exactly what I wanted to do, and how." He was one of a key group of enthusiasts who became active participants in the world they admired by bridging the space between the players and the audience.

And in every crowd and every audience there may be someone who is responding differently from everybody else—someone who is having his own epiphany, someone who sees his tribe not on the bleachers around him but on the stage in front of him.

Billy Connolly is one of the most original and one of the funniest comedians in the world. He was born in a working-class area of Glasgow, Scotland, in 1942. He struggled through school, which he mostly disliked, and left as soon as he could to become an apprentice welder in the Glasgow shipyards. He served his time there, learning his trade and also absorbing the ways and customs of working life on the banks of the river Clyde. From an early age, Connolly loved music and taught himself to play the guitar and the banjo. Like Bob Dylan, growing up at the same time and an ocean away, he was captivated by folk music and spent whatever time he could listening and playing at folk clubs around Scotland. He also loved the pubs and the banter of Glasgow nightlife, and made regular visits to the cinema, to Saturday-night dances, and to occasional live theater.

One night Connolly was watching the comedian Chick Murray on television. For more than forty years, Chick Murray had been a legend of comedy and music hall. His droll, acerbic wit epitomized the laconic take on life that typifies Scottish humor. Billy took his seat, ready for a riotous session with the great man. He had all of that. But he had something else—an epiphany. As he rolled around in his seat, he was acutely aware of the hysterical pleasure, the emotional release, and the lacerating insights that Murray was detonating around himself. For Billy in Glasgow, this was as much of a turning point as listening to Woody Guthrie was for Bob Dylan in Greenwich Village. He realized that it was possible to do this, and that he was going to do it. He began to separate from the crowd and to merge with his tribe.

Billy had always talked to his own small audiences between songs. Increasingly, he found himself talking more and singing less. He found too that the audiences were getting bigger. For many comedians of his generation, he went on to become the doyen of freewheeling stand-up comedy. His work has taken him far from the shipyards of the Clyde into packed theaters around the world, into award-winning movies as an actor, and into the minds and affections of millions of people.

Like most of the people in this book, he found his way not only when he found his Element but also when he found his tribe.

CHAPTER SIX

What Will They Think?

FINDING YOUR ELEMENT can be challenging on a variety of levels, several of which we've already discussed. Sometimes, the challenge comes from within, from a lack of confidence or fear of failure. Sometimes the people closest to you and their image and expectations of you are the real barrier. Sometimes the obstacles are not the particular people you know but the general culture that surrounds you.

I think of the barriers to finding the Element as three concentric "circles of constraint." These circles are *personal*, *social*, and *cultural*.

This Time It's Personal

Given the way his life has worked out, it's interesting that several of Chuck Close's teachers and classmates considered him a slacker when he was a child. The kids thought so because he had physical problems that made him poor at sports and even the most rudimentary playground games. The teachers probably thought so because he tested poorly, seemed lazy, and rarely finished his exams. It turned out later that he was dyslexic, but the diagnosis for this didn't exist when he was younger. To many outsiders, it didn't seem that Chuck Close was trying very hard to do anything with his life, and most thought that he wouldn't amount to much.

On top of his learning disorder and his physical maladies,

Close also faced more tragedy than any young boy should ever encounter. His father uprooted the family regularly and then died when Chuck was eleven. Around this time, his mother, a classical pianist, developed breast cancer, and the Close family lost their home when the medical bills overwhelmed them. Even his grandmother became terribly ill.

What got Close through all of this was his passion for art. "I think early on my art ability was something that separated me from everybody else," he said in an interview. "It was an area in which I felt competent and it was something that I could fall back on." He even devised innovative ways to use art to overcome the restrictions of his conditions. He created puppet shows and magic acts—what he called "entertaining the troops"—to get other kids to spend time with him. He supplemented his schoolwork with elaborate art projects to show teachers that he wasn't "a malingerer."

Ultimately, his interest in art and his innate gifts allowed him to blossom into one of the singular talents in American culture. After graduating from the University of Washington and getting his MFA at Yale—several of his earlier teachers had told him that college would be out of the question for him—Close set off on a career that was to establish him as one of America's most celebrated artists. His signature style involved a grid system he devised to create huge photorealistic images of faces alive with texture and expression. His method has drawn widespread attention from the media, and his paintings hang in top museums around the world. Through ceaseless dedication to his passion and his craft, Chuck Close overcame considerable constraints to find his Element and rise to the pinnacle of his profession.

But that's only the beginning of the story.

In 1988, Chuck was making an award presentation in New York when he felt something wrong inside his body. He made his way to the hospital, but within hours, he was a quadriplegic, the victim of a blood clot in his spinal column. One of the greatest artists of his generation could no longer even grasp a paintbrush. Early rehabilitation efforts proved frustrating, and this latest roadblock in a life filled with roadblocks seemed to be the one that would at last stifle his ambitions.

One day, however, Close discovered that he could hold a paintbrush with his teeth and actually manipulate it well enough to create tiny images. "I suddenly became encouraged," he said. "I tried to imagine what kind of teeny paintings I could make with only that much movement. I tried to imagine what those paintings might look like. Even that little bit of neck movement was enough to let me know that perhaps I was not powerless. Perhaps I could do something myself."

What he could do was create an entirely new form of artwork. When he later regained some movement in his upper arm, Close began using rich colors to make small paintings that fit together to create a large mosaic image. His new work was at least as popular as his older work and earned him additional acclaim and notoriety.

Throughout his life, Chuck Close has had endless reasons to give in to his problems and to give up as an artist. He chose instead to push on beyond every limit his life presented and to stay in his Element no matter what new obstacles reared up in his way. He would not let any of these things prevent him from being who he felt he was meant to be.

Chuck Close is not alone in overcoming physical obstacles to pursue his passion. We'll meet some other people who've done this, and some of them may surprise you. The problems they face are not only physical, though physical disabilities can be torturous and aggravating in themselves. They also faced problems arising from their own attitudes to their disability, and from the effects on their feelings of other people's attitudes to their disabilities. To overcome these physical and psychological barriers, people with disabilities of every sort must summon enormous reserves of self-belief and determination to do things that other people can do without a second thought.

Can*do*Co is a professional contemporary dance company based in Great Britain that includes disabled and nondisabled dancers. Over the years, the dancers have included single and double amputees, paraplegics in wheelchairs, and people with a wide range of other conditions. The vision of the company, founded in 1982, is to inspire audiences and support participants "to achieve their highest aspirations in line with the Company's ethos that dance is accessible to everyone." Can*do*Co works to broaden the perception of dance through its performances and through its education and training program. The directors of the company say that Can*do*Co has always aimed high—"High in quality of movement, high in integrity of dance as an art form and high in expectations of ourselves as performers. Our focus is on dance not disability, professionalism not therapy." One of a growing number of "integrated" companies in dance, theater, and music, their ambitions have been fulfilled through numerous international awards from professional dance critics and festivals around the world.

"To truly appreciate the Can*do*Co Dance Company," one reviewer noted, "it has been said that one should discard all conventional notions of the dancing body. Why talk about swift and articulate footwork with pointed toes, when legs are of no consequence? [In these performances] representations of the perfect and physically complete body are thrown out of the window, introducing less-than-whole figures with no less talent than their able-bodied counterparts . . . those who expected the Can*do*Co dancers to perform gravity-defying stunts with crutches and wheelchairs would have been sorely disappointed. Instead, their performance was a visual and psychological confrontation that was not so much a slap in the face, but a lingering thought that warms the heart and caresses the mind."

Whether you're disabled or not, issues of attitude are of paramount importance in finding your Element. A strong will to be yourself is an indomitable force. Without it, even a person in perfect physical shape is at a comparative disadvantage. In my experience, most people have to face internal obstacles of self-doubt and fear as much as any external obstacles of circumstance and opportunity.

The scale of these anxieties is clear from the burgeoning worldwide market for self-help courses and books, many of which focus on just these issues. For me, the best in breed is Susan Jeffers's landmark book *Feel the Fear and Do It Anyway*®. It has been translated into thirty-five languages and has sold millions of copies. In it, Jeffers writes with passion and eloquence about the gnawing fears that hold so many people back from living their lives in full and contributing to the world. These fears include the fear of failure, the fear of not being good enough, the fear of being found wanting, the fear of disapproval, the fear of poverty, and the fear of the unknown.

Fear is perhaps the most common obstacle to finding your Element. You might ask how often it's played a part in your own life and held you back from doing the things you desperately wanted to try. Dr. Jeffers offers a series of well-tested techniques to move from fear to fulfillment, of which the most powerful is explicit in the title of her book.

Social: It's For Your Own Good

Fear of disapproval and of being found wanting are often entangled in our relationships with the people closest to us. Your parents and siblings, and your partner and children if you have them, are likely to have strong views on what you should and shouldn't do with your life. They may be right, of course. And they can have positive roles as mentors in encouraging your real talents. However, they can also be very wrong.

People can have complex reasons for trying to clip other people's wings. Your taking a different path might not meet their interests, or might create complications in their lives that they feel they can't afford. Whatever the reasons, someone keeping you from the thing you love to do—or from even looking for it—can be a deep source of frustration.

There may be no conscious agenda from others at all. You may simply find yourself enmeshed in a self-sustaining web of social roles and expectations that forms a tacit boundary to your ambitions. Many people don't find their Element because they don't have the encouragement or the confidence to step outside their established circle of relationships.

Sometimes, of course, your loved ones genuinely think you would be wasting your time and talents doing something of which they disapprove. This is what happened to Paulo Coelho. Mind you, his parents went further than most to put him off. They had him committed repeatedly to a psychiatric institution and subjected to electroshock therapy *because they loved him*. The next time you feel guilty about scolding your children, you can probably take some comfort in not resorting to the Coelho parenting system.

The reason Coelho's parents institutionalized him was that he had a passionate interest as a teenager in becoming a writer. Pedro and Lygia Coelho believed this was a waste of a life. They suggested he could do a bit of writing in his spare time if he felt the need to dabble in such a thing, but his real future lay in becoming a lawyer. When Paulo continued to pursue the arts, his parents felt they had no choice but to commit him to a mental institution to drive these destructive notions from his head. "They wanted to help me," Coelho has said. "They had their dreams. I wanted to do this and that but my parents had different plans for my life. So there was a moment when they could not control me anymore and they were desperate."

Coelho's parents put Paolo in an asylum three times. They knew their son was extremely bright, believed he had a promising career ahead of him, and did what they felt they had to do to put him on the right track. Yet not even such an extreme approach to intervention stopped Paulo Coelho from finding his Element. In spite of the intense family opposition, he continued to pursue writing.

His parents were right in assuming he had a promising future ahead of him, but that future had nothing to do with the legal profession. Coelho's novel *The Alchemist* was a major international best seller, selling more than forty million copies around the world. His books have been translated into more than sixty languages, and he is the best-selling Portuguese-language writer in history. His creative reach extends to television, newspapers, and even popular music; he has written lyrics for several hit Brazilian rock songs.

It's entirely possible that Paulo Coelho would have made an excellent lawyer. His dream was to write, though. And even though his parents tried extraordinarily hard to put him on "the right course," he kept his focus on his Element.

Few of us are encouraged to conform to our family's expectations as firmly as Paulo Coelho was. But many people face barriers from family and friends: "Don't take a dance program, you can't make a living as a dancer," "You're good at math, you should become an accountant," "I'm not paying for you to be a philosophy major," and the rest.

When people close to you discourage you from taking a particular path, they usually believe they are doing it for your own good. There are some with less noble reasons, but most believe they know what's best. And the fact is that the average office worker probably does have more financial security than the average jazz trumpeter. But it is difficult to feel accomplished when you're not accomplishing something that matters to you. Doing something "for your own good" is rarely for your own good if it causes you to be less than who you really are.

The decision to play it safe, to take the path of least resistance, can seem irresistible, particularly if you have your own doubts and fears about the alternatives. And for some people it seems easier to avoid ruffling feathers and have the approval of parents, siblings, and spouses. But not for everyone.

Some of the people in this book had to pull away from their families, for a while at least, to become the person they needed to be. Their decision to take the less comfortable route and accept the price of troubled relationships, tense family holidays, and, in Coelho's case, even lost brain cells eventually led them to considerable levels of fulfillment and accomplishment. What each of them managed to do was weigh the cost of disregarding their loved ones against the cost of relinquishing their dreams.

When Arianna Stasinopoulos was a teenager in Greece in the 1960s, she had a sudden and passionate dream. Leafing through a magazine, she saw a picture of Cambridge University in England. She was only thirteen years old, but she decided on the spot that she had to be a student there. Everybody she told about this, including her friends and her father, said it was a ridiculous idea. She was a girl, it was too expensive, she had no connections there, and this was one of the most prestigious universities in the world. No one took her seriously. No one except Arianna herself, that is. And one other person.

Her mother decided that they had to find out if Arianna's dream was even remotely possible. She made some inquiries and learned that Arianna could apply for a scholarship. She even found some cheap air tickets "so we could go to England and see Cambridge in person. It was a perfect example of what we now call visualization." It was a long flight to London, and it rained the entire time they were in Cambridge. Arianna and her mother didn't meet anyone from the university; they simply walked around and imagined what it would be like to be there. With her dream reinforced, Arianna applied as soon as she was eligible.

To her delight and everyone's astonishment (except her mother's), Cambridge accepted Arianna—and she won a scholarship. At the age of sixteen, she moved to England and went on to graduate from Cambridge University with an M.A. in economics. At twenty-one, she became the first woman president of the famed debating society, the Cambridge Union.

Now based in the United States, Arianna Huffington is the author of eleven books on cultural history and politics, a nationally syndicated columnist, and cohost of *Left, Right & Center*, National Public Radio's popular political roundtable program. In May 2005, she launched the *Huffington Post*, a news and blog site that has become "one of the most widely read and frequently cited media brands on the Internet." In 2006, *Time* magazine put her on their list of the world's hundred most influential people.

For all her success, Huffington knows that the biggest obstacles to achievement can be self-doubt and the disapproval of other people. She says this is especially true for women. "I am struck by how often, when I asked women to blog for the *Huffington Post*, they had a hard time trusting that what they had to say was worthwhile, even established writers. . . . So often, I think, we as women stop ourselves from trying because we don't want to risk failing. We put such a premium on being approved of, we become reluctant to take risks.

"Women still have an uneasy relationship with power and the traits necessary to be a leader. There is this internalized fear that if we are really powerful, we are going to be considered ruthless or pushy or strident—all those epithets that strike right at our femininity. We are still working at trying to overcome the fear that power and womanliness are mutually exclusive."

Huffington says there were two key factors in pursuing her early dream. The first was that she didn't really understand what she was getting herself into. "My first taste of leadership came in a situation in which I was a blissfully ignorant outsider. It was in college, when I became president of the Cambridge Union debating society. Since I had grown up in Greece, I had never heard of the Cambridge Union or the Oxford Union and didn't know about their place in English culture, so I wasn't weighed down with the kinds of overwhelming notions that may have stopped British girls from even thinking about trying for such a position. . . . In this way, it was a blessing that I started my career outside my home environment. It had its own problems in that I was ridiculed for my accent and was demeaned as someone who spoke in a funny way. But it also taught me that it is easier to overcome people's judgments than to overcome our own self-judgment, the fear we internalize."

The second factor was the unwavering support of her mother. "I don't think that anything I've done in my life would have been possible without my mother. My mother gave me that safe place, that sense that she would be there no matter what happened, whether I succeeded or failed. She gave me what I am hoping to be able to give my daughters, which is a sense that I could aim for the stars combined with the knowledge that if I didn't reach them, she wouldn't love me any less. She helped me understand that failure was part of any life."

Groupthink

Positively or negatively, our parents and families are powerful influences on us. But even stronger, especially when we're young, are our friends. We don't choose our families, but we do choose our friends, and we often choose them as a way of expanding our sense of identity beyond the family. As a result, the pressure to conform to the standards and expectations of friends and other social groups can be intense.

Judith Rich Harris is a developmental psychologist who has looked at the influences on young people of their friends and peer groups. She argues that three main forces shape our development: personal temperament, our parents, and our peers. The influence of peers, she argues, is much stronger than that of parents. "The world that children share with their peers," she says, "is what shapes their behavior and modifies the characteristics they were born with, and hence determines the sort of people they will be when they grow up."

Children get their ideas of how to behave by identifying with the group and taking on its attitudes, behaviors, speech, and styles of dress and adornment. "Most of them do this automatically and willingly. They want to be like their peers, but just in case they have any funny ideas, their peers are quick to remind them of the penalties of being different. . . . The nail that sticks up gets hammered down."

Since breaking the rules is a sure way to find ourselves out of the group, we may deny our deepest passions to stay connected with our peers. At school, we disguise an interest in physics because our circle finds it uncool. We spend afternoons playing basketball when what we really want to do is master the five mother sauces. We never mention our fascination with hip-hop because the people we travel with consider something so "street" to be beneath them. Being in your Element may depend on stepping out of the circle.

Shawn Carter was born in the housing projects in Brooklyn, New York. Now known as Jay-Z, he is one of the most successful musicians and businesspeople of his generation, and an icon to millions of people around the world. To become all of that, he first had to confront the disapproval and the skepticism of the friends and peers he grew up with on the Brooklyn streets. "When I left the block, everyone was saying I was crazy," he has said of his early success. "I was doing well for myself on the streets, and cats around me were like, 'These rappers are hos. They just record, tour, and get separated from their families, while some white person takes all their money.' I was determined to do it differently."

His role model was the music entrepreneur Russell Simmons, and like him, Jay-Z now heads a diverse business empire that's rooted in his success as a musician but goes beyond it to include a clothing line and a record label. All of this has generated a huge personal fortune for Jay-Z and the renewed respect of many of the friends in Brooklyn he had to move aside to make his way.

In extreme cases, peer groups can become trapped in what psychologist Irving Janis has called "groupthink," a mode of thinking "that people engage in when they are deeply involved in a cohesive in-group, when the members' strivings for unanimity override their motivation to realistically appraise alternative courses of action." The prevailing belief here is that the group knows best, that a decision or a direction that seems to represent

the majority of the group stands beyond careful examination—
even when your instincts suggest otherwise.

There are several famous—and sometime infamous—studies
of the effects of groupthink, including the Solomon Asch conformity experiments. In 1951, psychologist Asch brought together
college students in groups of eight to ten, telling them he was studying visual perception. All but one of the students were "plants."
They knew the nature of the experiment, and Asch had instructed
them to give incorrect answers the majority of the time. The
real subject—the only one who Asch had not prepared ahead of
time—answered each question only after hearing most of the
other answers in the group.

Asch showed the students a card with a line on it. He then
held up another card with three lines of different lengths and
asked them to say which one was the same length as the line on
the other card. One was an obvious match but the planted students had been instructed by Asch to say that the match was one
of the other lines. When it was time for the subject to answer, the
effects of groupthink kicked in. In a majority of cases, the subject answered with the group, and against clear visual evidence, at
least once during the session.

When interviewed later, most of the subjects said they knew
they were giving the wrong answers but did so because they didn't
want to be singled out. "The tendency to conformity in our society is so strong," Asch wrote, "that reasonably intelligent and
well-meaning young people are willing to call white black. This is
a matter of concern. It raises questions about our ways of education and about the values that guide our conduct."

Management writer Jerry B. Harvey gives another famous example, known as the Abilene Paradox: On a hot afternoon in
Coleman, Texas, the story goes, a family is comfortably playing
dominoes on a porch, until the father-in-law suggests they take a

trip to Abilene, fifty-three miles north, for dinner. As Harvey describes it, "The wife says, 'Sounds like a great idea.' The husband, despite having reservations because the drive is long and hot, thinks that his preferences must be out of step with the group and says, 'Sounds good to me. I just hope your mother wants to go.' The mother-in-law then says, 'Of course I want to go. I haven't been to Abilene in a long time.' The drive *is* hot, dusty, and long. When they arrive at the cafeteria, the food is as bad. They arrive back home four hours later, exhausted. One of them dishonestly says, 'It was a great trip, wasn't it.'

"The mother-in-law says that, actually, she would rather have stayed home, but went along since the other three were so enthusiastic. The husband says, 'I didn't want to go. I only went to satisfy the rest of you.' The wife says, 'I just went along to keep you happy. I would have to be crazy to want to go out in the heat like that.' The father-in-law says that he only suggested it because he thought the others might be bored.

"The group sits back, perplexed that they together decided to take a trip which none of them wanted. They each would have preferred to sit comfortably, but did not admit to it when they still had time to enjoy the afternoon."

This is a benign but dramatic illustration of the consequences of groupthink. Every member of the group agreed to do something they didn't want to do because they thought the others were committed to doing it. The result was that no one came away happy.

Allowing groupthink to inform our decisions about our futures can lead to equally unpleasant—and much more consequential—results. Accepting the group opinion that physics is not cool, playing basketball is better than learning to be a chef, and hip-hop is beneath you is counterproductive not only to the individual but to the group. Perhaps, like those in the Abilene Paradox, others in the circle secretly disagree too but are afraid to stand alone against the group. Groupthink can diminish the group as a whole.

The major obstacles to finding the Element often emerge in school. This is partly because of the hierarchy of subjects, which means that many students never discover their true interests and talents. But within the general culture of education, different social groups form distinctive subcultures. For some groups the code is that it's just not cool to study. If you're doing science, you're a geek; if you're doing art or dance, you're effete. For other groups, doing these things is absolutely essential.

The power of groups is that they validate the common interests of their members. The danger of groupthink is that it dulls their individual judgment. The group thinks in unison and behaves en masse. In this respect, schools of people are like schools of fish.

A Single Ant Can't Ruin a Picnic

You've probably seen images of huge schools of fish swimming in tight formation that instantly move in a new direction like a single organism. Perhaps you've seen swarms of insects crossing the sky that spontaneously swoop and swirl like an orchestrated cloud. It's an impressive display that seems like controlled and intelligent behavior. But the individual herrings or mosquitoes are not acting on free will, as we think of it in humans. We don't know what may be on their minds as they go along with the crowd, but we do know that when they do it, they act almost as a single creature. Researchers are now understanding more about how this happens.

The probability is that fish make those dramatic tight shifts in direction by following the movements of the fish that lie directly in their field of perception. What appears to be a masterwork of choreography is probably little more than an especially elegant version of follow-the-leader. To illustrate the point, there are now computer programs that simulate the effects of swarms and schools with remarkable accuracy.

A similar principle seems to drive the operations of one of the oldest and most successful creatures on earth, the ant. If you've seen an ant wandering aimlessly across your kitchen floor in search of a morsel to eat, you don't get a sense of a highly developed intelligence at work. Yet the work of ant colonies is a miracle of efficiency and success. Ants depend on what's known as swarm intelligence, the nature of which is currently the subject of intense study. While they have yet to understand fully how ants have developed such sophisticated teamwork, researchers do know that ants achieve their goals by fulfilling their own very specific roles with military precision.

For instance, when looking for food, one ant starts on a path, leaving a trail of pheromones. The next ant follows this trail, leaving a trail of its own. In this way, a large collection finds its way to the food source and carries it back as a team to the colony. Each ant works toward a global goal, while no one ant takes the lead. In fact, there seems to be no hierarchy at all within ant colonies. Even the queen's one function seems to be to lay eggs. These patterns of coordinated group behavior in fish, ants, mosquitoes, and most other creatures are principally to do with protection and security, with mating and survival, and with getting food and not becoming food themselves.

It's much the same with human beings. We aggregate as groups for the same essential and primal purposes. The upside for us is that groups can be tremendously supportive. The downside is that they encourage uniformity of thought and behavior. The Element is about discovering yourself, and you can't do this if you're trapped in a compulsion to conform. You can't be yourself in a swarm.

Culture: Right and Thong

Beyond the specific social constraints we may feel from families and friends, there are others that are implicit in the general culture. I define culture as the values and forms of behavior that characterize different social groups. Culture is a system of permissions. It's about the attitudes and behaviors that are acceptable and unacceptable in different communities, those that are approved of and those that are not. If you don't understand the cultural codes, you can look just awful.

I'll always remember a man I saw who got it miserably wrong on a beach in Malibu in California. He strutted slowly into our midst, a vision of the unexpected that caused a beach full of strangers to form a deep bond of helpless camaraderie. He was about forty. My guess was that he was some sort of executive, and I could imagine that in certain settings he cut a distinguished figure. But here, he did not. In a land of physical culture and treadmills, he was pale, hairy, and inhabited a sagging body that clearly spent its days at a desk and its nights on a barstool. One can forgive a man for all of these things. But not for wearing a nylon, leopard-print thong.

The thong clung to his groin like an oxygen mask. A stretch of elastic held it in place, skirting his waist and threading tightly between his bare buttocks. He paraded down the length of the beach, apparently delighted that every eye was turning to him in a slow Mexican wave of amazement. He gave the impression of a self-appointed role model of physical attraction and sexual magnetism bathing in the bright sunlight of popular acclaim.

This wasn't the majority opinion, however. "At least he might have waxed," said the man next to me.

Why was this so hypnotically amusing for us all? It wasn't just that he had such an outrageously high opinion of his attractiveness. It was also that he was so far out of context. The outfit and attitude might have worked in the south of France, but in Malibu, for various reasons, it was all wrong. There's an unspoken code for men on California beaches. It's a curious mixture of peacock display and public modesty. Oiled torsos and rippling muscles are fine, but naked buttocks are not. All over America, there's this intricate mixture of prurience and prudishness.

Shortly afterward, my wife, Terry, and I were in Barcelona. There are beaches there that line the harbor in the city center, and every lunchtime during the summer the local offices spill out and young men and women head to the city beaches and sunbathe topless, in thongs at the very most. In Spain, that's completely accepted. It would be odd there to see someone in a pair of knee-length shorts and a T-shirt. The culture simply accepts that people can wander around virtually naked on the beach.

All social cultures promote what I'd describe as "contagious behavior." One of the best examples is language, and more particularly accents and dialects. These are wonderful illustrations of the impulse to copy and conform. It would be odd for someone born and raised in the Highlands of Scotland or the Badlands of Montana not to speak the local dialect of English with the local accent. We'd be amazed, of course, if a child born there spontaneously started speaking French or Hebrew. But we'd be just as taken aback if the child spoke the local language in an entirely different dialect or accent from everyone else. The natural instinct of children is to copy and imitate, and as they grow they absorb not only the sounds they hear but the sensibilities they express and the culture they convey. Languages are the bearers of the cultural genes. As we learn a language, accents, and ways of speaking, we also learn ways of thinking, feeling, and relating.

The cultures in which we are raised do not only affect our values and outlook. They also shape our bodies and may even restructure our brains. Language, again, is a prime example. As we learn to speak, our mouths and vocal organs adapt to make the sounds our languages use. If you grow up speaking only one or two languages, it can be physically difficult to create the sounds that other languages require and that other cultures take for granted—those guttural French sounds, or the lispy sounds of Spanish, or the tonal sounds of some Asian languages. To speak a new language, we may have to retrain our bodies to make and understand the new sounds. But the effects of culture may go deeper still—into the actual structures of the brain.

In the last few years there has been a series of fascinating studies into differences in visual perception between people from the West and from East Asia. These studies suggest that the cultures we grow up in affect the basic processes by which we see the world around us. In one such study, Westerners and Asians were asked to look at a series of photographs and to describe what they saw. A number of marked differences emerged. In essence, Westerners tend to focus more on the foreground of the pictures and on what they consider the subject. Asians focus more on the whole image, including the relationships between the different elements. For example, one photograph showed a jungle scene with a tiger. Typically, the Western observers, when asked what they saw, said, "A tiger." To Western readers of this book, that may seem reasonable enough. However, Asian observers typically said, "It's a jungle with a tiger in it," or "It's a tiger in a jungle." The difference is significant, and it relates to larger cultural differences in the Western and Asian worldviews.

In Asian art there is often much less emphasis on portraiture and the individual subject of the sort that is common in Western art. In Asian cultures, there is less emphasis on the individual and more on the collective. Western philosophy since the ancient Greeks has emphasized the importance of critical reasoning, logical analysis, and the separation of ideas and things into categories. Chinese philosophy is not based as much on logic and deductive reasoning and tends to emphasize relationships and holism. These differences in perception may lead to differences in memory and judgment. At least one study suggests that over time they may also lead to structural differences in the brain.

Researchers in Illinois and Singapore monitored brain activity in young and elderly volunteers as they looked at a series of images with different subjects and backgrounds. Using functional magnetic resonance imaging (fMRI), they focused on the part of the brain known as the lateral occipital complex, which processes visual information about objects. All the younger participants showed similar brain activity, but there were marked differences in neural responses between the older Western and Asian observers. In the Westerners, the lateral occipital complex remained active, while in the Asian participants it responded only minimally.

Dr. Michael Chee is a professor with the Cognitive Neuroscience Laboratory in Singapore and coauthor of the study. He concluded, "The parts of the brain involved in processing background and objects are engaged differently across the two sets of elderly people coming from different geographical and—by inference—cultural backgrounds." Dr. Denise Park is professor of psychology at the University of Illinois and a senior researcher on the project. In her view, these different results may be because East Asian cultures "are more interdependent and individuals spend more time monitoring the environment and others. Westerners focus on individuals and central objects because these cultures tend to be independent and focused more on the self than others." She says that these studies show that culture can sculpt the brain.

Whether and to what extent this happens is now attracting a wider field of researchers. What is already clear is that what we actually see of the world is affected by culture, not only what we think of what we see. Culture conditions all of us in ways that are imperceptible.

Swimming Against the Tide

All cultures have an unwritten "survival manual" for success, to quote cultural anthropologist Clotaire Rapaille. The rules and guidelines are transparent to most of us (if not to the thong man), and those who move from one culture to another can gain insight into the different rules and guidelines relatively easily. This survival manual comes from generations of adaptation to the particular climate in which the culture resides. But in addition to helping those within the culture thrive, it also sets out a series of constraints. Such constraints can inhibit us from reaching our Element because our passions seem inconsistent with the culture.

The great social movements are those that are stimulated when the boundaries are broken. Rock music, punk, hip-hop, and other great shifts in the social culture usually derive their energy from young people looking for some alternative way of being. Youthful rebellion often expresses itself through distinctive styles of speech and dress codes, which usually turn out to be just as conformist and orthodox within their subculture as they are at odds with the dominant culture they're trying to escape. It's very hard to pass as a hippie if you're wearing an Armani suit.

All cultures—and subcultures—also embody systems of constraints that can inhibit individuals from reaching their Element if their passions are in conflict with their context. Some people born in one culture end up adopting another because they prefer its sensibilities and ways of life, like cultural cross-dressers; a French person may become an Anglophile, or an American a Francophile. Like people who change religions, they can become more zealous about their adopted culture than those who were born into it.

The urban culture may not be best for someone who wants to run a small shop where he knows everyone's name. Parts of heartland American culture are not prime territory for those who want careers as scathing political comics. This is why Bob Dylan had to get out of Hibbing, and why Arianna Stasinopoulos wanted to leave Greece. Finding your Element sometimes requires breaking away from your native culture in order to achieve your goals.

Zaha Hadid, the first woman ever to win the Pritzker Prize for Architecture, grew up in Baghdad in the 1950s. Iraq was a different place then, much more secular and more open to Western thought. During this time, there were many women in Iraq developing ambitious careers. But Hadid wanted to be an architect, and she found no female role models of this sort in her homeland. Driven by her passions, Hadid moved first to London and then to America, where she studied with the greatest architects of her time, honed a revolutionary style, and, after a rocky start—her work requires considerable risky conceptual leaps, which many clients were loath to make at first—built some of the most distinctive structures in the world.

Her work includes the Rosenthal Center for Contemporary Art in Cincinnati, Ohio, which the *New York Times* called "the most important new building in America since the Cold War." Moving out of her culture and into a milieu that celebrated invention gave Hadid the opportunity to soar. If she'd stayed in Iraq, she might have had a good career, at least until political circumstances changed for women. But she would not have found her

Element in architecture, because her native culture simply didn't afford women that option.

The contagious behavior of schools of fish, insect swarms, and crowds of people is generated by close physical proximity. For most of human history, cultural identities have also been formed through direct contact with the people who are physically nearest to us: small villages, the local community. Large movements of people once were limited to invasions, military conquests, and trade, and these were the main ways in which cultural ideas were disseminated and different languages and ways of life imposed on other communities.

All of this has changed irreversibly in the last two hundred years or so with the growth of global communications. We now have patterns of contagious behavior being generated on a massive scale through the Web. Second Life has millions of people online from different parts of the world potentially affecting how they each think and taking on new virtual identities and roles.

Many of us now live like Russian dolls nestled in multiple layers of cultural identity. I was amused to read recently, for example, that nowadays being British "means driving home in a German car, stopping off to pick up some Belgian beer and a Turkish kebab or an Indian takeaway, to spend the evening on Swedish furniture, watching American programs on a Japanese TV." And the most British thing of all? "Suspicion of anything foreign."

The complexities and fluidity of contemporary cultures can make it easier to change context and break away from the pressures of groupthink and feeling stereotyped. They can also make for a profound sense of confusion and insecurity. The message here isn't as simplistic as "Don't let anything get in your way." Our families, friends, culture, and place in the human community are all important to our sense of fulfillment, and we have certain responsibilities to all of them. The real message here is that, in seeking your Element, you're likely to face one or more of the three levels of constraint—personal, social, and cultural.

Sometimes, as Chuck Close found, reaching your Element requires devising creative solutions to strong limitations. Sometimes, as we learned from Paulo Coelho, it means maintaining a vision in the face of vicious resistance. And sometimes, as Zaha Hadid showed us, it means walking away from the life you've known to find an environment more suited to your growth.

Ultimately, the question is always going to be, "What price are you willing to pay?" The rewards of the Element are considerable, but reaping these rewards may mean pushing back against some stiff opposition.

CHAPTER SEVEN

Do You Feel Lucky?

BEING GOOD AT SOMETHING and having a passion for it are essential to finding the Element. But they are not enough. Getting there depends fundamentally on our view of ourselves and of the events in our lives. The Element is also a matter of attitude.

When twelve-year-old John Wilson walked into his chemistry class at Scarborough High School for Boys on a rainy day in late October 1931, he had no way of knowing that his life was about to change completely. The class experiment that day was to show how heating a container of water would bring oxygen bubbling to the surface, something students at this school and at schools all around the world had been doing for a very long time. The container the teacher gave John to heat, however, was not like the containers students everywhere had used. Somehow, this container mistakenly held something more volatile than water. It turned out that the container had the wrong solution because a laboratory assistant had been distracted and put the wrong label on the bottle. And when John heated it with a Bunsen burner, the container exploded, shattering glass bottles in the vicinity, destroying a portion of the classroom, and pelting the students with razor-edged shards. Several students came away from this accident bleeding.

John Wilson came away from it blinded in both eyes.

Wilson spent the next two months in the hospital. When he

returned home, his parents attempted to find a way to deal with the catastrophe that had befallen their lives. But Wilson did not regard the accident as catastrophic. "It did not strike me even then as a tragedy," he said once in an interview with the *Times* of London. He knew he had the rest of his life to live, and he did not intend to live it in an understated way. He learned braille quickly and continued his education at the esteemed Worcester College for the Blind. There, he not only excelled as a student but also became an accomplished rower, swimmer, actor, musician, and orator.

From Worcester, Wilson studied law at Oxford. Away from the protected environs of a school set up for blind students, he needed to contend with a busy campus and the very active streets in the vicinity. Rather than relying on a walking stick, though, he relied on an acute sense of hearing and what he called his "obstacle sense" to keep him out of harm's way. At Oxford, he received his law degree and set out to work for the National Institute for the Blind. His real calling, however, was still waiting for him.

In 1946, Wilson went on a fact-finding tour of British territories in Africa and the Middle East. What he found there was rampant blindness. And unlike the accident that cost him his eyesight, the diseases that affected so many of these people were preventable with the proper medical attention. For Wilson, it was one thing to accept his own fate and quite another to allow something to continue when it could be fixed so easily. This moved him to action.

The report Wilson delivered upon his return led to the formation of the British Empire Society for the Blind, now called Sight Savers International. Wilson himself served as the director of the organization for more than thirty years and accomplished remarkable things during his tenure.

His work often led him to travel more than fifty thousand

miles a year, but he considered this an essential part of the job, believing that he needed to be present in the places where his organization's work was being done. In 1950, he and his wife lived in a mud hut in a part of Ghana known as "the country of the blind" because a disease that came from insect bites had blinded 10 percent of the population. He set his team to work on developing a preventative treatment for the disease, commonly known as "river blindness." Using the drug Mectizan, the organization inoculated the children in the seven African countries stricken with the disease and all but eradicated it. By the early 1960s, river blindness was overwhelmingly under control. It is no exaggeration to say that generations of African children can thank the efforts of John Wilson for their sight.

Under Wilson's direction, the organization conducted three million cataract operations and treated twelve million others at risk of becoming blind. They also administered more than one hundred million doses of vitamin A to prevent childhood blindness and distributed braille study packs to afflicted people throughout Africa and Asia. In all, tens of millions can see because of the commitment John Wilson made to preventing the preventable.

When Wilson retired, he and his wife devoted their considerable energies to Impact, a program of the World Health Organization that works on the prevention of all types of disabling diseases. Knighted in 1975, he also received the Helen Keller International Award, the Albert Schweitzer International Prize, and the World Humanity Award. He continued to be an active and prominent voice for the cause of preventing blindness and all avoidable disability until his death in 1999.

John Coles, in his biography *Blindness and the Visionary: The Life and Work of John Wilson*, wrote, "By any standards, his achievements rate comparison with those of other great humanitarians." Others have compared his accomplishments with those of Mother Teresa.

Many people, faced with the circumstances Sir John Wilson encountered, would have bemoaned their existence. Perhaps they would have considered themselves cursed by ill fortune and frustrated in their attempts to do anything significant with their lives. Wilson, however, insisted that blindness was "a confounded nuisance, not a crippling affliction," and he modeled that attitude in the most inspiring possible way.

He lost his sight and found a vision. He proved dramatically that it's not what happens to us that determines out lives—it's what we make of what happens.

Attitude and Aptitude

There is a risk in giving examples of people who have found their Element. Their stories can be inspiring, of course, but they can also be depressing. After all, these people seem blessed in some way; they've had the good fortune to do what they love to do and to be very good at doing it. One could easily ascribe their good fortune to luck, and certainly many people who love what they do say that they've been lucky (just as people who don't like what they're doing with their lives often say they've been unlucky). Of course, some "lucky" people have been fortunate to find their passions and to have the opportunities to pursue them. Some "unlucky" people have had bad things happen to them. But good and bad things happen to all of us. It's not what happens to us that makes the difference in our lives. What makes the difference is our attitude toward what happens. The idea of luck is a powerful way of illustrating the importance of our basic attitudes in affecting whether or not we find our Element.

Describing ourselves as lucky or unlucky suggests that we're simply the beneficiaries or victims of chance circumstances. But if being in your Element were just a matter of chance, all you could do is cross your fingers and hope to get lucky as well. There's much more to being lucky than that. Research and experience show that lucky people often make their luck because of their attitudes.

Chapter 3 looked at the concept of creativity. The real message there is that we all create and shape the realities of our own lives to an extraordinary extent. Those who simply wait for good things to happen really would be lucky to encounter them. All of the people I've profiled in this book have taken an active role in "getting lucky." They've mastered a combination of attitudes and behavior that led them to opportunities and that give them the confidence to take them.

One of these is the ability to look at situations in different ways. There's a difference between what we are able to perceive— our field of perception—and what we actually do perceive. As I mentioned in the last chapter, there are significant cultural differences in how people perceive the world around them. But two different people with the same cultural orientations may still see the same scene in completely different ways, depending upon their preconceptions and their sense of mission. Best-selling author and top motivational speaker Anthony Robbins demonstrates this with a simple activity. In his three-day seminars, he asks the thousands of people in attendance to look around and count how many items of green clothing they can see. He gives them a few minutes to do this and then asks them for their findings. He then asks them how many items of red clothing they saw. Most people can't even begin to answer the question because Robbins told them to look for items of green clothing, and they only focused on those.

In his book *The Luck Factor*, psychologist Richard Wiseman writes about his study of four hundred exceptionally "lucky" and "unlucky" people. He found that those who considered themselves lucky tended to exhibit similar attitudes and behaviors. Their unlucky counterparts tended to exhibit opposite traits.

Wiseman has identified four principles that characterize lucky people. Lucky people tend to maximize chance opportunities. They are especially adept at creating, noticing, and acting upon these opportunities when they arise. Second, they tend to be very effective at listening to their intuition, and do work (such as meditation) that is designed to boost their intuitive abilities. The third principle is that lucky people tend to expect to be lucky, creating a series of self-fulfilling prophecies because they go into the world anticipating a positive outcome. Last, lucky people have an attitude that allows them to turn bad luck to good. They don't allow ill fortune to overwhelm them, and they move quickly to take control of the situation when it isn't going well for them.

Dr. Wiseman performed an experiment that speaks to the role of perception in luck. He set up a nearby café with a group of actors told to behave the way people normally did in that setting. He also put a five-pound note on the sidewalk just outside the café. He then asked one of his "lucky" volunteers to go down to the shop. The lucky person saw the money on the ground, picked it up, walked into the shop, and ordered a coffee for himself and the stranger at the next chair. He and the stranger struck up a conversation and wound up exchanging contact information.

Next, Dr. Wiseman sent one of his "unlucky" volunteers to the café. This person stepped right over the five-pound note, bought coffee, and interacted with no one. Later, Wiseman asked both subjects if anything lucky happened that day. The lucky subject talked about finding the money and making a new contact. The unlucky subject couldn't think of anything.

One way of opening ourselves up to new opportunities is to make conscious efforts to look differently at our ordinary situations. Doing so allows a person to see the world as one rife with possibility and to take advantage of some of those possibilities if they seem worth pursuing. What Robbins and Wiseman show us is that if we keep our focus too tight, we miss the rest of the world swirling around us.

Another attitude that leads to what many of us would consider "good luck" is the ability to reframe, to look at a situation that fails to go according to plan and turn it into something beneficial.

If things had worked out differently, there is a very good chance that I would not be writing this book at all now and you would therefore not be reading it. I might be running a sports bar in England and regaling anyone who'd listen with tales of my glittering soccer career. I grew up in Liverpool as one of a large family of boys and one sister. My father had been an amateur soccer player and boxer, and like everyone in my extended family, he was devoted to our local soccer team, Everton. It was the dream of every household in the neighborhood to have one of their own kids play for Everton.

Until I was four, everyone in my family assumed the Everton soccer player in our clan would be me. I was strong, very active, and I had a natural aptitude for soccer. This was in 1954, the year in which the polio epidemics reached their peak in Europe and America. One day, my mother came to collect me from nursery school to find that I was howling in pain from a piercing headache. I never cried much as a child, so my misery concerned her deeply. Our doctor came to the house and decided I had the flu. By the next morning, it became clear that his diagnosis was off. I woke up completely paralyzed—I could not move at all.

I spent the next few weeks on the emergency list in the polio isolation unit of our local hospital. I'd completely lost the use of my legs and much of my body. For eight months, I found myself in the hospital surrounded by other kids who were struggling with sudden paralysis. Some of them were in iron lungs. Some of them didn't survive.

Very slowly, I began to recover some use of my left leg and, thankfully, the full use of my arms and the rest of my body. My right leg remained completely paralyzed. I eventually left the hospital at the age of five in a wheelchair, wearing two braces.

This pretty much put an end to my planned career in soccer— although, given the way Everton has been playing lately, I might still have a shot at making the team.

This blow was devastating to my parents and everyone in my family. As I grew up, one of their biggest concerns was how I would make a living. My father and mother recognized from the outset that I needed to make the best use of my other talents, though it wasn't clear at that point what those talents might be. Their first priority was for me to get the best education possible. As I moved through school, I was under extra pressure to study and do well in my exams. This was not easy. After all, I was one of a large, very close family living in a house that was constantly full of visitors, noise, and laughter.

On top of this, the house was in Merseyside in the early '60s. Rock music—loud rock music—was everywhere. My brother Ian played drums in a band that rehearsed every week in our house right next door to the room where I was trying to find some relevance in algebra and Latin. In the battle for my attentions between the books and the beat, the books were losing badly.

Still, as much as any boy could, I understood that there was a future to consider and that I needed to do the most with what I had. Soccer was no longer an option, and as much as I loved music, I didn't have any musical talent to speak of. With the benign pressure of my father, I eventually got through school. I went on to college, and it was there that the interests that have shaped my life began to take form.

I don't know what kind of soccer player I would have been. I do know that catching polio opened many more doors for me than the one it so firmly closed at the time. I certainly didn't see this when it happened, and neither did anyone in my family. But my parents' ability to reframe our situation by doing their best to focus me on my schoolwork, and my ability to reframe my circumstance, turned a disaster into a completely unexpected set of opportunities, which continue to evolve and multiply.

Someone else who was denied a career in soccer went in a very different direction. Vidal Sassoon is one of the most celebrated names in hairdressing. In the 1960s, his clients included the biggest stars and iconic models of the time, such as Mary Quant, Jean Shrimpton, and Mia Farrow. His revolutionary creations included the bob, the five-point geometric cut, and the Greek goddess style, taking over from the beehive styles of the 1950s.

When Vidal was a child in the East End of London, his father abandoned his mother. An aunt took them all in, and Vidal and four other children lived together in her two-bedroom tenement flat. Things got so bad that eventually his mother sent Vidal and his brother to an orphanage, and it was nearly six years before she was able to get them home again. As a teenager, he had a passionate ambition to be a soccer player, but his mother insisted that he apprentice as a hairdresser. She thought that would be a more secure job for him.

"I was fourteen years old," he said, "and in England unless you were privileged, that was when you left school and started to earn a living. I was apprenticed to this wonderful man called Adolph Cohen on Whitechapel Road and what a disciplinarian he was! I was fourteen, it was 1942, and the war was on. Bombs were dropping practically every night, the Luftwaffe was giving London hell, and we still had to come in with our nails clean, our trousers pressed, and our shoes polished. Those two years with him definitely gave me the structure I needed in my life: the inconvenience of discipline.

"I took some time out after that because I still wasn't sure if I wanted to be a hairdresser. I loved football so much. In the end, I suppose it was the prospect of all the pretty girls and, of course, my mother that swung it for me. At first I couldn't get a proper job in the West End of London at a big salon like Raymond's because I had a cockney accent. That's the way it was in those days."

For three years, he took voice lessons to improve how he sounded so he could get a job at one of the better salons. "I knew I had to learn how to project myself, so I got a job teaching in different salons in the evenings. I used my tips to take a bus to the West End and go to the theater. I'd catch the matinee and see great Shakespearean actors like Laurence Olivier and John Gielgud and try to copy their voices."

He went regularly to London's many art museums and began to educate and inspire himself with the history of painting and architecture. "I really think that was what set me on my course. I was developing my own vision for hairdressing. The shapes in my head were always geometric. I have always been working toward a bone structure so as to define a woman rather than just make her 'pretty pretty.' I knew hair dressing could be different, but it took a lot of work and nine years to develop the system we use in our salons."

In 1954, he and a partner opened a very small salon on the third floor of a building in London's fashionable Bond Street. "Bond Street was magic to me because it meant the West End. It was where I couldn't get a job earlier. The West End meant I was going to make it. I was determined to change the way things were done or leave hairdressing. For me it wasn't a case of bouffants and arrangements. It was about structure and how you train the eye."

In the first week, they took in only fifty pounds, but after two years they had built the business to a point where they could move to the "right" end of Bond Street and compete with the top salons.

"London was a fascinating place in the sixties. There was this incredible energy. We were not going to do things the way our parents did. I was always looking for different ways of doing things. Everything was changing: our music, clothes, and art. So it was clear to me that there could be something different for hair."

And then one day, something caught his eye that was to transform his vision and the whole field of hairdressing. "One Saturday, one of the guys was drying a client's hair and just using a brush and drier without any rollers. I thought about it over the weekend, and on the Monday I asked him why he had dried her hair like that. He said he'd been in a hurry and didn't want to wait for her to come out of the dryer. 'Hurry or not,' I said, 'you've discovered something, and we are going to work on this.' For us, that's how blow drying started."

Vidal Sassoon was to create a revolution in cutting and styling hair that changed the industry and the way that women looked around the world.

"I always had shapes in my head. I remember cutting Grace Cruddington's hair into the 'five point haircut' and flying to Paris with her in 1964. I wanted to actually show it to the magazine editors. I knew we'd got something but you had to see it, see the way it moved and swung. It was all about scissors. Our motto was 'eliminate the superfluous.' We made pages and pages in *Elle* magazine. They'd been going to feature curls but they loved what we'd done. That led on to more photo sessions and tours. Then in 1965, I was invited to do a show in New York and about five newspapers covered it. They gave us the front page of the beauty section in the *New York Times* the following day. The papers and magazines were full of pictures of our new geometric cuts. We'd done it! We'd brought America 'the bob.'"

He opened the first Sassoon school in London in 1967. Now they are all over the world. "My philosophy has always been to share knowledge. Our academy and education centers are filled with energy. That's what helps young people to push the boundaries of their creativity. I tell them, if you have a good idea, go for it, do it your way. Take good advice, make sure it is good advice, then do it your way. We've been around for a long time and to me 'longevity is a fleeting moment that lasts forever.'"

Vidal Sassoon created a new look and a whole new approach to fashion and style. He not only took the opportunities that he saw, he created a million more in the way he responded to them.

Perhaps the most important attitude for cultivating good fortune is a strong sense of perseverance. Many of the people in this book faced considerable constraints in finding the Element and managed to do it through sheer, dogged determination. None more so than Brad Zdanivsky.

At nineteen, Brad knew that he loved to climb. He'd been climbing trees and boulders since he was a kid and had moved on to scale some of the highest peaks in Canada. Then, while returning home from a long drive after a funeral, he fell asleep at the wheel of his car and plunged nearly two hundred feet off a cliff.

The accident left him a quadriplegic, but he remained a rock climber in his heart. Even as he waited at the bottom of the cliff for help to arrive, knowing that he couldn't move, he recalls wondering if it were possible for a quadriplegic to climb. After eight months of rehab, he began to talk to fellow climbers about designing some kind of gear that would get him back onto a mountain. With the help of several people, including his father, he created a device with two large wheels at the top and a smaller one on the bottom. Seated in this rig, he uses a pulley system with his shoulders and thumbs that allows him to scale about a foot at a time. The technique is excruciatingly slow, but Zdanivsky's persistence has been rewarded. Before his injury, his goal had been to climb the two-thousand-foot Stawamus Chief, one of the largest granite monoliths in the world. In July 2005, he reached that goal.

We all shape the circumstances and realities of our own lives, and we can also transform them. People who find their Element are more likely to evolve a clearer sense of their life's ambitions and set a course for achieving them. They know that passion and aptitude are essential. They know too that our attitudes to events and to ourselves are crucial in determining whether or not we find and live our lives in the Element.

CHAPTER EIGHT

Somebody Help Me

AFTER I CAUGHT POLIO, I went to a special school for the physically handicapped. This was standard procedure back then in Britain; the education authorities removed any children with disabilities from mainstream state schools and sent them to one of these special schools. So I found myself from the age of five traveling by special bus every day from our working-class area of Liverpool across the city to a small school in a relatively affluent area. The Margaret Beavan School had about a hundred or so pupils aged from five to fifteen with various sorts of disability, including polio, cerebral palsy, epilepsy, asthma, and, in the case of one of my best friends there, hydrocephalus.

We weren't especially conscious of each other's disabilities, though many of us wore braces, used crutches, or were in wheelchairs. In that setting, the nature of anyone's disability was more or less irrelevant. Like most kids, we formed our friendships based on people's personalities. One of my classmates had cerebral palsy and severe spasticity. He couldn't use his hands and spoke with tremendous difficulty. The only way he could write was by gripping a pencil between his toes and arching his leg over the desk. For all of that, he was a funny and entertaining guy once you got used to his strained efforts at speaking and could understand what he was actually saying. I enjoyed my time at the school and had all the childhood excitements and frustrations that I knew my brothers and sister were having at their "normal" schools. If anything, I seemed to like my school more than they liked theirs.

One day when I was ten, a visitor appeared in the classroom. He was a well-dressed man with a kind face and an educated voice. He spent some time talking to the teacher, who seemed to me to take him very seriously. Then he wandered around the desks talking to the kids. I suppose there were about a dozen of us in the room. I remember speaking with him for a little while, and that he left soon afterward.

A day or so later, I received a message to go to the headmaster's office. I knocked on the large paneled door, and a voice called me in. Sitting next to the head teacher was the man who'd come into my classroom. He was introduced to me as Mr. Strafford. I learned later that he was Charles Strafford, a member of a distinguished group of public officials in the United Kingdom, Her Majesty's Inspectors of Schools. The government had appointed these senior educators to report independently on the quality of schools around the country. Mr. Strafford had particular responsibility for special schools in the northwest of England, including Liverpool.

We had a short conversation during which Mr. Strafford asked me some general questions about how I was getting on at the school and about my interests and family. A few days later, I received another message to go to the headmaster's study. This time I wound up in another room and met a different man who asked me a series of questions in what I later understood was a general IQ test. I remember this vividly because I made a mistake during the test that really irritated me. The man read a series of statements and asked me to comment on them. One of them was this: "Scientists in America have discovered a skull which they believe belonged to Christopher Columbus when he was fourteen." He asked me what I thought of that, and I said that it could not have been Christopher Columbus's skull because he didn't go to America when he was fourteen.

The moment I left the room, I realized what a stupid answer that was and turned to knock on the door to tell the man that I knew the real flaw in the statement. I heard him speaking to someone else, though, and decided not to interrupt. The next day I saw him crossing the playground and was about to accost him with the answer. But I worried that he would assume that I'd spoken with my dad overnight and that he'd told me the real answer. I decided it was a waste of time to correct things. Fifty years later, I'm still annoyed about this. I know; I should get over it.

My error turned out to be insignificant to whatever the testers were looking for in me. Shortly afterward, the school moved me to a different class of children who were several years older than me. Apparently, Mr. Strafford had spoken with the head teacher about me and said that he saw a particular spark of intelligence that the school wasn't developing as fully as they could. He thought the school could challenge me more and that I had the potential to pass a test known at the time as the eleven-plus examination.

In Britain back then, high school education took place in two different types of school: secondary modern schools and grammar schools. The grammar schools offered a more prestigious, academic education, and they were the primary routes to professional careers and universities. Secondary modern schools offered a more practical education for kids to take up manual and blue-collar jobs. The whole system was a deliberate piece of social engineering designed to provide the workforce needed for the industrial economy in the UK. The eleven-plus was a series of IQ tests developed to identify the academic aptitudes needed for a grammar school education. Passing the eleven-plus was, for working-class kids, the best path to a professional career and an escape from a possible lifetime of manual work.

The teacher in my new class was the redoubtable Miss York. She was a small woman in her forties, kind but with a reputation for being intellectually rigorous and demanding. Some of the teachers at the school had relatively low expectations of what we kids were likely to achieve in our lives. I think they saw the purpose of "special education" mainly as pastoral. Miss York did not. She expected of her "special" pupils what she would expect of any others: that they work hard, learn, and do their absolute best. Miss York coached me relentlessly in math, English, history, and a variety of other subjects. Periodically she would give me past eleven-plus exams to practice on, encouraging me to excel at these. She remains one of the most impressive teachers I have ever met.

Eventually, with a group of other children from my school and other special schools in the area, I sat down to take the actual eleven-plus exam. For weeks afterward, Miss York, Mr. Strafford, my parents, and I waited anxiously for the brown envelope from the Liverpool Education Committee to arrive with the potentially life-changing result of the test. One morning in the early summer of 1961, we heard the letterbox clatter, and my mother ran to the front door. Tense with excitement, she carried the letter into the small kitchen where we were having breakfast and handed it to me to open. With a deep breath, I took out the small folded piece of paper inside the envelope with its typed message. I had passed.

We could hardly believe it. The house erupted in wild excitement. I was the first member of my family to pass this test, and the only pupil at the school who passed it that year. From that moment on, my life moved in a completely new direction. I received a scholarship to the Liverpool Collegiate School, one of the best in the city. In one leap, I moved from the special school into the upper ends of mainstream state education. There, I began to develop the interests and capacities that have shaped the rest of my life.

Charles Strafford became a close friend of my family and a frequent visitor to our packed, usually frenetic family home in Liverpool. He was a sophisticated, urbane man with a passion for helping people find the chances they deserved. A professional educator with a love of literature and classical music, he played the timpani, sang in choirs, and conducted music ensembles in Mersey-side. He had a refined taste for good wines and brandies and lived in a finely furnished town house in northern England. He'd served as a major during World War II and had been part of the Normandy campaign. He kept a second home in Ranville in the Calvados region of northern France, where he had become a key figure in the local French community. Ranville now boasts a road named after him, the allée Charles Strafford. I visited him there in my university days, and he introduced me to local society and to the pleasures of French cuisine and calvados apple brandy, for which I am equally grateful.

For me, Charles Strafford was a window into another world. Through hands-on, practical assistance, he facilitated my early journey from the back row of special education to what has become a lifelong passion for full-scale educational reform. He was an inspirational role model for seeing the potential in other people and for creating opportunities for them to show what they can really do. Aside from my parents, he was my first true mentor and taught me the invaluable role mentors play in helping us reach our Element.

The Life-Changing Connection

Finding our Element often requires the aid and guidance of others. Sometimes this comes from someone who sees something in us that we don't see in ourselves, as was the case with Gillian Lynne. Sometimes it comes in the form of a person bringing out the best in us, as Peggy Fury did with Meg Ryan. For me, Charles Strafford saw that I would only reach my potential if my educators offered me greater challenges. He took the necessary steps to assure that it happened.

I didn't know it at the time, but the person who was to mentor me for most of my adult life this far was also at school in Liverpool at the time, just a few miles away from me. I met Terry years later, when I was living and working in London in my late twenties. I was back in Liverpool for a week to run a course for teachers. She was teaching drama in a difficult, low-income area of the city. We had an instant connection—which had absolutely nothing to do with teaching, education, or the Element—and we've been together ever since. She's one of the finest mentors I know, not just to me but to friends, family, and everyone who works with her and for her. She knows intuitively the power and importance of mentors because they have been so important in her own life. While I was being mentored by Charles, she had a childhood mentor of her own. This is how she tells it:

"I went to an all-girls Catholic high school run by an order of nuns known as the Sisters of Mercy—a misnomer if ever there was one. This was the 'swinging sixties,' and we weren't doing any swinging, but we were doing a lot of praying and in particular, I was praying for a way out. By the time I was seventeen my only ambition was to leave home, move away from the suburbs and get to the bright lights of London fast. From there I was planning on getting to America and marrying Elvis Presley.

"My academic career had been one abject failure after another, but I loved to act and I loved to read. Then in my last year at school for the first time I had an inspirational English teacher, Sister Mary Columba, a tiny young woman who had a passion for W. B. Yeats and a passion for teaching. At the very first seminar, she picked me to read a poem to the class and, as I did, the hairs on the back of my neck tingled. I still have never read anything more beautiful or powerful:

> Had I the heavens' embroidered cloths
> Enwrought with golden and silver light,
> The blue and the dim and the dark cloths
> Of night and light and the half light,
> I would spread the cloths under your feet;
> But I, being poor, have only my dreams;
> I have spread my dreams under your feet;
> Tread softly because you tread on my dreams.

"For the first time I really wanted to learn more and over the next two years she guided me to a love of Dickens and E. M. Forster to Wilfred Owen, Shakespeare, and Synge. We were a small tutorial group and every one of us was intensely engaged in her classes. She encouraged my writing, she made me give of my best and with her guidance I was able to challenge others intellectually and to shine.

"These books opened me to a world of possibilities and what intrigued me most was how open-minded she was. After all, she was a Catholic nun and here we were discussing love and sex and the occult. No subject was taboo. We would spend hours discussing any theme that was thrown up, from the Oedipus complex in *Coriolanus* to the infidelity in *Howards End*. For a girl who had rarely been out of Liverpool this was heady stuff.

"I was her top pupil that year and I passed my English exams cum laude. At her suggestion I went on to study drama and literature at college. From then on I never doubted my ability to debate. I had friends for life in the writers we studied and I know that without her wonderful mentoring I would still be looking for Elvis."

Mentors often appear in people's lives at opportune times, though, as we saw with Eric Drexler and Marvin Minsky, sometimes "mentees" take an active role in choosing their mentors. Warren Buffett, a man who has himself inspired legions of investors, points to Benjamin Graham (known as the father of security analysis) as his mentor. Graham taught Buffett at Columbia University—giving Buffett the only A-plus he ever bestowed in twenty-two years of teaching—and then offered Buffett a job at his investment company. Buffett stayed there several years before heading off on his own. In his book *Buffett: The Making of an American Capitalist*, Roger Lowenstein writes, "Ben Graham opened the door, and in a way that spoke to Buffett personally. He gave Buffett the tools to explore the market's manifold possibilities, an approach that fit his student's temper. Armed with Graham's techniques, Buffett could dismiss his oracles and make use of his native talents. And steeled by the example of Graham's character, Buffett would be able to work with his trademark self-reliance."

In a different domain entirely, the singer Ray Charles was a guiding light to countless people for his remarkable musical talent and his ability to overcome adversity. His story starts, though, with a man who taught him to tap into the music that was deep inside him.

In an interview with the Harvard Mentoring Project posted on www.WhoMentoredYou.org, Charles recalled, "Wiley Pittman, he was a cat. I mean, if it hadn't been for him, I don't think

I'd be a musician today. We lived next door to him. He had a little café, a general store, and he had a piano in there. Every afternoon around 2:00 p.m., 3:00 p.m., he'd start to practice. I was three years old and—I don't know why I loved him, I can't explain that—but any time he'd start practicing and playing that boogie woogie—I loved that boogie woogie sound—I would stop playing as a child, I didn't care who was out there in the yard, my buddies, or whoever, I would leave them, and go inside and sit by him and listen to him play.

"From time to time, I'd start hittin' the keys with my whole fists and finally he would say to me, 'Look kid, you don't hit the keys with your whole fist like this if you like music so much,' and he knew how much I liked music because I'd stop everything I was doing and listen to him.

"So he started to teach me how to play little melodies with one finger. And, of course, I realize today that he could've said, 'Kid, get away from me, can't you see I'm practicing?' But he didn't. He took the time. Somehow, he knew in his heart, 'this kid loves music so much, I'm going to do whatever I can to help him learn how to play.'"

Marian Wright Edelman, founder and president of the Children's Defense Fund, discovered her mentor when she went away to school at Spelman College, a place she describes as "a staid women's college that developed safe, young women who married Morehouse men, helped raise a family, and never kicked up dust." While she was there, she met the history professor Howard Zinn. They were in the South in the late 1950s, and Zinn felt it was important to motivate his students to play an active part in the civil rights struggle.

Inspired by Zinn, Edelman engaged in the early civil rights protests that opened the door to a national movement. Her essential role as a voice for change and justice, and the extraordinary work she has done for children for more than three decades, found its path through the mentorship of Howard Zinn.

I came upon the stories about Ray Charles and Marian Wright Edelman while reading about National Mentoring Month, a campaign orchestrated by the Harvard Mentoring Project of the Harvard School of Public Health, MENTOR/National Mentoring Partnership, and the Corporation for National and Community Service. Sponsors for the campaign (eight years old, as of January 2009) include many huge corporations. In addition, a large number of major media companies serve as partners, doing everything from offering hundreds of millions of dollars of free public service announcements to incorporating mentoring stories into the plots of television shows.

Public/Private Ventures, a national nonprofit organization focused on improving "the effectiveness of social policies, programs, and community initiatives, especially as they affect youth and young adults," performed a landmark impact study on mentoring beginning in 2004. Randomly pairing 1,100 fourth- through ninth-graders in more than seventy schools around the country with volunteers from Big Brothers Big Sisters of America, they reached some encouraging findings about the value of mentoring. The mentored students improved in overall academic performance, quality of class work, and delivery of homework. They also got into serious trouble in school less often and were less likely to skip school.

It was good to see these results, but they didn't surprise me at all. Many of these kids probably did better in school simply because they appreciated someone taking an interest in them. This is an essential point, and I'll come back to it later on when I look at the issues and challenges of education. At the very least, good mentoring raises self-esteem and sense of purpose. But mentoring takes an elevated role for people when it involves directing or inspiring their search for the Element. What the psychologist saw with Gillian Lynne and what Wiley Pittman saw with Ray Charles was the opportunity to lead someone toward his or her heart's fulfillment. What Howard Zinn saw with Marian Wright Edelman and Ben Graham saw with Warren Buffett was rare talent that could blossom into something extraordinary if nurtured. When mentors serve this function—either turning a light on a new world or fanning the flames of interest into genuine passion—they do exalted work.

The Roles of Mentors

Mentors connect with us in a variety of ways and remain with us for varying lengths of time. Some are with us for decades in an evolving role that might start as teacher/student and ultimately evolve into close friendship. Others enter our lives at a critical moment, stay with us long enough to make a pivotal difference, and then move on. Regardless, mentors tend to serve some or all of four roles for us.

The first role is *recognition*. Charles Strafford served that function in my life, identifying skills that my teachers had not yet noticed. One of the fundamental tenets of the Element is the tremendous diversity of our individual talents and aptitudes. As we've discussed earlier, some tests are available that aim to give people a general indication of their strengths and weaknesses based on a series of standardized questions. But the real subtlety and nuances of individual aptitudes and talents are far more complex than any existing tests can detect.

Some people have general aptitudes for music, or for dance, or for science, but more often than not, their aptitudes turn out to be much more specific within a given discipline. A person may have an aptitude for a particular type of music or for specific instruments: the guitar, not the violin; the acoustic guitar, not the electric guitar. I don't know of any test or software program that can make the kinds of subtle, personal distinctions that differentiate an interest from a potential burning passion. A mentor who has already found the Element in a particular discipline can do precisely that. Mentors recognize the spark of interest or delight and can help an individual drill down to the specific components of the discipline that match that individual's capacity and passion.

Lou Aronica, my coauthor on this book, spent the first twenty years of his professional life working for book publishers. His first job out of college was for Bantam Books, one of New York's publishing powerhouses. Not long after he started at the company, he noticed a wizened, gnomish man wandering the halls. The man didn't seem to have any particular job, but everyone seemed to pay attention to him. Lou finally asked about the man and learned that he was Ian Ballantine, who'd not only founded Bantam Books and later Ballantine Books but was in fact the person who introduced the paperback book to the United States in the 1940s. Over the next couple of years, Lou passed Ballantine in the hall numerous times, nodding to him politely, and feeling a bit intimidated in the presence of a man who was such a legend in his chosen profession.

Lou got his first "real" job at Bantam around this time, a position in the editorial department, trying to piece together a science fiction and fantasy publishing program. One day not long after this, Lou was sitting at his desk when Ian Ballantine strolled in and sat down. This part was surprising enough to Lou. The next several minutes, however, left him stunned. "Ian had a distinctive way of speaking," Lou told me. "You got the sense that every thought was a pearl, but his language was so circuitous that it seemed the pearl still had the oyster around it." What became clear as Ballantine continued to speak, though, was that—much to Lou's astonishment—the publishing legend wanted to take Lou under his wing. "He never actually said, 'Hey, I'll be your mentor.' Ian didn't make declarative statements like that. But he suggested he might enjoy dropping by regularly, and I made it clear that he could drop by whenever he wanted and that I'd be happy to go halfway across the world to get to him if he didn't feel like coming to me."

Over the next several years, Lou and Ian spent a considerable amount of time together. Ballantine taught Lou much about the history and, more importantly, the philosophy of book publishing. One of Ballantine's lessons to Lou was to "zig when everyone else is zagging," his way of suggesting that the fastest path to success is often to go against the flow. This struck a special chord with Lou. "From the time I started in the business, I'd been hearing about the 'conventions' of book publishing. It seemed there were a lot of rules about what you could and couldn't do, which didn't seem to make much sense to me, since readers don't read by rules. Ian didn't believe any of that, and he'd been overwhelmingly more successful than the people spouting these rules were. Right then, I decided to become a publisher who would publish books I loved with only a nodding glance to 'the rules.' "

The approach served Lou well. He had his first book imprint by the time he was twenty-six and became deputy publisher at Bantam and then publisher at Berkley Books and Avon Books before turning his attentions to writing. Before Ian Ballantine chose to mentor him, Lou knew he wanted a career in books. But in addition to teaching him the nuances of the industry, Ballantine helped him identify the particular part of publishing that truly brought him to his Element.

The second role of a mentor is *encouragement*. Mentors lead us to believe that we can achieve something that seemed improbable or impossible to us before we met them. They don't allow us to succumb to self-doubt for too long, or the notion that our dreams are too large for us. They stand by to remind us of the skills we already possess and what we can achieve if we continue to work hard.

When Jackie Robinson came to play major-league baseball in Brooklyn for the Dodgers, he experienced levels of abuse and hardship worthy of Greek tragedy from those who believed a black man shouldn't be allowed to play in a white man's league. Robinson bore up under most of this, but at one point, things got so bad that he could barely play the game. The taunts and threats rattled his concentration so badly that he faltered at the plate and in the field. After a particularly bad moment, Pee Wee Reese, the Dodger shortstop, called a time-out, walked over to Robinson, and offered him encouragement, telling him he was a great ballplayer destined for the Hall of Fame. Years later, during Robinson's Hall of Fame induction ceremony, he spoke about that moment. "He saved my life and my career that day," Robinson said from the podium at Cooperstown. "I had lost my confidence, and Pee Wee picked me up with his words of encouragement. He gave me hope when all hope was gone."

The third role of a mentor is *facilitating*. Mentors can help lead us toward our Element by offering us advice and techniques, paving the way for us, and even allowing us to falter a bit while standing by to help us recover and learn from our mistakes. These mentors might even be our contemporaries, as was the case with Paul McCartney.

"I remember one weekend John and I took the bus across town to see someone who knew how to play B7 on the guitar," Paul told me. "The three basic chords you needed to know were E, A, and B7. We didn't know how to do B7 and this other kid did. So we got the bus to see him, learned the chord, and came back again.

So then we could play it too. But basically, mates would show you how to do a particular riff. I remember one night watching a TV show called *Oh Boy!* Cliff Richard and the Shadows were on, playing 'Move It.' It had a great riff. I loved it but didn't know how to play it. Then I worked it out and ran over to John's house saying, 'I've got it. I've got it.' That was our only education experience—showing each other how to do things.

"To start with, we were just copying and imitating everyone. I was Little Richard and Elvis. John was Jerry Lee Lewis and Chuck Berry. I was Phil from the Everly Brothers and John was Don. We just imitated other people and taught each other. This was a big point for us when we were planning the policies at LIPA—the fact that it's important for students to rub up against people who have actually done or are doing the thing that the students are learning. They don't really need to tell you much, just show you what they do."

The fourth role of a mentor is *stretching*. Effective mentors push us past what we see as our limits. Much as they don't allow us to succumb to self-doubt, they also prevent us from doing less with our lives than we can. A true mentor reminds us that our goal should never be to be "average" at our pursuits.

James Earl Jones is known as a superlative actor and one of the great "voices" in contemporary media. Yet most of us never would have heard that voice had it not been for a mentor. One can only imagine what Darth Vader might sound like if Donald Crouch hadn't entered Jones's life.

As a child, Jones suffered from crippling self-consciousness, largely because he stuttered and found it very difficult to speak in front of people. When he got to high school, he found himself in an English class taught by Crouch, a former college professor who had worked with Robert Frost. Crouch discovered that Jones wrote poetry, a fact that Jones kept to himself for fear of ridicule from the other boys in school. "He questioned me about why, if I loved words so much, couldn't I say them out loud?" Jones says in the book *The Person Who Changed My Life: Prominent Americans Recall Their Mentors.*

"One day I showed him a poem I had written, and he responded to it by saying that it was too good to be my own work, that I must have copied it from someone. To prove that I hadn't plagiarized it, he wanted me to recite the poem, by heart, in front of the entire class. I did as he asked, got through it without stuttering, and from then on I had to write more and speak more. This had a tremendous effect on me, and my confidence grew as I learned to express myself comfortably out loud.

"On the last day of school we had our final class outside on the lawn, and Professor Crouch presented me with a gift—a copy of Ralph Waldo Emerson's *Self-Reliance.* This was invaluable to me because it summed up what he had taught me—self-reliance. His influence on me was so basic that it extended to all areas of my life. He is the reason I became an actor."

Mentors serve an invaluable role in helping people get to the Element. It might be overstating things to suggest that the only way to reach the Element is with the help of a mentor, but it is only a mild overstatement. We all encounter multiple roadblocks and constraints on the journey toward finding what we feel we were meant to do. Without a knowledgeable guide to aid us in identifying our passions, to encourage our interests, to smooth our paths, and to push us to make the most of our capacities, the journey is considerably harder.

Mentorship is of course a two-way street. As important as it is to have a mentor in your life, it is equally important to fulfill these roles for other people. It is even possible that you'll find that your own real Element is as a mentor to other people.

Anthony Robbins is one of the world's most successful personal coaches and mentors, often credited with laying the foundations for the personal coaching profession. This sector is growing exponentially around the world and has become a multimillion-dollar industry. All of this speaks eloquently to the appetite for mentoring and coaching and to the profound roles these can fulfill in many of our lives. More and more people are discovering that being a mentor, for them, is being in the Element.

This happened for David Neils. His own mentor was Mr. Clawson, a neighbor who came up with multiple successful inventions. When Neils was a child, he would go to visit the neighbor while he worked. Instead of chasing the kid away, Clawson asked for Neils's advice and criticism about his work. This interaction charged Neils with a sense of self-worth and an understanding that his opinions mattered. As an adult, Neils founded the International Telementor Program, an organization that facilitates mentoring by electronic means between professionals and students. Since 1995, the program has helped more than 15,000 students around the world receive professional guidance. David Neils literally made mentoring his life's work.

More Than Heroes

I'm sure that several of the mentors mentioned here, including many of the Big Brothers and Big Sisters, became heroes to those they mentored. We all have personal heroes—a parent, a teacher, a coach, even a schoolmate or colleague—whose actions we idolize. In addition, we all have heroes we've never met who stir our imaginations with their deeds. We consider Lance Armstrong a hero for the way he overcame a life-threatening illness to dominate a physically grueling sport, and Nelson Mandela one for his critical role in ending apartheid in South Africa. In addition, we forever associate people with heroic acts—Rosa Parks's triumphant stand against bigotry, Neil Armstrong's first step on the moon.

These people inspire us and lead us to marvel at the wonders of human potential. They open our eyes to new possibilities and fire our aspirations. They might even drive us to follow their examples in our lives, moving us to dedicate ourselves to public service, exploration, breaking barriers, or lessening injustice. In this way, these heroes perform a function similar to mentors.

Yet mentors do something more than heroes in our search for the Element. Heroes may be remote from us and inaccessible. They may live in another world. They may be dead. If we meet them, we may be too awestruck to engage properly with them. Heroes may not be good mentors to us. They may be competitive or refuse to have anything to do with us. Mentors are different. They take a unique and personal place in our lives. Mentors open doors for us and get involved directly in our journeys. They show us the next steps and encourage us to take them.

CHAPTER NINE

Is It Too Late?

SUSAN JEFFERS is the author of *Feel the Fear and Do It Anyway®* and many other best-selling books. She didn't begin her writing career until she was well into her forties. How she did it is a remarkable story.

As a child, Susan loved to read. The best time of the day for her was when she could curl up with a book in the quiet of her room. "I was always curious, and my father was a great one for explaining things. Sometimes he would go into so much detail my eyes would roll back. I remember hearing something on the radio once that I didn't understand. The word was *circumcision*. True to form, he didn't give me a short explanation! He was like a teacher. I think he missed his calling. He'd always wanted a boy, and I was treated to all the things he would have done with a son. I got to go to a lot of wrestling matches!"

Susan went off to college, where she met and soon married her first husband. She dropped out when she got pregnant with the first of her two children. After four years at home, she decided she had to go back to college. This decision created much anxiety: "The years at home had shattered my confidence, and I wasn't sure I would succeed." She eventually found her feet at college and even graduated summa cum laude. When she learned of this honor, she began phoning everyone she knew. "Finally I dropped the phone and began crying as I realized that the one person I was trying to reach was my father, who had died a few years earlier. He would have been so proud."

With the encouragement of one of her teachers, Susan enrolled in graduate school and ultimately received her doctorate in psychology. Then, through an unexpected turn of events, she was asked to become the executive director of the Floating Hospital in New York City. She hesitated at first, as it was a very big job and she didn't know if she could handle it. But finally, she agreed.

By then, she was having trouble in her marriage, and she filed for divorce. This was a difficult time for Susan. "Even having my doctorate in psychology didn't help. While my job was rewarding beyond my wildest dreams, I was miserable. I soon got tired of feeling sorry for myself and knew I had to find a new way of 'being' in the world. And that is when my spiritual journey began."

During the ten years she ran the Floating Hospital, Susan became what she calls a "workshop addict." In her free time, she studied Eastern philosophies and attended all manner of personal growth and New Age workshops. "I discovered that it was fear that was creating my 'victim mentality' and negative attitude. It was stopping me from taking responsibility for my experience of life. It was also fear that was keeping me from being a truly loving person. Little by little, I learned how to push through fear and move myself from the weakest to the strongest part of who I am. Ultimately, I felt a sense of power that I had never felt before."

Sitting at her desk one day, the thought came into her mind to go down to the New School for Social Research, a place she had never been. Since she was learning to trust her intuition, she decided to check it out. "I thought maybe they had a workshop I needed to take. When I arrived, I looked at the directory and noticed the Department of Human Resources, which sounded relevant to my interests. I made my way to their offices. There was no one in the reception area. Then I heard a woman in the office to the right say, 'Can I help you?' I walked in and blurted out, 'I'm here to teach a course about fear.' Where that came from, I hadn't a clue! She looked at me in shock and said, 'Oh my goodness, I've been searching for someone to teach a course on fear and this is the last day to put it in the catalogue and I have to leave in fifteen minutes.' Satisfied with my credentials she said, 'Quickly write a course title and a seventy-five-word course description. Without any forethought, I titled the course 'Feel the Fear and Do It Anyway' and wrote the course description. She was pleased and placed my course information on her assistant's desk with a note to include it in the catalogue. She thanked me profusely and quickly exited. Alone, I stood thinking to myself, 'What just happened?' I believe strongly in the Law of Attraction, but to me this was mind blowing."

Susan was nervous as she faced the first session of the twelve-week course. The two hours went well, but she then was confronted with a new fear. "I thought, 'That's it. That's all I know about this subject. So what am I going to teach next week? And the ten more sessions to follow?' But every week I found I had more to say. And my confidence level grew. I realized I had learned so much over the years about pushing through fear. And my students were drinking it up. Ultimately, they were amazed at how shifting their thinking really changed their lives. Teaching this course convinced me that the techniques that had transformed my life were the same techniques that could transform anyone regardless of age, sex, or background."

Susan eventually decided to write a book based on the course she had taught. She faced many roadblocks. And after four agents and fifteen rejections from various publishers, she reluctantly put the proposal in a drawer. One of the worst rejection letters she received said, "Lady Di could be bicycling nude down the street giving this book away, and no one would read it!"

During this period, she decided to leave the Floating Hospital and focus on becoming a serious writer. "I remember riding in a cab one evening. The driver asked me what I did. I heard myself say, 'I'm a writer.' I suppose until that moment I had thought of myself as a psychologist or an administrator, but there it was. I was a writer."

After three years of writing articles for magazines, she was going through the drawer that held her much-rejected book proposal. "I picked it up and had a profound sense that I held something in my hands that many people needed to read. So I set out with much determination to find a publisher who believed in my book the same way I did. This time, I succeeded. What's more, I succeeded beyond my wildest dreams."

Feel the Fear and Do It Anyway® has sold millions of copies. It is available in a hundred countries, and it has been translated into more than thirty-five languages. Susan has written seventeen more books that are also making their way around the world. Susan was indeed a writer; the *Times* of London even dubbed her the "Queen of Self-Help." She is a sought-after public speaker and has been a guest on many radio and television shows internationally. About *Feel the Fear and Do It Anyway*®, she says, "My Web site receives e-mails from all over the world from people telling me how my book has helped their lives. Some have actually credited it with *saving* their lives. I'm so happy I never gave up. My father would really have been proud."

Is It Too Late?

We all know people who feel locked into their lives. They sincerely wish they could do something more meaningful and fulfilling, but at age thirty-nine or fifty-two or sixty-four, they feel that the opportunity has passed. Perhaps you feel that it's too late—that it's unrealistic to pivot your life suddenly in a new direction. Perhaps you feel that you've missed the one opportunity you had to pursue your heart's desire (maybe due to one of the constraints we discussed earlier). Perhaps you didn't have the confidence to follow the passion earlier, and now believe that the moment is gone.

There is abundant evidence that opportunities to discover our Element exist more frequently in our lives than many might believe. In the course of writing this book, we have come upon literally hundreds of examples of people following their passions later in their lives. For example, Harriet Doerr, the best-selling author, only dabbled in writing while she raised her family. When she was sixty-five, she returned to college to get a degree in history. But the writing courses she took along the way raised her prose skills to a new level, and she wound up enrolled in Stanford's creative writing program. She eventually published her first novel, the National Book Award–winning *Stones for Ibarra*, in 1983, at the age of seventy-three.

While less than half that age at thirty-six, Paul Potts still seemed stuck in an obscure and unfulfilling life. He'd always known he had a good voice and he'd pursued operatic training. However, a motorcycle accident cut short his dreams of the stage. Instead, he became a mobile telephone salesman in South Wales and continued to struggle with a lifelong self-confidence problem. Then he heard about auditions for the talent competition television show *Britain's Got Talent*, created by Simon Cowell of *American Idol* fame. Potts got the opportunity to sing Puccini's "Nessun Dorma" on national television, and his beautiful voice brought down the house, leaving one of the judges in tears. Over the next few weeks, Potts became an international sensation— the YouTube video of his first performance has been downloaded more than eighteen million times. He ultimately won the competition and got the opportunity to sing in front of the Queen. Carphone Warehouse's loss has been a gain for opera fans around the world, as Potts released his first album, *One Chance*, in late 2007. Singing had always been his Element.

"My voice," he said, "has always been my best friend. If I was having problems with bullies at school, I always had my voice to fall back on. I don't really know why people bullied me. I was always a little bit different. So I think that's the reason sometimes that I struggled with self-confidence. When I'm singing I don't have that problem. I'm in the place where I should be. All my life I felt insignificant. After that first audition, I realized that I am somebody. I'm Paul Potts."

Julia Child, the chef credited with revolutionizing American home cooking and originating the television cooking show, worked first as an advertising copywriter and then in various roles for the U.S. government. In her mid-thirties, she discovered French cuisine and began professional training. It was not until she was nearly fifty that she published *Mastering the Art of French Cooking*, and her storied career took off.

At sixty-five, Maggie Kuhn was a church organizer who had no intention of leaving her job. Unfortunately, her employers made retirement mandatory at her age. Angry at the way her employer showed her the door, she decided to start a support group with friends in similar situations. Their attempts to address the common problems of retirees pushed them toward higher and higher levels of activism, culminating in the creation of the Gray Panthers, a national advocacy group.

We've all heard that fifty is the new thirty and that seventy is the new forty (if this algorithm extends in both directions, it would explain the adolescent behavior of some thirty-somethings I know). But there are some important changes that we should take seriously. Life expectancy has increased in our lifetimes. It has more than doubled in the past hundred years, and is growing at an accelerated rate. Quality of health for older people has improved. According to a MacArthur Foundation study, nearly nine in ten Americans ages sixty-five to seventy-four say they are living disability-free. Many older people in the developed world have much greater financial stability. In the 1950s, 35 percent of older Americans lived in poverty; today that figure is 10 percent.

There's a great deal of talk these days about the "second middle age." What we once considered middle age (roughly thirty-five to fifty) presaged a rapid descent toward retirement and imminent death. Now, the end of this first middle age marks a series of benchmarks (a certain level of accomplishment in your work, kids going off to college, reduction in necessary capital purchases). What comes after this is a second stretch where healthy, accomplished people can set off to reach their next set of goals. It's certainly either chastening or inspirational—I'm not sure which—to hear boomer rock stars prove their predictions wrong about what they'd be doing "when I'm sixty-four" or still trying to get some "satisfaction."

If we have an entire extra "middle age" these days, certainly we get additional opportunities to do more with our lives as part of the package. Thinking that we need to fulfill our grandest dreams (or at least be in the process of fulfilling them) by the time we're thirty is outmoded.

I don't mean to say, of course, that we all can do anything at any time in our lives. If you're about to turn one hundred, it's unlikely that you're going to nail the leading role in *Swan Lake*, especially if you have no previous dance background. At fifty-eight, with a wobbly sense of balance, I'm getting used to the idea that I'll probably never take the speed-skating gold at the Winter Olympics (particularly since I've never actually seen a pair of ice skates in real life). Some dreams truly are "impossible dreams."

However, many aren't. Knowing the difference is often one of the first steps to finding your Element, because if you can see the chances of making a dream come true, you can also likely see the necessary next steps you need to take toward achieving it.

One of the most basic reasons for thinking that it's too late to be who you are truly capable of being is the belief that life is linear. As if we're on a busy one-way street, we think we have no alternative but to keep going forward. If we missed something the first time, we can't double back and take another look because it takes all of our effort just to keep up with traffic. What we've seen in many of the stories in this book, though, are clear indications that human lives are not linear. Gordon Parks's explorations and mastery of multiple disciplines were not linear. Chuck Close certainly has not lived a linear life; disease caused him to reinvent himself.

Sir Ridley Scott had a decidedly nonlinear approach toward entering the film world. He told me that when he first left art school, "I had absolutely no thoughts about making films. Films were something I would go to on a Saturday. It was impossible to think of how you would make that leap into film from the life I was leading.

"I then decided that fine art wasn't for me. I needed something more specific. I needed a target, a brief. So I moved around and tried other forms of art practice and finally I found my feet with Mr. Ron Store in printing. I loved the printing process. I loved having to grind stones for each color of the lithograph. I used to work late every day, go to the pub for two pints of beer, and get the last bus home. I did that for four years, five nights a week. I adored it."

A short while after this, he started moonlighting at the BBC. "I was always trying to break the boundaries of what I was doing, maximizing the budgets. They sent me on a year's travel scholarship, and when I went back, I went straight in as a designer. After two years at the BBC, I was put into the director's course."

From there, though, he made another leap, this time into advertising, because it was "fantastically fun. Advertising has always been a dirty word in relation to fine art and painting and you know, that side of things. I unashamedly grabbed it with both hands."

Directing commercials led to directing television. Only after that did Ridley Scott become immersed in the film world that would define his life's work. If he'd believed at any point along this journey that he had to follow a straight path in his career, he never would have found his true calling.

Human lives are organic and cyclical. Different capacities express themselves in stronger ways at different times in our lives. Because of this, we get multiple opportunities for new growth and development, and multiple opportunities to revitalize latent capacities. Harriet Doerr started to explore her writing skill before life took her in another direction. That skill was waiting for her decades later when she turned back to it. Maggie Kuhn discovered her inner advocate when the opportunity arose, though she was probably entirely unaware that she had this talent until that moment.

While physical age is absolute as a way of measuring the number of years that have passed since you were born, it is purely relative when it comes to health and quality of life. Certainly, we are all getting older by the clock. But I know plenty of people who are the same age chronologically and generations apart emotionally and creatively.

My mother died at the age of eighty-six, very suddenly and very quickly from a stroke. Right up to the end of her life, she looked ten or fifteen years younger than her birth date suggested.

She had an insatiable curiosity about other people and the world around her. She danced, read, partied, and traveled. She entertained everyone she met with her wit, and she inspired them with her sense of style, her energy, and her sheer pleasure in being alive—in spite of multiple hardships, struggles, and crises in her life.

I'm one of her seven children, and she was one of seven as well—so when we gathered in one place with our extended family, we were a substantial crowd. My mother took care of us during times when there were few modern conveniences and little help apart from what she could drag reluctantly from us when we were not actually creating work for her. When I was nine, we all faced a catastrophe. My father, who was the pillar of the family, and had been so distraught at my getting polio, had an industrial accident. He broke his neck, and for the rest of his life was a quadriplegic.

He was himself an extraordinary man who remained firmly at the center of our family life. He was sharply funny, deeply intelligent, and an inspiration to everyone who came within range of him. So, too, was my mother. Her energy and zest for life never diminished. She was always taking on new projects and learning new skills. At family gatherings, she was always the first on the dance floor. And in the last years of her life, she was studying ballroom dancing and making dollhouses and miniatures. For both my mother and my father there was always a clear, substantial difference between their chronological ages and their real ages.

There's no shortage of people who achieved significant things in their later years. Benjamin Franklin invented the bifocal lens when he was seventy-eight. That's how old Grandma Moses was when she decided to get serious about painting. Agatha Christie wrote *The Mousetrap*, the world's longest-running play, when she was sixty-two. Jessica Tandy won the Oscar for Best Actress at age eighty. Vladimir Horowitz gave his last series of sold-out piano recitals when he was eighty-four.

Compare these accomplishments with the premature resignation of people you know in their thirties or forties, who behave as if their lives have settled into a dull routine and who see little opportunity to change and evolve.

If you're fifty, exercise your mind and body regularly, eat well, and have a general zest for life, you're likely younger—in very real, physical terms—than your neighbor who is forty-four, works in a dead-end job, eats chicken wings twice a day, considers thinking too strenuous, and looks at lifting a beer glass as a reasonable daily workout.

Dr. Henry Lodge, coauthor of *Younger Next Year*, makes the point sharply. "It turns out," he says, "that 70% of American aging is not real aging. It's just decay. It's rot from the stuff that we do. All the lifestyle diseases . . . the diabetes, the obesity, the heart disease, much of the Alzheimer's, lots of the cancers, and almost all of the osteoporosis, those are all decay. Nature doesn't have that in store for any of us. We go out and buy it off the rack."

The people at realage.com have pulled together a set of metrics designed to calculate your "real age" as opposed to your chronological age. It takes into consideration a wide range of factors regarding lifestyle, genetics, and medical history. What's fascinating about this is that their work suggests that it's actually possible to make yourself younger by making better choices.

One way to improve your real age is to take better care of yourself physically, through exercise and nutrition. I know this, because I live in California, where everyone seems to have stock in Lycra, and dairy products have the same health status as cigarettes. I try my best to live healthily, too. I aim to do sit-ups every day and to avoid dessert. But it's not only about working out and eating in.

One of the fundamental precepts of the Element is that we need to reconnect with ourselves and to see ourselves holistically. One of the greatest obstacles to being in our Element is the belief that our minds somehow exist independently of our bodies, like tenants in an apartment, or that our bodies are really just a form of transport for our heads. The evidence of research, and of common sense, is not only that our physical health affects our intellectual and emotional vitality, but that our attitudes can affect our physical well-being. But equally important is the work you do to keep your mind young. Laughter has a huge impact on aging. So does intellectual curiosity. Meditation can also provide significant benefits to the physical body.

The answer to the question, Is it too late for me to find the Element? is simple: No, of course not. Even in the cases where the physical degradations that come with age make certain achievements impossible, the Element is still within reach. I'll never get that speed-skating gold, but if the sport meant that much to me (it doesn't), I could find a way to gain access to that tribe, perhaps using the skills I already have and those I could acquire to make a meaningful contribution to that world.

Keeping Things Plastic

What this really comes down to is our capacity to continue to develop our creativity and intelligence as we enter new stages in our lives. Obviously, it happens in dramatic ways when we're very young. The infant brain is tremendously active and enormously plastic. It is a ferment of potential. It has somewhere near one hundred billion neurons, and it can make a nearly infinite variety of possible connections, building what scientists call "neural pathways" out of what we encounter in the world. Our brains are pre-programmed to some degree by our genetics, but our experiences deeply affect how we evolve as individuals and how our brains develop.

Consider, for instance, how we learn language. Learning to speak is one of the most miraculous achievements in a child's life. It happens for most of us within our first few years. No one teaches language to us—certainly not our parents. They couldn't possibly do that because spoken language is too complex, too subtle, and too full of variations for anyone to teach it formally to a child. Of course, parents and others guide and correct young children as they learn to speak and they may encourage and applaud them. But babies don't learn to speak by instruction. They learn by imitation and inference. We are all born with a deep, instinctive capacity for language, which is activated almost as soon as we draw breath.

Babies instinctively recognize meanings and intentions in the sounds and tones they hear from other humans around them. Babies born into households with dogs as pets will respond to the noises and growls that dogs make. However, they don't confuse these sounds with human language. Most children don't opt for barking as a way of communicating—with the possible exception of the terrible twos and a couple of years in late adolescence.

There doesn't seem to be any obvious limit to our capacity for languages. Children born into multilingual households are likely to learn each of these languages. They don't reach a point of saturation and say, "Please keep my grandmother out of here. I can't handle another dialect." Young children tend to learn all the languages to which they are exposed and to slip effortlessly between them. I recall meeting three school-age brothers a few years ago. Their mother was French, their father was American, and they lived in Costa Rica. They were fluent in French, English, and Spanish as well as an amalgam they created from the three that they used exclusively when speaking with each other.

On the other hand, if you are born into a monolingual household, the odds are that you won't seek out other languages to learn, at least until you need to choose one in middle school. Learning a new language at that point is a much more difficult thing to do because you've already paved a large number of neural pathways with regard to language (in other words, you've made a huge number of yes/no decisions about what to call a particular item, how to form sentences, and even how to shape your mouth when speaking). Trying to speak a foreign language for the first time in your thirties is even tougher.

The neuroscientist Susan Greenfield illustrates the amazing plasticity of the young brain in a cautionary tale of a six-year-old boy in Italy, who was blind in one eye. The cause of his blindness was a mystery. As far as the ophthalmologists could tell, his eye was perfectly normal. They eventually discovered that when he was a baby, he had been treated for a minor infection. The treatment included having the eye bandaged for two weeks. This would have made little difference to the eye of an adult. But in a young baby, the development of the eye-to-brain neural circuits is a delicate and critical process. Because the neurons serving the bandaged eye were not being used during this crucial period of development, they were treated by the brain as though they weren't there at all. "Sadly," said Greenfield, "the bandaging of the eye was misinterpreted by the brain as a clear indication that the boy would not be using the eye for the rest of his life." The result was that he was permanently blinded in that eye.

Young brains are in a constant process of evolution and change, and extremely reactive to their environment. During early stages of development, our brains go through a process that cognitive scientists call "neural pruning." Essentially, this involves trimming away neural pathways that we determine at an unconscious level to have little long-term value to us. This pruning is of course different for every individual, but it is a tremendously necessary part of development. It serves the same function in our brains as pruning does to a tree—it gets rid of the unnecessary branches to allow for continued growth and increased overall strength. It shuts down pathways that we'll never use again in order to make room for the expansion of pathways that we will use regularly. As a result, the enormous natural capacities with which we are all born become shaped and molded, expanded or limited, through a constant process of interaction between internal biological processes and our actual experiences in the world.

The best news in all of this is that the physical development of the brain is not a straightforward, one-way linear process. Our brains don't stop developing when we get our first set of car keys (though the insurance companies would like to suggest as much). Harvard neurobiologist Gerald Fischbach has performed extensive research in brain cell counting and has determined that we retain the overwhelming majority of our brain cells throughout our lives. The average brain contains more neurons than it could possibly use in a lifetime, even given our increased life expectancies.

In addition, research indicates that, as long as we keep using our brains in an active way, we continue to build neural pathways as we get older. This gives us not only the ongoing potential for creative thought, but also an additional incentive for continuing to stretch ourselves. There is strong evidence to suggest that the creative functions of our brain stay strong deep into our lives: we can recover and renew many of our latent aptitudes by deliberately exercising them. Just as physical exercise can revitalize our muscles, mental exercise can revitalize our creative capabilities.

There's extensive research going on now regarding neurogenesis, the creation of new brain cells in adult humans. It's becoming clear that, contrary to what we believed for more than a century, the brain continues to generate new cells, and certain mental techniques (such as meditation) can even accelerate this.

We can admire the remarkable work done by people like Georgia O'Keeffe, Albert Einstein, Paul Newman, and I. M. Pei late in their lives, but we should not consider this work remarkable *because* they did it late in life. These people were simply high achievers who kept their brains sharp so they could continue to be high achievers. That they accomplished what they did at advanced ages should not surprise us nearly as much as it often does.

I mentioned earlier that it's unlikely that a centenarian will take the lead in *Swan Lake*. It's not impossible, just unlikely. The reason, of course, is that, at least until medical science takes several leaps forward, some of our capacities *do* deteriorate with age, especially physical athleticism. There's not much point in denying this, though some of us try desperately to do so, to the point of embarrassing ourselves in public.

However, this isn't true of all of our capacities. Like a good wheel of Parmigiano-Reggiano, some of them actually improve over time. There seem to be seasons of possibility in all of our lives, and they vary according to what we're doing. It's widely accepted that our abilities in mathematics, for example, tend to grow and peak in our twenties and thirties. I don't mean the ability to work out the food bill or to calculate the odds of your team winning the Super Bowl. I'm speaking about the kind of higher math done by world-class mathematicians, the Terence Taos of the world. Most math geniuses have done their most original work by the time the rest of us have signed up for our first mortgages— which is something we probably wouldn't do if we were better at math. The same is true of learning the technical skills of playing a musical instrument.

But in other ways and in other areas, maturity can be a genuine advantage, especially, for example, in the arts. Many writers, poets, painters, and composers have produced their greatest work as their insights and sensitivities deepened with age. One can say the same about disciplines as diverse as law, cooking, teaching, and landscape design. In fact, in any discipline where experience plays a significant role, age is an asset rather than a liability.

It follows, then, that "too late" arrives at various times, depending on where your search for the Element takes you. If it's toward internationally competitive gymnastics, it might be too late by the time you're fifteen. If it's toward developing a new style of fusion cuisine, "too late" might never come. For most of us, we're not even close to "too late."

Engaged Forever

One of the results of seeing our lives as linear and unidirectional is that it leads to a culture (true of most Western cultures, in fact) of segregating people by age. We send the very young to nursery schools and kindergartens as a group. We educate teenagers in batches. We move the elderly into retirement homes. There are some good reasons for all of this. After all, as Gail Sheehy noted decades ago, there are predictable passages in our lives, and it makes some sense to create environments where people can experience those passages in an optimal way.

However, there are also good reasons to challenge the routines of what really amounts to age discrimination. An inspiring example is a unique educational program in the Jenks school district of Tulsa, Oklahoma.

The state of Oklahoma has a nationally acclaimed early-years reading program, providing reading classes for three- to five-year-olds throughout the state. The Jenks district offers a unique version of the program. This came about when the owner of another institution in Jenks—one across the street from one of the elementary schools—approached the superintendent of schools. He'd heard about the reading program and wondered if his institution could offer some help. The superintendent responded positively to the idea and, after clearing some bureaucratic hurdles, welcomed the other institution's help.

The other institution is the Grace Living Center, a retirement home.

Over the next few months, the district established a preschool and kindergarten classroom in the very heart of Grace Living Center. Surrounded by clear glass walls (with a gap at the top to allow the sounds of the children to filter out), the classroom sits in the foyer of the main building. The children and their teachers go to school there every day as though it were any other classroom. Because it's in the foyer, the residents walk past it at least three times a day to get to their meals.

As soon as the class opened, many of the residents stopped to look through the glass walls at what was going on. The teachers told them that the children were learning to read. One by one, several residents asked if they could help. The teachers were glad to have the assistance, and they quickly set up a program called Book Buddies. The program pairs a member of the retirement home with one of the children. The adults listen to the children read, and they read to them.

The program has had some remarkable results. One is that the majority of the children at the Grace Living Center are outperforming other children in the district on the state's standardized reading tests. More than 70 percent are leaving the program at age five reading at third-grade level or higher. But the children are learning much more than how to read. As they sit with their book buddies, the kids have rich conversations with the adults about a wide variety of subjects, and especially about the elders' memories of their childhoods growing up in Oklahoma. The children ask things about how big iPods were when the adults were growing up, and the adults explain that their lives really weren't like the lives that kids have now. This leads to stories about how they lived and played seventy, eighty, or even ninety years ago. The children are getting a wonderfully textured social history of their home-towns from people who have seen the town evolve over the decades. Parents are so pleased with this extracurricular benefit that a lottery is now required because the demand for the sixty available desks is so strong.

Something else has been going on at the Grace Living Center, though: medication levels there are plummeting. Many of the residents on the program have stopped or cut back on their drugs.

Why is this happening? Because the adult participants in the program have come back to life. Instead of whiling away their days waiting for the inevitable, they have a reason to get up in the morning and a renewed excitement about what the day might bring. Because they are reconnecting with their creative energies, they are literally living longer.

There's something else the children learn. Every now and then, the teachers have to tell them that one of their book buddies won't be coming any more; that this person has passed. So the children come to appreciate at a tender age that life has its rhythms and cycles, and that even the people they become close to are part of that cycle.

In a way, the Grace Living Center has restored an ancient, traditional relationship between the generations. The very young and the very old have always had an almost mystical connection.

They seem to understand each other in a fundamental, often un-spoken way. Our practice in the West is often to keep these generations apart. The Book Buddies program shows in a simple yet profound way the enrichment possible when generations come together. It shows too that the elderly can revive long-lost energies if the circumstances are right and the inspiration is there.

There's Time

What everyone from Susan Jeffers to Julia Child to the book buddies teach us is that remarkable, life-enhancing things can happen when we take the time to step out of our routines, rethink our paths, and revisit the passions we left behind (or never pursued at all) for whatever reason. We can take ourselves in fresh directions at nearly any point in our lives. We have the capacity to discover the Element at practically any age. As the actor Sophia Loren once said, "There *is* a fountain of youth: it is your mind, your talents, the creativity you bring to your life and the lives of the people you love. When you learn to tap this source, you will truly have defeated age."

CHAPTER TEN

For Love or Money

G ABRIEL TROP is an accomplished academic scholar. When I met him, he was at Berkeley studying for a Ph.D. in German literature. This work means a great deal to him, but it is not the only thing about which he is passionate. He also has an overwhelming attraction to music. "If I were to lose the use of my hands," he said to me, "my life would be over."

Yet Gabriel has never entertained the thought of becoming a professional musician. In fact, for a long time he didn't want to be involved in music at all. In his first years of high school, Gabriel would look pityingly at the music students, struggling across the campus with their bulky instrument cases, turning up at school for rehearsals hours before anyone else had to be there. That wasn't a life for him, especially the part about getting to school extra early. He vowed secretly to avoid music.

However, one day, in the music class that was part of his school's standard curriculum, he was tinkling idly on the piano and realized that he found it easy to pick out tunes. With a sinking feeling, he realized too that he actually enjoyed doing it. He tried to disguise his obvious pleasure from the music teacher, who had wandered over to listen. He must not have done this particularly well, because the teacher told Gabriel that he had a good ear and suggested that Gabriel go into the music storeroom to see if any of the instruments there appealed to him.

A friend of Gabriel's played the cello, and for this reason and no other, Gabriel decided to try out one of those in the storeroom. He found that he loved the shape and size of the instrument and the deep, sonorous noise it made when he plucked the strings. One cello in particular, had "a wonderful smell of middle school varnish." He decided to break his vow and to give the cello a chance. When he began practicing, he took it very casually. But he quickly found that he loved playing this instrument, and that he was spending more and more time doing so.

From there, Gabriel practiced so often and with such intensity that within a couple of months he was playing reasonably well. Within a year, he was the principal cellist in the school orchestra. This meant, of course, that he arrived at school early in the morning, dragging his bulky instrument case across the campus to the pitying looks of the nonmusicians he had left behind.

Gabriel also loves literature, the German language, and academic work. At some point, he had to make a hard decision between music and academics as his primary focus in life. After a long internal struggle, he chose German literature because he felt that doing so would allow him to continue to spend time as a cellist, while if he dedicated himself to a profession in music, the time required to do so would have made it nearly impossible for him to explore German poetry in depth. "I chose literature because it seemed to me compatible with an intensity of music playing, and if I were to be a professional musician, my attachment to literature would have been disproportionately sidetracked. So this arrangement was really the one I could find where I could remain a dedicated cellist and sustain a high degree of involvement with literary language."

Still, he plays for hours every day and continues to perform (he recently played a cello concerto with the University of California Berkeley Symphony Orchestra). He doesn't know how he would survive without regular immersion in the practice and enjoyment of music. To call this a hobby, he says, would be ridiculous. Music is elemental in his life, and in music, he has found his Element.

In the truest meaning of the word, Gabriel is an amateur musician. And he wouldn't have it any other way.

For the Love of It

At the most basic levels, professionals in any field are simply those people who earn their living in that field, while amateurs are people who don't. But the terms *amateur* and *professional* often imply something else—something about quality and expertise. People often think of amateurs as second-rate, as those who perform well below professional levels. Amateurs are the ones who gesticulate too wildly in the local theater production, who score over a hundred on the golf course, or who write cute stories about pets in the town's free newspaper. When we call something "amateurish," we use the word as a pejorative. We're suggesting that the thing upon which we're commenting is nowhere near professional, that the effort is something of an embarrassment.

Sometimes it's perfectly reasonable to draw sharp distinctions between professionals and amateurs. There can, after all, be enormous differences of accomplishment between them. If I had to have a vasectomy, I'd greatly prefer to put myself in the hands of someone who did this sort of thing for a living rather than someone who occasionally dabbled in it. But often the differences between professionals and amateurs have less to do with quality than with choice. Many people, like Gabriel, do perform at professional levels in the fields they love. They simply choose not to make their living that way. They aren't professionals in this field because they don't make money that way. They are, by definition, amateurs. But nothing about their skill is "amateurish."

The word amateur derives from the Latin word *amator*, which means lover, devoted friend, or someone who is in avid pursuit of an objective. In the original sense, an amateur is someone who does something for the love of it. Amateurs do what they do because they have a passion for it, not because it pays the bills. True amateurs, in other words, are people who have found the Element in something other than their jobs.

In "The Pro-Am Revolution," a report for the British think tank Demos, Charles Leadbeater and Paul Miller underline the rise of a type of amateur that works at increasingly higher standards and generates breakthroughs sometimes greater than those made by professionals—hence the term *Pro-Am*. In many cases, new technology is providing a wider group with apparatus once unaffordable to the amateur—CCD chips for telescopes, Pro Tools for musicians, sophisticated video editing software for home computers, and so on. Leadbeater and Miller point to the emergence of hip-hop, a musical genre that started with the distribution of handmade tapes.

They note that the Linux computer operating system is a collaborative work created by a large community of programmers in their spare time. The Jubilee 2000 debt campaign, which has resulted in the relief of tens of billions of dollars in debt from Third World countries, started with the petitions of people with no professional lobbying experience. And an amateur astronomer using a ten-inch telescope is credited with the discovery of a supernova.

"A Pro-Am pursues an activity as an amateur, mainly for the love of it, but sets a professional standard," Leadbeater and Miller say. "Pro-Ams are unlikely to earn more than a small portion of their income from their pastime but they pursue it with the dedication and commitment associated with a professional. For Pro-Ams, leisure is not passive consumerism but active and participatory; it involves the deployment of publicly accredited knowledge and skills, often built up over a long career, which has involved sacrifices and frustrations."

Leadbeater and Miller call Pro-Ams "a new social hybrid," noting that they pursue their passions outside of the workplace, but with an energy and dedication rarely given to acts of leisure. Pro-Ams find this level of intensity restorative, often helping to compensate for less-than-inspiring jobs.

Some people do truly remarkable work as amateurs. Arthur C. Clarke was a best-selling science fiction writer, author of, among other novels, *2001: A Space Odyssey* and *Rendezvous with Rama*. He'd already begun his writing career when he became an officer in the British Royal Air Force. While there, he observed scientists in the air force's radar division and became fascinated with their work. In 1945 he published an article in *Wireless World* magazine entitled "Extra-Terrestrial Relays: Can Rocket Stations Give World-Wide Radio Coverage?" In it, he posited the use of satellites in geostationary orbit to broadcast television signals around the globe.

Most scientists dismissed this proposition as yet another work of science fiction. However, Clarke had a very keen interest in the subject, and he had studied it carefully. His proposal was solid technically and, as we all now know, utterly prescient. The specific geostationary orbit Clarke proposed is now known as the Clarke orbit, and hundreds of satellites use it. And while Clarke made his living in the upper stratospheres of the *New York Times* best-seller list, it's the work he did as an amateur (specifically a letter to the editors of *Wireless World* that preceded his article) that sits in the National Air and Space Museum.

Susan Hendrickson hasn't had a particular profession at all. She dropped out of high school, became a skilled scuba diver, taught herself to identify rare marine specimens, became an expert at finding amber insect fossils, and has lived a multifaceted life as an explorer and adventurer. In 1990, Hendrickson joined an archaeological expedition in South Dakota led by the Black Hills Institute of Geological Research. The work started extremely slowly. The group explored six outcrops and made no significant discoveries. Then one day, while the rest of her team was in town, Hendrickson decided to explore the only other mapped outcrop. There, she came upon a few small bones. These bones would lead to the uncovering of the largest and most complete fossil skeleton of a *Tyrannosaurus rex* ever discovered—and one of the few female *T. rex*es ever found.

The skeleton is now on display at the Field Museum in Chicago. Her name: Tyrannosaurus Sue, after the amateur archaeologist who unearthed her.

In his book *The Amateurs*, David Halberstam wrote about four athletes in their pursuit of Olympic gold in 1984. Unlike the track champions or basketball players who could leverage Olympic success into huge professional contracts (the Olympic Committee didn't allow NBA stars to participate back then) or endorsement deals, the subjects Halberstam followed—scullers—had no chance of cashing in on their victories. They were doing it purely for the love of the sport and the sense of accomplishment that would come from being the best.

The book focuses most closely on Christopher "Tiff" Wood. Halberstam calls Wood "the personification of the amateur. He had put aside career, marriage, pleasure in his single-minded pursuit of excellence in a sport that few of his fellow countrymen cared about and that was, therefore, absolutely without commercial rewards." At thirty-one, Wood was old for the sport (at least at the Olympic level), but he was on a mission. He'd been an alternate at the 1976 Olympics and never got to compete. He was the captain of the 1980 team that was supposed to go to Moscow. But, as a protest over the Soviet invasion of Afghanistan, America chose not to attend those games.

The 1984 Olympics would be Wood's last chance for a gold medal. Within the small but devoted sculling community, he'd become something of a favorite son. Tiff Wood, as it turns out, did not come away with the gold. That fact, though, is only a sidebar to the story. What comes across in Halberstam's depiction of Wood and the other scullers is the passion and satisfaction associated with a purely amateur pursuit. Tiff Wood discovered the Element through his nonprofessional efforts. His job was just a job. Rowing was his life.

To be in your Element, it isn't necessary to drop everything else and do it all day, every day. For some people, at some stages in their lives, leaving their current jobs or roles to pursue their passions simply isn't a practical proposition. Other people choose not to do that for a whole range of reasons. Many people earn their living doing one thing, and they then create time and space in their lives to do the thing they love. Some people do this because it makes greater sense emotionally. Others do it because they feel they have no alternative but to pursue their passions "on the side."

A couple of years ago, I was leasing a new car from a dealership in Santa Monica. As it turned out, this was not easy. There was a time when the only decision you had to make when buying a car was whether to have it or not. Now you have to take a full-scale multiple-choice test to navigate your way between the hundreds of finishes, trims, accessories, and performance features that stand between you and the version you actually want. I'm not good at this kind of excessive decision-making. I need help deciding what to wear in the morning, where there's much less choice and the stakes are far lower. By the time I'd made up my mind about the car, my salesman, Bill, and I had bonded and were planning our annual reunion.

While we were waiting for the final paperwork—another lengthy process—I asked him what he did when he wasn't working. Without missing a beat, he said he was a photographer. I asked him what he photographed, assuming he meant family weddings and pets. He said he was a sports photographer. I asked him what sports he covered. "Just surfing," he said. I was intrigued and asked him why. He said that he'd been a surfer when he was younger and simply loved the beauty and dynamics of the sport. He went to the beach at Malibu after work, weekends, holidays—whenever he could—just to take pictures. He'd been doing this for years and had accumulated thousands of dollars' worth of cameras, tripods, and specialized lenses. Over longer holidays, he traveled to Hawaii and Australia to catch the big surf on camera.

I asked him if any of his pictures had been published. He said they had, and pulled open the drawer of his desk. It was full of high-production, glossy surfing magazines. He had pictures in every one of them. His work was very, very good.

I asked him if he'd ever thought of doing this type of work for a living. "I'd love to," he said, "but there isn't enough money in it." Nonetheless, surfing photography was his passion, and one of the things that made his life worthwhile. As I leafed through these amazing, professional images, I asked him what his boss at the dealership thought of them. "He doesn't know anything about them," Bill told me. "It's not really relevant to how I do my job, is it?"

I'm not sure he was right about that. I actually think it might have had a great deal to do with how Bill did his job, as is likely the case with all people who discover the Element in a pursuit other than their jobs. My guess is that the satisfaction and excitement Bill found photographing surfers made it so much easier for him to be effective at what he thought of as the relative drudgery of helping customers choose from dozens of paint samples, finish options, and decisions about running boards. The creative outlet he found in his photography made him that much more patient and helpful in his day job.

The need for an outlet of this sort manifests itself in many forms. One that I find fascinating is the emergence of the corporate rock band. Unlike the company softball team, which tends to fill its roster with young people from the mailroom, these bands tend to include a lineup of senior executives (unless someone in the mailroom is a great bass player) who once dreamed of being rock stars before settling into other careers. The passion with which many of these amateur musicians play shows that such an avocation offers a level of fulfillment they can't find in their work, regardless of how accomplished they are at their jobs.

For four years now, there has been a rock festival of sorts put together in New York to benefit the charity A Leg to Stand On. What distinguishes this rock benefit show from all others is that every member of every band (with the exception of a couple of ringers) is in the hedge fund business. "By day, most of the performers manage money," states one of the press releases for Hedge Fund Rocktoberfest, "but when they turn off their trading screens, they turn on the music."

"By 11 p.m., everyone is either thinking about their 4 a.m. train ride the next morning or the fact that the Tokyo markets are now open," noted Tim Seymour, one of the performers. But while the show is on, it's pure revelry, with managers covering classic hits or even donning skimpy outfits to serve as backup singers. The contrast between the day job and this is dramatic and, by all indications, liberating for everyone who participates.

Transformation

Finding the Element is essential to a balanced and fulfilled life. It can also help us to understand who we really are. These days, we tend to identify ourselves by our jobs. The first question at parties and social gatherings is often, "What do you do?" We dutifully answer with a top-line description of our professions: "I'm a teacher," "I'm a designer," "I'm a driver." If you don't have a paid job, you might feel somewhat awkward about this and find the need to give an explanation. For so many of us, our jobs define us, even to ourselves—and even if the work we do doesn't express who we really feel we are. This can be especially frustrating if your job is unfulfilling. If we're not in our Element at work, it becomes even more important to discover that Element somewhere else.

To begin with, it can enrich everything else you do. Doing the thing you love and that you do well for even a couple of hours a week can make everything else more palatable. But in some circumstances, it can lead to transformations you might not have imagined possible.

Khaled Hosseini immigrated to America in 1980, got a medical degree in the 1990s, and set off on a career practicing internal medicine in the Bay Area. In his heart, though, he knew he wanted to be a writer and that he wanted to tell the story of life in Afghanistan prior to the Soviet invasion. While continuing his medical practice, he began work on a novel about two boys growing up in Kabul. That novel became *The Kite Runner*, a book that has sold more than four million copies and generated a recent film.

Hosseini's pursuit of his most intense interests, even while he was working hard at another profession, transformed him in profound ways. The success of *The Kite Runner* has allowed him to go on an extended sabbatical from medicine and to concentrate on writing full-time. He published his second novel, the best-selling *A Thousand Splendid Suns*, in 2007. "I enjoyed practicing medicine and was always honored that patients put their trust in me to take care of them and their loved ones," he said in a recent interview. "But writing had always been my passion, since childhood. I feel ridiculously fortunate and privileged that writing is, at least for the time being, my livelihood. It is a dream realized."

Like Khaled Hosseini's, Miles Waters's first career was in the medical profession. He began practicing as a dentist in England in 1974. And like Hosseini, Waters had a burning passion for an entirely different field. In Waters's case, it was popular music. He'd played in bands at school and started writing songs along the way. In 1977, he scaled back his dental practice to spend more time at songwriting. It took him several years to make inroads, but he eventually wrote several hit songs and began to earn a living in the music field. He quit dentistry for a period and worked full-time as a writer and producer, contributing to an album by Jim Capaldi (from the legendary rock band Traffic) that featured work from Eric Clapton, Steve Winwood, and George Harrison. He's traveled in the same circles as Paul McCartney and Pink Floyd's David Gilmour. These days, he shuttles between music and dentistry, maintaining a practice while still composing and producing.

John Wood made a fortune as a marketing executive for Microsoft. During a trip to the Himalayas, though, he came upon a school in an impoverished village. The school taught four hundred and fifty students, but had only twenty books—and not one of these was a children's book. When Wood asked the school's headmaster how the school got by with such a paucity of books, the headmaster enlisted his aid. Wood began collecting books and raising money for this school and others, doing the work on nights and weekends while dealing with a hugely demanding day job. Finally, he walked away from Microsoft for his true calling— Room to Read, a nonprofit organization with the goal of extending literacy in poor countries. Several of his Microsoft colleagues thought he'd lost his mind. "It was incomprehensible to many of them," he said in an interview. "When they found out I was leaving to do things like delivering books on the backs of donkeys, they thought I was crazy." Room to Read has been transformational not only for Wood, but for thousands and thousands of others. The nonprofit organization has created more than five thousand school libraries in six countries with plans to extend that reach to ten thousand libraries and fifteen countries by 2010.

Beyond Leisure

There's an important difference between leisure and recreation. In a general sense, both words suggest processes of physical or mental regeneration. But they have different connotations. Leisure is generally thought of as the opposite of work. It suggests something effortless and passive. We tend to think of work as something that takes our energy. Leisure is what we do to build it up again. Leisure offers a respite, a passive break from the challenges of the day, a chance to rest and recharge. Recreation carries a more active tone—literally of re-creating ourselves. It suggests activities that require physical or mental effort but which enhance our energies rather than depleting them. I associate the Element much more with recreation than with leisure.

Dr. Suzanne Peterson is a management professor at the W. P. Carey School of Business and Center for Responsible Leadership at Arizona State University and a consultant for an executive coaching firm. She's also a championship dancer, twice winning the

Holiday Dance Classic in Las Vegas and grabbing the 2007 Hot-lanta US Open Pro-Am Latin Championship, among others.

Suzanne took some dance classes when she was a teenager, but she never seriously considered dance as a career. Suzanne knew from the time she was in high school that she wanted to be an executive. "I didn't grow up knowing exactly what I wanted to be, but I knew that I wanted to wear business suits, speak to large groups of people and have them listen to me, and have a title. I always saw myself as being able to wear great business suits for some reason. And I liked the idea that I could visualize myself in front of groups of people and have something important to say. But dancing was not a passion when I was young. It was something you did because what else do girls do as a hobby if they don't want to play soccer and baseball?"

Her rediscovery of dance and the intense excitement that accompanied it this time around came nearly accidentally. "I was just looking for a hobby and my achievement and motivation got the best of me. I was about twenty-six, and I was in graduate school. At this time, salsa and swing dancing were getting popular, so I'd just go into the social dance studio and I would watch. I'd mimic what the teachers were doing. Slowly but surely I started taking group lessons and then some private lessons. The next thing I know, it's this huge part of my life. So it really was a progression based on my belief that I had the requisite talent for it and sort of the basic ability level. But probably my academic side allowed me to study it and focus on it just like any other subject.

"And I literally would study it like any other academic science. Huge visualization. I would sit on planes and I would visualize myself going through all the dances. So anytime I couldn't physically practice, I would mentally practice. I could feel the music. I could feel the emotions. I could see the facial expressions. And I would come the next day to the dance studio after being gone and I would be better. And my dance partner would say, 'How did you get better overnight? Weren't you traveling to Philadelphia?' and I would say, 'Oh, I practiced on the plane.' And I literally would practice up to two hours in my head totally uninterrupted.

"I went into dancing the same way I go into my career—you give 110 percent and you go in strong and powerful. And I realized that when you do that in dancing, it's too much. You lose the femininity and, all of a sudden, you're in everybody's face so much. The business side is power and confidence and all these things. And the dancing is vulnerability and sensuality, everything soft. You go from one to the other and I enjoy them equally."

Suzanne in fact seems to have found her Element in multiple ways. She loves her profession, and she loves what she does for recreation. "If I'm really teaching something about leadership that I'm passionate about, I get the same exact feeling except that it's just a different emotion. I mean I feel confident and powerful and very connected to the audience and I want to make a difference. And then in the dancing I feel more vulnerable, a little less confidence. But they're both escapes in different ways and I get completely engulfed in them and get very moved by them emotionally."

Ultimately, though, her life has added meaning because she's chosen a recreational pursuit that is fulfilling, rather than simply entertaining. "It's taught me more about communication than studying communication ever could. You realize the effect that you have on another person. If you were in a bad mood, that person knows it in a second just touching your hand. And so in my head I could feel the perfect connection that's in a partnership, the perfect communication. I would feel extremely happy.

"It's a flow experience. I mean it's a complete release. I don't think about anything. I don't think about anything good in my life. I don't think about anything bad in my life. Literally, I would not get distracted if gunshots went off. It's really amazing."

Suzanne's sister, Andrea Hanna, is an executive assistant working in Los Angeles. Like Suzanne, she's found a pursuit beyond her job that adds dimension to her life.

"I didn't like writing until my senior year of high school," she told me. "My English teacher told us to write a compelling college entrance essay about anything of our choice. Like most assignments, I dreaded the idea of sitting down and writing a five-paragraph essay that was just going to end up covered in red pen. Nonetheless, I finally sat down and wrote about how unprepared I felt for college but how excited I was to start a new chapter of my life. This was the first essay I had ever written for school that had humor in it. It was also the first essay where I was able to write about something I was an expert on: me. To my surprise, my teacher loved it and read it in front of the class. She also entered it into a writing contest. I won first place and was asked to read my paper in front of a large group of professional women writers. I even got my picture in the paper! It was exciting for me and gave me a boost of confidence as I entered college.

"I have always been told I have a very strong writer's voice. People always tell me, 'I can hear you while I read this.' In college I started sending friends the occasional comedic e-mail recapping our weekends. I would turn each one of my friends into a character and embellished the story just enough to get the laugh I wanted. My e-mails started getting circulated amongst groups of friends and pretty soon I would get a reply from someone I wouldn't know telling me how great my writing was. It felt great to be so good at something that came so naturally for me.

"The summer between my sophomore and junior year, I got a job as a receptionist at a radio station. Within a month, I had started writing funny advertising spots for the station. The station manager loved my ideas and put them on air. All my friends would tune in to hear my funny commericals, many of which I starred in myself. It felt really good to hear my work produced and get the response I had sought out to get.

"As my work got recognized, I started realizing I had a talent for something that could possibly be a career. I entered the entertainment industry right after college. I had several jobs working for television writers and film producers, learning the ropes. After years of coffee runs and executive car washes, I realized that many of these 'dream jobs' were some of the least creative jobs out there. At one point, I dreamt of being a writer for *Saturday Night Live*, but learned weekly deadlines and high-stress environments take any enjoyment out of it for me. I began to think, *why does a paycheck validate my talent?* When it comes down to it, I just love to make people laugh and if one of my sketches, short stories, or funny e-mails makes someone crack up, well that's really enough for me. I became a much happier person when I came to that realization.

"When I think about it, I think the main reason I enjoy writing comedy is because I feel witty and smart when I am doing it. For so many years I felt stupid because I never excelled at school. My writing gives me confidence and makes me feel like a more complete version of myself."

The objective of this form of recreation is to bring a proper balance into our lives—a balance between making a living and making a life. Whether or not we can spend most of our time in our Element, it's essential for our well-being that we connect with our true passions in some way and at some point. More and more people are doing this through formal and informal networks, clubs, and festivals to share and celebrate common creative interests. These include choirs, theater festivals, science clubs, and music camps. Personal happiness comes as much from the emotional and spiritual fulfillment that this can bring as from the material needs we meet from the work we may have to do.

The scientific study of happiness is a relatively new field. It got off to something of a false start with Abraham Maslow six decades ago, when he suggested that we spend more time understanding the psychology of our positive traits rather than focusing exclusively on what makes us mentally ill. Unfortunately, most of his contemporaries found little inspiration in his words. The concept gained a great deal of traction, though, when Martin Seligman became president of the American Psychological Association and, coining the term *Positive Psychology*, announced that the goal of his yearlong term in office was to provoke further exploration into what made human beings flourish. Since then, scientists have conducted dozens of studies on happiness. "Happy individuals seem to have a whole lot more fun than the rest of us ever do," Dr. Michael Fordyce said in his book *Human Happiness*. "They have many more activities they enjoy doing for fun, and they spend much more of their time, on a given day or week, doing fun, exciting, and enjoyable activities."

Discovering the Element doesn't promise to make you richer. Quite the opposite is possible, actually, as exploring your passions might lead you to leave behind that career as an investment banker to follow your dream of opening a pizzeria. Nor does it promise to make you more famous, more popular, or even a bigger hit with your family. For everyone, being in their Element, even for part of the time, can bring a new richness and balance to their lives.

The Element is about a more dynamic, organic conception of human existence in which the different parts of our lives are not seen as hermetically sealed off from one another but as interacting and influencing each other. Being in our Element at any time in our lives can transform our view of ourselves. Whether we do it full-time or part-time, it can affect our whole lives and the lives of those around us.

The Russian novelist Aleksandr Solzhenitsyn saw this clearly. "If you want to change the world," he said, "who do you begin with, yourself or others? I believe if we begin with ourselves and do the things that we need to do and become the best person we can be, we have a much better chance of changing the world for the better."

CHAPTER ELEVEN

Making the Grade

MANY OF THE PEOPLE we've met in this book didn't do well at school, or at least didn't enjoy being there. Of course, many people do do well in their schools and love what they have to offer. But too many graduate or leave early, unsure of their real talents and not knowing what direction to take next. Too many feel that what they're good at isn't valued by schools.

Too many think they're not good at anything.

Sometimes, getting away from school is the best thing that can happen to a great mind. Sir Richard Branson was born in England in 1950. He attended Stowe School, and he was very popular there, making friends easily and excelling at sports. He was so good at athletics, in fact, that he became the captain of the soccer and cricket teams. He also showed an early flair for business. By the time he was fifteen, he'd started two enterprises, one selling Christmas trees and the other selling small Australian birds known as budgerigars. Neither business was particularly successful, but Richard had an obvious aptitude for this kind of thing.

What he didn't seem to have an affinity for was school. His grades were poor, and he disliked the whole business of attending classes. He tried to make a go of it, but it just wasn't a comfortable fit. At the age of sixteen, he decided he'd had enough and left, never to return.

Richard's experience at school confounded those who taught

him. Clearly he was bright, clearly he was industrious, clearly he was personable and capable of putting his mind to good use—but equally clearly, he was completely unwilling to conform to the school's standards. Commenting on Richard's decision to drop out, his head teacher said, "By the time he is twenty-one, Richard will either be in jail or be a millionaire, and I have no idea which it will be."

Out in the real world now, Richard needed to find something to do with his life. Sports were not an option; he wasn't skilled enough to be a professional athlete. However, something else stirred his passions at least as much, and he had a strong feeling that he was *very* good at this—he would become an entrepreneur.

Richard Branson soon started his first real enterprise, a magazine called *Student*. He followed this in 1970 with a mail-order business selling records. The mail-order business ultimately became a chain of record stores—you might know them now as Virgin Megastores. This was the first of his enterprises to carry the Virgin name. But it was hardly the last. Not long after he launched the stores, he started Virgin Records. Then, in the 1980s, he took on an entirely new business with Virgin Atlantic Airways, starting the airline with virtually no cash outlay and one 747 that he leased from Boeing. Today, his empire also includes Virgin Cola, Virgin Trains, Virgin Fuel, and, one of his most ambitious ventures, Virgin Galactic, the first commercial endeavor to send people into space. His decision to forgo school and become an entrepreneur was inspired. And his head teacher's prophecy did turn out to be true—at least the part about his becoming a millionaire by the time he was twenty-one.

Branson eventually learned that one of the reasons for his poor academic performance was dyslexia. Among other things, this caused him to have serious difficulties understanding math. Even now, in spite of the billions he is worth, he still can't navigate his way around a profit-and-loss sheet. For a long time, he couldn't even grasp the difference between net and gross income. One day, in exasperation, his director of finance took him aside after a Virgin board meeting and said, "Richard, think of it this way: if you go fishing and throw a net into the sea, everything you catch in the net is yours to keep. That's your 'net' profit. Everything else is the gross."

"Finally," Richard said, "I got the difference."

Branson's flamboyant style of entrepreneurship and huge success in so many fields earned him a knighthood in 1999. None of this seemed remotely likely when he was struggling to make passing grades at school. Perhaps it should have been, though.

"The fact is," he told me, "all the great entrepreneurs of my generation really struggled at school and couldn't wait to get out and make something of themselves."

Paul McCartney didn't find school nearly as uninspiring as Richard Branson did. In fact, Paul actually considered becoming a teacher until he decided to become a Beatle instead. Still, one subject that left him entirely unengaged was music.

"I didn't like music at school because we weren't really taught it. Our class was just thirty teenage Liverpool lads. The music teacher would come in and put an old LP of classical music on this old turntable and then walk out. He'd spend the rest of the lesson in the common room having a cigarette. So as soon as he'd gone, we turned the gramophone off and posted a guy at the door. We got the playing cards and cigarettes out and spent the whole lesson playing cards. It was great. We just thought of music as card-playing lessons. Then when he was coming back, we put the record back on, right near the end. He asked us what we thought, and we'd say 'It was great that, sir!' I really can't remember anything else about music at school. Honestly. That's all we ever did.

"The music teacher completely failed to teach us anything

about music. I mean, he had George Harrison and Paul McCartney in his classes as kids and he couldn't interest us in music. George and I both went through school and no one ever thought we had any kind of musical talent at all. The only way it would ever show then was if you were in a little band or something. Sometimes people would get guitars out at the end of term. John was in a band like that in his school. But otherwise, no one would ever notice you were interested in music. And nobody taught us anything about it."

Finding our Element is essential for us as individuals and for the well-being of our communities. Education should be one of the main processes that take us to the Element. Too often, though, it serves the opposite function. This is a very serious issue for all of us. In many systems, the problems are getting worse.

What do we do about this?

This Looked-Down-Upon Thing

I receive many e-mail messages from students around the world. This is one from a seventeen-year-old student in New Jersey who watched the speech I gave at the TED Conference in 2006 (TED stands for Technology, Entertainment, and Design):

> Here I am sitting quietly unable to sleep in my room. It's currently 6:00 a.m., and this is the period of my life that is supposed to change me forever. After a few weeks, I will be a senior and colleges seem to be the main topic of my life right now . . . and I hate it. It's not that I don't want to go to college, it's just that I had thoughts of doing other things that wouldn't suppress my ideas. I was so dead confident about something I wanted to do and devote my time with, but to everyone around me it seems like getting a Ph.D. or some boring job is key to being

successful in life. To me I thought that spending your time on something boring and meaningless was a bad idea. This is the one opportunity in my life . . . heck it's the one life I'll ever get and if I don't do something drastic, I will never get a chance to do it. I hate it when I get some funny look from my parents or my friends' parents when I tell them I want to pursue something completely different than the trite old medical- or business-related job.

Somehow, I stumbled upon a video with a guy talking about ideas I've had in my head for some time now and it utterly shook me to euphoria. . . . If everyone wants to be a pharmacist, in the future, a job in the medical field won't be such a prestigious profession. I don't want money, I don't want some lousy "expensive" car. I want to do something meaningful with my life, but support is something I rarely get. I just want to tell you that you've personally made me believe once again that I can follow my dream. As a painter, a sketcher, a music writer, a sculptor, and a writer, I truly thank you for giving me hope. My art teacher always gives me stares when I would do something odd. I once poured my paintbrush cleaning water on top of a paint ing my teacher said was "completed and ready to be graded." Boy, would you have loved the look on her face. These boundaries are so clearly set in school and I want to break free and create the ideas that come from my head at three in the morning. I hate drawing plain old shoes or trees and I don't like having this "grading" of art. Since when should someone "grade" art? I bet if Pablo Picasso handed in one of his pieces to his old art teacher, she'd absolutely flip and fail him. I asked my teacher if I could incorporate sculpture with canvas and have both intertwined together and have my sculpture give the illusion that the painting was alive and coming towards the viewer. . . . Her response was that it wasn't allowed! I am going to take an AP art studio class my senior year and they tell me that I can't do three-dimensional art? It's insane and we need people like you to come down to New Jersey and give a speech or two about this looked-down-upon thing called creativity.

It pains me when the minute I say I want to be an artist when I grow up, all I get are laughs or frowns. Why can't people do the things they love to do? Is happiness a mansion, some big-screen television screen, watching numbers scroll go by as you cringe when S&P goes down a point? . . . This world has turned into an overpopulated, scary, and competitive place. Thank you for those nineteen minutes and twenty-nine seconds of pure truth. Cheers.

This student is railing against two things that most people eventually discover in their education. One is the hierarchy of disciplines in schools that we discussed in the first chapter. The other is that conformity has a higher value than diversity.

Conformity or Creativity

Public education puts relentless pressure on its students to conform. Public schools were not only created in the interests of industrialism—they were created *in the image* of industrialism. In many ways, they reflect the factory culture they were designed to support. This is especially true in high schools, where school systems base education on the principles of the assembly line and the efficient division of labor. Schools divide the curriculum into specialist segments: some teachers install math in the students, and others install history. They arrange the day into standard units of time, marked out by the ringing of bells, much like a factory announcing the beginning of the workday and the end of breaks. Students are educated in batches, according to age, as if the most important thing they have in common is their date of manufacture. They are given standardized tests at set points and compared with each other before being sent out onto the market. I realize this isn't an exact analogy and that it ignores many of the subtleties of the system, but it is close enough.

This system has had many benefits and successes. It has done well for many people whose real strength is conventional academic work, and most people who go through thirteen years of public education are at least moderately literate and capable of making change for a twenty. But dropout rates, especially in the United States, are extraordinarily high, and levels of disaffection among students, teachers, and parents are higher still. Increasingly, the structure and character of industrial education are creaking under the strain of the twenty-first century. A powerful symptom of the problem is the declining value of a college degree.

When I was a student, my contemporaries and I repeatedly heard the story that if we worked hard and did well—and certainly if we went to college and received a degree—we'd have a secure job for the rest of our lives. Back then, the idea that a person with a college degree would be out of work was preposterous. The only reason that a college-educated person would not have a job was if he or she didn't want a job.

I left college in 1972 and I, for one, did *not* want a job. I'd been going to school since I was five, and I wanted a break. I wanted to find myself, so I decided to go to India, where I thought I might be. I didn't get to India, as it happens. I only got as far as London, where there are a lot of Indian restaurants. But I never doubted that whenever I decided to get a job, I would just go out and get one.

It's not like that now. Students leaving college are no longer guaranteed a job in the field for which they may be qualified. Many graduates leaving top universities are finding themselves doing relatively unskilled work or heading home again to figure out their next move. In fact, in January 2004, the number of unemployed American college graduates actually exceeded the number of unemployed high school dropouts. It's difficult to believe that this would be possible, but in fact, it is.

Problems for college graduates exist in many places in the world. A report from the Association of Graduate Recruiters in the UK noted that 3.4 percent fewer college-level job openings were available in 2003 than in the previous year. An average of forty-two people applied for each of these jobs, as opposed to thirty-seven the year before, meaning that the scramble for good jobs is becoming more frantic, even with a high-level education. China, which boasts the world's fastest-growing economy, has seen huge numbers of college graduates (some estimates have it at 30 percent of the more than three million who graduate annually) going unemployed. What will happen when their economy slows down?

It is still true, though, that anybody starting out in the job market is better off having a college education than not having one. A recent U.S. Census Bureau report indicates that college graduates can expect to earn in excess of $1 million more than people with only high school degrees over their lifetimes. Those with professional degrees can earn greater than $3 million more.

But the plain fact is that a college degree is not worth a fraction of what it once was. A degree was once a passport to a good job. Now, at best, it's a visa. It only gives you provisional residence in the job market. This is not because the standards of college degrees are lower than they used to be. That's very hard to judge. It's mainly because so many more people have them now. In the industrial period, most people did manual and blue-collar work, and only a minority actually went to college. Those who did found that their degree certificates were like Willy Wonka's golden ticket. Now, with so many people graduating college, four-year degrees are more like the shiny paper in which they wrap the chocolate bars.

Why are there so many more college graduates? The first reason is that, in the developed world at least, the new economies of the twenty-first century are driven more and more by innovations in digital technologies and information systems. They depend less on manual work and more and more on what my uncle used to call "head work." So higher levels of education are essential for more and more people.

The second reason is that there are simply more people in the world now than ever before. The population of the world, as I noted earlier, has doubled in the last thirty years from three to six billion and may be heading for nine billion by the middle of the century. Putting these factors together, some estimates suggest that more people will be graduating from higher education in the next thirty years than the total number since the beginning of history.

According to the Organisation for Economic Co-operation and Development (OECD), in the decade from 1995 to 2005, the graduation rates of the countries with the most powerful economies grew 12 percent. More than 80 percent of young Australians graduate from college now, while nearly the same percentage of Norwegians do. More than 60 percent of American students get college degrees. In China, more than 17 percent percent of college-age students go to college, and this percentage is increasing rapidly. Not long ago, it was closer to 4 percent.

One of the results of this huge growth in higher education is that the competition to get into many universities—even those beyond the vaunted first tier—has become increasingly intense.

This pressure is driving a new profession of commercial coaches and college preparatory cramming programs. This is especially true in Japan, where "cram schools" exist all over the country. There are actually chains of them. These operations teach preschoolers, sometimes even one-year-olds, to prepare for entrance exams to prestigious elementary schools (the necessary first step toward placement in a high-level Japanese university). There, small children perform drills in literature, grammar, math, and a wide variety of other subjects to gain an edge on their "competition." So much for recess and arts and crafts. It's a common belief that a potential Japanese executive's future is largely determined by the time he or she enters first grade.

This is also the case in the United States and in other parts of the world. In cities like Los Angeles and New York, there is fierce competition for places in particular kindergarten schools. Children are being interviewed at the age of three to see if they are suitable material. I assume that earnest selection panels are thumbing through the résumés of these toddlers, assessing their achievements to date—"You mean this is it? You've been around for almost thirty-six months, and this is all you've done? You seem to have spent the first six months doing nothing but lying around and gurgling."

Cram schools exist all over the globe. In England, cram schools focus on getting kids through college entrance exams, as do SAT prep courses in the United States. In India, cram schools known as "tutorials" help students drive through competitive tests. In Turkey, the *dershane* system pushes students toward getting ahead, with extensive programs for students on weekends and after school during the week.

It's difficult to believe that an education system that places this kind of pressure on children is of benefit to anyone—the children or their communities. Most countries are making efforts to reform education. In my view, they are going about it in exactly the wrong way.

Reforming Education

Nearly every system of public education on earth is in the process of being reformed—in Asia, the Americas, Europe, Africa, and the Middle East. There are two main reasons. The first is economic. Every region in the world is facing the same economic challenge—how to educate their people to find work and create wealth in a world that is changing faster than ever. The second reason is cultural. Communities throughout the world want to take advantage of globalization, but they don't want to lose their own identities in the process. France wants to stay French, for example, and Japan wants to stay Japanese. Cultural identities are always evolving, but education is one of the ways in which communities try to control the rate of change. This is why there's always such heat generated around the content of education.

The mistake that many policymakers make is to believe that in education the best way to face the future is by improving what they did in the past. There are three major processes in education: the curriculum, which is what the school system expects students to learn; pedagogy, the process by which the system helps students to do it; and assessment, the process of judging how well they are doing. Most reform movements focus on the curriculum and the assessment.

Typically, policymakers try to take control of the curriculum and specify exactly what students should learn. In doing this, they tend to reinforce the old hierarchy of subjects, putting greater emphasis on the disciplines at the top of the existing hierarchy (the back-to-basics drive we discussed earlier). In practice, this means that they push other disciplines—and the students who excel at them—even further to the margins of education. In the United States, for example, more than 70 percent of school districts have cut back or eliminated arts programs because of No Child Left Behind.

Next, they put greater emphasis on assessment. This is not wrong in itself. The problem is the method used. Typically, reform movements rely increasingly on the proliferation of standardized tests. One of the principal effects is to discourage innovation and creativity in education, the very things that make schools and students thrive. Several research studies show the negative impact of unrestricted standardized testing on student and teacher morale. There's lots of anecdotal evidence too.

A friend recently told me that his eight-year-old announced in October that her teacher "hadn't done any teaching" since the school year began. She said this was because her school insisted that the teacher focus on preparing for the upcoming statewide standardized tests. My friend's daughter found the endless review in preparation for these tests boring, and she would have preferred that her teacher "teach" instead of doing this. Interestingly, when my friend and his wife had their semiannual meeting with the teacher, the teacher complained bitterly that she gets to spend much less time on a reading program she loves because the school administration forces her to prep her students for the district-wide tests that come up every marking period. Good teachers find their own creativity suppressed.

Third, policymakers penalize "failing" schools. In the case of No Child Left Behind, schools that fail to meet guidelines five years in a row, regardless of circumstances such as socioeconomics, face the termination of teachers and principals, school closures, and the takeover of schools by private organizations or the state. These schools struggle to conform to the hierarchy and the culture of standardization, fearfully eschewing nearly all efforts at creativity or adaptation to the specific needs and talents of the students.

Let me be clear here. I'm not against standardized tests in principle. If I go for a medical examination, I want some standardized tests. I want to know what my blood sugar and cholesterol levels are in comparison with everybody else's. I want my doctor to use a standard test and a standard scale, and not ones that he thought up in the car on the way to work. But the tests in themselves are only useful as part of a diagnosis. The doctor needs to know what to make of the results in my particular case, and to let me know what I should do about them given my particular physiology.

It's the same in education. Used in the right way, standardized tests can provide essential data to support and improve education. The problem comes when these tests become more than simply a tool of education and turn into the focus of it.

Whatever its educational effects, standardized testing is now big business. There's a considerable profit motive associated with increasing reliance on standardized tests. According to the Government Accountability Office (GAO), in the United States individual states will spend in the range of $1.9 billion and $5.3 billion each between 2002 and 2008 to implement the tests mandated by No Child Left Behind. This number includes direct costs only. Indirect costs could make these figures ten times larger. Most of this money goes to private testing companies that create, administer, and grade the tests. Standardized testing has become a booming industry. Using the GAO figures, these testing companies may generate considerably more than $100 billion in business over seven years.

You'll notice that I haven't yet mentioned teaching. The reason is that policymakers, for the most part, don't seem to understand its fundamental importance in raising standards in education. My own extremely strong belief, based on decades of work in the field, is that the best way to improve education is not to focus primarily on the curriculum, nor on assessment, important though these things are. The most powerful method of improving education is to invest in the improvement of teaching and the status of great teachers. There isn't a great school anywhere that doesn't have great teachers working in it. But there are plenty of poor schools with shelves of curriculum standards and reams of standardized tests.

The fact is that given the challenges we face, education doesn't need to be reformed—it needs to be transformed. The key to this transformation is not to standardize education but to personalize it, to build achievement on discovering the individual talents of each child, to put students in an environment where they want to learn and where they can naturally discover their true passions. The key is to embrace the core principles of the Element. Some of the most invigorating and successful innovations in education around the world illustrate the real power of this approach.

Transforming Education

In the first part of my career, I worked particularly in the field of drama education. I did this because I was always deeply impressed by the power of drama to invigorate the imaginations of children and to promote a strong sense of collaboration, self-esteem, and community feeling in classrooms and schools. Children learn best when they learn from each other and when their teachers are learning with them. As I mentioned earlier, when I met my wife and partner, Terry, she was teaching drama in an elementary school in Knowsley, a low-income and difficult part of the city of Liverpool. Nonetheless, the school was achieving remarkable results. The reasons were simple. First, the school was led by an inspirational head teacher who understood the lives the children were leading. He also understood the real processes by which they could be excited to learn. Second, he hired staff members, like Terry, who were passionate in their disciplines and gifted at connecting with the children. This is Terry's account of the school's approach:

"I passionately believe that, when it is properly integrated into the curriculum, drama can transform the culture of a school. I know this from my own experience as a teacher in one of the poorest areas of Liverpool. We actually kept clean clothes at the school for some of the kids to wear while attending classes. They would change into them in the morning and change out of them to go home. We discovered that if they were just given the clothes, within a week, they would be in just as bad a state as the rest of their things, or they would mysteriously disappear.

"Some of the children lived in terrible circumstances at home. I remember that in one of our creative writing classes, one of the girls wrote a story about dead babies. We were struck by the vividness of this story, and the school contacted social services to check what was happening at home. They discovered that her premature baby sister's body was rotting under her bed. We had overcrowded classrooms and every imaginable social problem, but we also had a world-class group of committed teachers and a visionary headmaster.

"He believed in playing to our strengths and that teaching should be child-centered. He called a staff meeting to discuss how we could redesign the school day and asked each of us to talk about our subject specialization and what we loved to teach best. At that time it was usual for children to stay with their class teacher all day. Over the course of a few months of meetings we came up with a plan. In the mornings, we would teach our class reading, writing, and math, and then in the afternoon we would teach our favorite subject. This meant that over the course of a week each teacher was teaching the whole school.

"As a drama teacher, my job was to look at the topics each year group was studying in all subjects and to bring them to life in the hall. Another teacher would take art, another geography, another history, and so on. Then we would pick the topics for each year group. When the ten-year-olds read the story of the French Revolution, they built a guillotine with the help of the science teacher, and then we constructed trials, held executions, and even spoke some French. We "decapitated" a few teachers, too.

"When the topic was archaeology in Roman times, we performed adapted versions of *Julius Caesar*. Because they had become comfortable with the process, when it came time to put on the school plays, the kids were confident and desperate to be involved, to perform, sew costumes, build sets, write, sing, and dance. They couldn't wait to get to their lessons. It was a lot of fun, and it was so fulfilling to see how kids developed social skills and interacted.

"They were using their imaginations in ways they never had before. Kids who had never excelled at anything suddenly found they could shine. Kids who couldn't sit still didn't have to, and quite a few discovered they could act, entertain, write, debate, and stand up with confidence to address an entire group. The standard of all their work improved dramatically. There was great support from parents, and the governors used the school as a model. It was all because of the head teacher, Albert Hunt, a wonderful man."

Unlike his experience with music classes, Paul McCartney had a wonderful experience with the teacher who introduced him to Chaucer because that teacher chose to do so in a way that he knew would reach the teenaged boy.

"The best teacher I had was our English teacher, Alan Durband. He was great. I was good with him too because he understood our mentality as fifteen- and sixteen-year-old boys. I did Advanced Level English with him. We were studying Chaucer and it was impossible to follow it. Shakespeare was hard enough but Chaucer was worse. It was like a completely foreign language. You know, 'Whan that Aprille with his shoures soote,' all that type of thing. But Mr. Durband gave us a modern English translation by Neville Coghill, which had the original Chaucer on one page and the modern version on the facing page, so you could get the story and what it was really about.

"And he told us that Chaucer was a really popular writer in his time and quite bawdy. He knew that would get us interested, and it did. He told us to read *The Miller's Tale*. We couldn't believe how bawdy it was. The bit when she pokes her bum out of the window and he talks about kissing a beard . . . I was hooked. He really turned me on to literature. He understood that the key for us would be sex and it was. When he turned that key, I was hooked."

There are inspiring models of education at work throughout the world. In the northern Italian town of Reggio Emilia, a breakthrough method of preschool education arose in the early 1960s. Known now internationally as the Reggio approach, this program sees young children as intellectually curious, resourceful, and full of potential. The curriculum is child-directed; teachers take their lessons where student interests dictate. The setting of the school is vitally important and considered an essential teaching tool. Teachers fill the rooms with dramatic play areas, worktables, and multiple environments where the kids can interact, problem-solve, and learn to communicate effectively.

Reggio schools spend a great deal of time on the arts, believing that children learn multiple "symbolic languages" through

painting, music, puppetry, drama, and other art forms to explore
their talents in all of the ways in which humans learn. A poem
from founder Loris Malaguzzi underscores this:

> The child
> is made of one hundred.
> The child has
> a hundred languages
> a hundred hands
> a hundred thoughts
> a hundred ways of thinking
> of playing, of speaking.
> A hundred always a hundred
> ways of listening
> of marveling of loving
> a hundred joys
> for singing and understanding
> a hundred worlds
> to discover
> a hundred worlds
> to invent
> a hundred worlds
> to dream.
> The child has
> a hundred languages
> (and a hundred hundred more)
> but they steal ninety-nine.
> The school and the culture
> separate the head from the body.
> They tell the child:
> to think without hands
> to do without head
> to listen and not to speak
> to understand without joy

to love and to marvel
only at Easter and Christmas.
They tell the child:
to discover the world already there
and of the hundred
they steal ninety-nine.
They tell the child:
that work and play
reality and fantasy
science and imagination
sky and earth
reason and dream
are things
that do not belong together.

And thus they tell the child
that the hundred is not there.
The child says:
No way. The hundred *is* there.

Reggio teachers build the school year around weeklong short-term projects and yearlong long-term projects in which students make discoveries from a variety of perspectives, learn to hypothesize, and discover how to collaborate with one another, all in the context of a curriculum that feels a great deal like play. The teachers consider themselves researchers for the children, helping them to explore more of what interests them, and they see themselves as continuing to learn alongside their pupils.

For the past two decades, Reggio schools have received considerable acclaim, winning the LEGO Prize, the Hans Christian Andersen Prize, and an award from the Kohl Foundation. There are currently schools all over the world (including thirty American states) using the Reggio approach.

The town of Grangeton is very different from the town of Reggio Emilia. In fact, it isn't technically a town at all. It's actually an environment run by elementary school students at Grange Primary, in Long Eaton, Nottinghamshire, in central England. The town has a mayor and a town council, a newspaper and a television studio, a food market and a museum, and children are in charge of every bit of it. Head teacher Richard Gerver believes that "learning has to mean something for young people." So when the school board hired him to turn around the flagging school, he took the dramatic approach of creating Grangeton. The goal was to inspire kids to learn by connecting their lessons to their place in the real world. "My key words are experiential and contextual," Gerver told me.

Gerver changed around the curriculum at the school entirely—and he did it while working within the guidelines created by national testing. The students at Grange are involved in rigorous classroom work, but all of it comes to them in a way that allows them to understand the practical applications. Math means more when put in the context of running a cash register and estimating profits. Literacy and writing skills gain additional meaning when employed in the service of an original film screenplay. Science comes alive when students use technology to make television shows. Music appreciation gains new purpose when children need to determine playlists for the radio station. Civics makes sense when the council has decisions to make. Gerver regularly brings industry professionals in to help the students with technical training. The BBC is actively involved here.

The children in the upper grades hold the positions with the greatest responsibility (and their curriculum is most heavily weighted toward the Grangeton model), but younger students take an active role nearly as soon as they get to the school. "At no stage are we giving them the message that we're teaching them to pass an exam," noted Gerver. "They are learning because they can see how it moves their community of Grangeton onwards—exams are a way of assessing their progress to that end. It's giving the children a completely different perspective of why they are here."

Attendance at Grange is well above national averages. Meanwhile, the students perform in exemplary fashion on the national tests. In 2004, 91 percent of them exhibited proficiency in English (a 30-point increase from 2002, the year before the program started), 87 percent exhibited proficiency in math (a 14-point increase), and 100 percent exhibited proficiency in science (a 20-point increase). "The project has had a remarkable impact on attitudes," said Gerver. "Where pupils were de-motivated and lackluster, particularly the boys and the potential high achievers, there is now real excitement and commitment. That ethos has fed dramatically into the classroom, where teachers have adapted and developed their teaching and learning to become more experiential and contextual. Children are more confident and as a result more independent. Learning at Grange has a real purpose for the children, and they feel part of something very exciting. The effect has also fed into staff and parents, who have begun to contribute so much to the project's further development."

A recent report from Ofsted, the British school inspection agency, noted of Grange, "Pupils love coming to school and talk enthusiastically about the many exciting experiences on offer, tackling these with eagerness, excitement, and confidence."

In the state of Oklahoma there is a groundbreaking program called A+ Schools that builds on a tremendously successful program that began in North Carolina. This program, now in use in more than forty schools across Oklahoma, emphasizes the arts as a way of teaching a wide variety of disciplines within the curriculum. Students might write rap songs to help them understand the salient themes in works of literature. They might use collages of different sizes to allow them to see the practical uses of math. Dramatic presentations might characterize key moments in history, while dance movements make essential points about science. Several of the schools hold monthly "informances" that combine live performance with academic detail.

A+ Schools encourage teachers to use learning tools such as mapping, thematic webbing (establishing connections between various subject areas), the development of essential questions, the creation and use of interdisciplinary thematic units, and cross-curricular integration. They build the curriculum around experiential learning. They use enriched assessment tools to help students maintain an ongoing grasp of how they are doing. They encourage collaboration between teachers of different disciplines, between students, and between the school and the community. They build an infrastructure that supports the program and its distinctive way of dealing with state-mandated curriculum. And they foster a climate where students and teachers can feel excited about the work they are doing.

The schools in the A+ program cut across wide demographic groups. There are urban schools and rural schools, large schools and small, schools in affluent areas and those in economically challenged ones. Consistently, though, the A+ schools show marked improvement on standardized tests and often exceed the test scores of schools with similar demographics that do not use the A+ program. One A+ school, Linwood Elementary School in Oklahoma City, has twice won the Oklahoma Title I Academic Achievement Award. In 2006, the school was one of only five in the country to receive the Excellence in Education Award from the National Center for Urban School Transformation.

Elemental Education

The fundamental theme of this book is that we urgently need to make fuller use of our own natural resources. This is essential for our well-being and for the health of our communities. Education is supposed to be the process that develops all resources. For all the reasons I have set out, too often it is not. Many of the people I've talked about in this book say that they went through the whole of their education without really discovering their true talents. It is no exaggeration to say that many of them did not discover their real abilities until after they left school—until they had recovered from their education. As I said at the outset, I don't believe that teachers are causing this problem. It's a systemic problem in the nature of our education systems. In fact, the real challenges for education will only be met by empowering passionate and creative teachers and by firing up the imaginations and motivations of the students.

The core ideas and principles of the Element have implications for each of the main areas of education. The curriculum of education for the twenty-first century must be transformed radically. I have described intelligence as being diverse, dynamic, and distinct. Here is what it means for education. First, we need to eliminate the existing hierarchy of subjects. Elevating some disciplines over others only reinforces outmoded assumptions of industrialism and offends the principle of diversity. Too many students pass through education and have their natural talents marginalized or ignored. The arts, sciences, humanities, physical education, languages, and math all have equal and central contributions to make to a student's education.

Second, we need to question the entire idea of "subjects." For generations, we have promoted the idea that the arts, the sciences, the humanities, and the rest are categorically different from each other. The truth is that they have much in common. There is great skill and objectivity in the arts, just as there is passion and intuition at the heart of science. The idea of separate subjects that have nothing in common offends the principle of dynamism.

School systems should base their curriculum not on the idea of separate subjects, but on the much more fertile idea of disciplines. Math, for example, isn't just a set of information to be learned but a complex pattern of ideas, practical skills, and concepts. It is a discipline—or rather a set of disciplines. So too are drama, art, technology, and so on. The idea of disciplines makes possible a fluid and dynamic curriculum that is interdisciplinary.

Third, the curriculum should be personalized. Learning happens in the minds and souls of individuals—not in the databases of multiple-choice tests. I doubt there are many children who leap out of bed in the morning wondering what they can do to raise the reading score for their state. Learning is a personal process, especially if we are interested in moving people toward the Element. The current processes of education do not take account of individual learning styles and talents. In that way, they offend the principle of distinctiveness.

Many of those whose stories I have told in this book would agree. For them the liberation came from meeting their passion and being able to pursue it. As Don Lipski says, "The main thing is to encourage kids to follow anything they have enthusiasm for. When I got interested in magic, I got great encouragement and support. I devoted myself to magic in the same way that I do artwork now. A kid may have a thing about baseball, not playing it but learning all the statistics of the players and knowing who should be traded to what team. It may seem useless, but maybe that kid will end up being the manager of a baseball team. If a kid is the only one in the class who's an opera fan, that should be validated and encouraged. Whatever it might be for, enthusiasm is the main thing that needs to be developed."

The Element has implications for teaching. Too many reform movements in education are designed to make education teacher-proof. The most successful systems in the world take the opposite view. They invest in teachers. The reason is that people succeed best when they have others who understand their talents, challenges, and abilities. This is why mentoring is such a helpful force in so many peoples lives. Great teachers have always understood that their real role is not to teach subjects but to teach students. Mentoring and coaching is the vital pulse of a living system of education.

The Element has implications for assessment. Education is being strangled persistently by the culture of standardized testing. The irony is that these tests are not raising standards except in some very particular areas, and at the expense of most of what really matters in education.

To get a perspective on this, compare the processes of quality assurance in education with those in an entirely different field—catering. In the restaurant business, there are two distinct models of quality assurance. The first is the fast-food model. In this model, the quality of the food is guaranteed, because it is all standardized. The fast-food chains specify exactly what should be on the menu in all of their outlets. They specify what should be in the burgers or nuggets, the oil in which they should be fried, the exact bun in which they should be served, how the fries should be made, what should be in the drinks, and exactly how they should be served. They specify how the room should be decorated and what the staff should wear. Everything is standardized. It's often dreadful and bad for you. Some forms of fast food are contributing to the massive explosion of obesity and diabetes across the world. But at least the quality is guaranteed.

The other model of quality assurance in catering is the Michelin guide. In this model, the guides establish specific criteria for excellence, but they do not say how the particular restaurants should meet these criteria. They don't say what should be on the menu, what the staff should wear, or how the rooms should be decorated. All of that is at the discretion of the individual restaurant. The guides simply establish criteria, and it is up to every restaurant to meet them in whatever way they see best. They are then judged not to some impersonal standard, but by the assessments of experts who know what they are looking for and what a great restaurant is actually like. The result is that every Michelin restaurant is terrific. And they are all unique and different from each other.

One of the essential problems for education is that most countries subject their schools to the fast-food model of quality assurance when they should be adopting the Michelin model instead. The future for education is not in standardizing but in customizing; not in promoting groupthink and "deindividuation" but in cultivating the real depth and dynamism of human abilities of every sort. For the future, education must be Elemental.

The examples I have just given point the way to the sorts of education we now need in the twenty-first century. A number of them build on principles that educational visionaries have been promoting for generations—principles often seen as eccentric, even heretical. And they were, then. The views of these visionaries were ahead of their times (hence my describing them as visionary). But the right time has arrived. If we are serious about educational transformation, we must understand the times and catch the new tide. We can ride it into the future, or be overwhelmed and sink back into the past.

The stakes could hardly be higher for education and for all who pass through it.

Afterword

FINDING THE ELEMENT in yourself is essential to discovering what you can really do and who you really are. At one level, this is a very personal issue. It's about you and people you know and care for. But there is a larger argument here as well. The Element has powerful implications for how to run our schools, businesses, communities, and institutions. The core principles of the Element are rooted in a wider, organic conception of human growth and development.

Earlier, I argued that we don't see the world directly. We perceive it through frameworks of ideas and beliefs, which act as filters on what we see and how we see it. Some of these ideas enter our consciousness so deeply that we're not even aware of them. They strike us as simple common sense. They often show up, though, in the metaphors and images we use to think about ourselves and about the world around us.

Sir Isaac Newton, the great physicist, composed his theories at the dawn of the mechanical age. To him the universe seemed like an enormous mechanical clock, with perfectly regular cycles and rhythms. Einstein and others have since shown that the universe is not like a clock at all; its mysteries are more complicated, subtle, and dynamic than even your favorite watch. Modern science has changed metaphors, and in doing so has shifted our understanding of how the universe works.

In our own time, though, we still routinely use mechanistic

and technological metaphors to describe ourselves and our communities. I often hear people talk about the mind as a computer; about mental inputs and outputs, about "downloading" their feelings or being "hardwired" or "programmed" to behave in certain ways.

If you work in any kind of organization, you may have seen an organizational chart. Typically, these are comprised of boxes with people's names or functions in them and patterns of straight lines showing the hierarchy between them. These charts tend to look like architectural drawings or diagrams of electrical circuitry, and they reinforce the idea that organizations are really like mechanisms, with parts and functions that only connect in certain sorts of ways.

The power of metaphors and analogies is that they point to similarities, and there are certainly some similarities in how lifeless computers and living minds actually work. Nonetheless, your mind clearly isn't a solid-state system in a metal box on your shoulders. And human organizations are not at all like mechanisms. They are made up of living people who are driven by feelings and motives and relationships. Organizational charts show you the hierarchy, but they don't capture how the organization feels or how it really works. The fact is that human organizations and communities are not like mechanisms: they are much more like organisms.

The Climate Crisis

I was in a natural history museum a while ago. It's a fascinating place. There are separate rooms devoted to different species of creatures. In one, there's a display of butterflies, all arranged beautifully in glass cases, pinned through the body, scrupulously labeled, and dead. The museum grouped them by type and size, with the big ones at the top and smaller ones at the bottom. In another room, there are beetles similarly arranged by type and size, and in another, there are spiders. Organizing these creatures into categories and putting them in separate cabinets is one way of thinking about them, and it's very instructive. But this is not how they are in the world. When you leave the museum, you do not see all the butterflies flying in formation, with the large ones in the front and the small ones at the back. You don't see the spiders scuttling along in disciplined columns with the small ones bringing up the rear, while the beetles keep a respectful distance. In their natural state, these creatures are all over each other. They live in complicated, interdependent environments, and their fortunes relate to one another.

Human communities are exactly the same, and they are facing the same sorts of crises that are now confronting the ecosystems of the natural environment. The analogy here is strong.

The relationships of living systems and our widespread failure to understand them was the theme of *Silent Spring*, Rachel Carson's hard-hitting book published in September 1962. She argued that the chemicals and insecticides that farmers were using to improve crops and destroy pests were having unexpected and disastrous consequences. As they drained into the ground, these toxic chemicals were polluting water systems and destroying marine life. By indiscriminately killing insects, farmers were also upsetting the delicate ecosystems on which many other forms of life depended, including the plants the insects propagated and the countless birds who fed on the insects themselves. As the birds died, their songs were silenced.

Rachel Carson was one of a number of pioneers who helped to shift our thinking about the ecology of the natural world. From the beginning of the industrial age, human beings seemed to see nature as an infinite warehouse of useful resources for industrial production and material prosperity. We mined the earth for coal and ore, drilled through the bedrock for oil and gas, and cleared the forests for pasture. All of this seemed relatively straightforward. The downside is that, three hundred years on, we may have brought the natural world gasping to its knees, and we now face a major crisis in the use of the earth's natural resources.

The evidence of this is so strong that some geologists say we are entering a new geological age. The last ice age ended ten thousand years ago. Geologists call the period since then the Holocene epoch. Some are calling the new geological period the Anthropocene age, from the Greek word for human, *anthropos.* They say the impact of human activity on the earth's geology and natural systems has created this new geologic era. The effects include the acidification of the oceans, new patterns of sediments, the erosion and corrosion of Earth's surface, and the extinction of many thousands of natural species of animals and plants. Scientists believe that this crisis is real, and that we have to do something profound within the next few generations if we're to avoid a catastrophe.

One climate crisis is probably enough for you. But I believe there's another one, which is just as urgent as and has implications just as far-reaching as the crisis we're seeing in the natural world. This isn't a crisis of natural resources. It is a crisis of human resources. I think of this as *the other climate crisis.*

The Other Climate Crisis

The dominant Western worldview is not based on seeing synergies and connections but on making distinctions and seeing differences. This is why we pin butterflies in separate boxes from the beetles—and teach separate subjects in schools.

Much of Western thought assumes that the mind is separate

from the body and that human beings are somehow separate from the rest of nature. This may be why so many people don't seem to understand that what they put into their bodies affects how it works and how they think and feel. It may be why so many people don't seem to understand that the quality of their lives is affected by the quality of the natural environment and what they put into it and what they take out.

The rate of self-inflicted physical illness from bad nutrition and eating disorders is one example of the crisis in human resources. Let me give you a few others. We're living in times when hundreds of millions of people can only get through their day by relying on prescription drugs to treat depression and other emotional disorders. The profits of pharmaceutical companies are soaring, while the spirits of their consumers continue to dive. Dependence on nonprescription drugs and alcohol, especially among young people, is also rocketing. So too is the rate of suicides. Deaths each year from suicide around the world are greater than deaths from all armed conflicts. According to the World Health Organization, suicide is now the third highest cause of death among people aged fifteen to thirty.

What is true of individuals is naturally true of our communities. I live in California. In 2006, the state of California spent $3.5 billion on the state university system. It spent $9.9 billion on the state prison system. I find it hard to believe that there are three times more potential criminals in California than potential college graduates, or that the growing masses of people in jails throughout the country were simply born to be there. I don't believe that there are that many naturally malign people wandering around, in California or anywhere else. In my experience, the great majority of people are well intentioned and want to live lives with purpose and meaning. However, very many people live in bad conditions, and these conditions can drain them of hope and purpose. In some ways, these conditions are becoming more challenging.

At the beginning of the Industrial Revolution, there was hardly anybody around. In 1750, there were one billion people living on the planet. It took the whole of human existence for the world population to reach one billion. I know that sounds a lot, and we've agreed that the planet is relatively small. But it's still big enough for a billion people to spread out in reasonable comfort.

In 1930, there were two billion people. It took just one hundred and eighty years for the population to double. But there was still plenty of room for people to lie down. It took only forty more years for us to get to three billion. We crossed that threshold in 1970, just after the Summer of Love, which I'm sure was a coincidence. After that came a spectacular increase. On New Year's Eve 1999, you were sharing the planet with six billion other people. The human population had doubled in thirty years. Some estimates suggest that we'll hit nine billion by the middle of the twenty-first century.

Another factor is the growth of cities. Of the one billion people on Earth at the dawn of the Industrial Revolution, only 3 percent lived in cities. By 1900, 12 percent of the almost two billion people lived in cities. By 2000, nearly half of the six billion people on Earth lived in cities. It's estimated that by 2050 more than 60 percent of the nine billion human beings will be city dwellers. By 2020, there may be more than five hundred cities on Earth with populations above one million, and more than twenty megacities, with populations in excess of twenty million. Already, Greater Tokyo has a population of thirty-five million. This is greater than the total population of Canada, a territory *four thousand* times larger.

Some of these massive cities will be in the so-called developed countries. They will be well planned, with shopping malls, information booths, and property taxes. But the real growth isn't happening in those parts of the world. It's happening in the so-called developing world—parts of Asia, South America, the Middle East, and Africa. Many of these sprawling cities will be mainly shantytowns, self-built with poor sanitation, little infrastructure, and barely any social support services. This massive growth in the size and density of human populations across Earth presents enormous challenges. It demands that we tackle the crisis in natural resources with urgency. But it demands too that we tackle the crisis in human resources and that we think differently about the relationships between these two. All of this points to a powerful need for new ways of thinking—and new metaphors about human communities and how they flourish or decay.

For more than three hundred years Western thought has been dominated by the images of industrialism and the scientific method. It's time to change metaphors. We have to move beyond linear, mechanistic metaphors to more organic metaphors of human growth and development.

A living organism, like a plant, is complex and dynamic. Each of its internal processes affects and depends on the others in sustaining the vitality of the whole organism. This is also true of the habitats in which we live. Most living things can only flourish in certain types of environment, and the relationships between them are often highly specialized. Healthy, successful plants take the nutrients they need from their environment. At the same time, though, their presence helps to sustain the environment on which they depend. There are exceptions, like the Leyland cypresses that just seem to take over everything in their path, but you get the idea. The same is true of all creatures and animals, including us.

Farmers base their livelihoods on raising crops. But farmers do not make plants grow. They don't attach the roots, glue on the petals, or color the fruit. The plant grows itself. Farmers and gardeners provide the conditions for growth. Good farmers know what those conditions are, and bad ones don't. Understanding the dynamic elements of human growth is as essential to sustaining human cultures into the future as the need to understand the ecosystems of the natural world on which we ultimately depend.

Aiming High

A few hundred miles away from my home in Los Angeles is Death Valley, one of the hottest, driest places on earth. Not much grows in Death Valley, hence the name. The reason is that it doesn't rain very much there—about two inches a year on average. However, in the winter of 2004–5, something remarkable happened. More than seven inches of rain fell on Death Valley, something that had not happened for generations. Then in the spring of 2005, something even more remarkable happened. Spring flowers covered the entire floor of Death Valley. Photographers, botanists, and just plain tourists traveled across America to see this remarkable sight, something they might never see again in their lifetimes. Death Valley was alive with fresh, vibrant growth. At the end of the spring, the flowers died away and slipped again beneath the hot desert sand, waiting for the next rains, whenever they would come.

What this proved, of course, was that Death Valley wasn't dead at all. It was asleep. It was simply waiting for the conditions of growth. When the conditions came, life returned to the heart of Death Valley.

Human beings and human communities are the same. We need the right conditions for growth, in our schools, businesses, and communities, and in our individual lives. If the conditions are right, people grow in synergy with the people around them and the environments they create. If the conditions are poor, people protect themselves and their anxieties from neighbors and the world. Some of the elements of our own growth are inside us. They include the need to develop our unique natural aptitudes and personal passions. Finding and nurturing them is the surest way to ensure our growth and fulfillment as individuals.

If we discover the Element in ourselves and encourage others to find theirs, the opportunities for growth are infinite. If we fail to do that, we may get by, but our lives will be duller as a result. This is not just a West Coast, California argument, even though I do live there now. I believed this in the damp, cold days of December in England, when these thoughts can be harder to come by. This is not a new view. It's an ancient view of the need for balance and fulfillment in our lives and for synergies with the lives and aspirations other people. It's an idea that is easily lost in our current forms of existence.

The crises in the worlds of nature and of human resources are connected. Jonas Salk was the pioneering scientist who developed the Salk polio vaccine. As somebody who contracted polio in the 1950s, I feel some affinity with his life's passion. Later in his life, Salk made a provocative observation, one that addresses the two forms of climate crisis. "It's interesting to reflect," he said, "that if all the insects were to disappear from the earth, within fifty years all other forms of life would end." He understood, as Rachel Carson did, that the insects we spend so much effort trying to eradicate are essential threads in the intricate web of life on Earth. "But," Salk went on, "if all human beings were to disappear from the earth, within fifty years all other forms of life would flourish."

What he meant is that we have now become the problem. Our extraordinary capacity for imagination has given rise to the most far-reaching examples of human achievement and has taken us from caves to cities and from marshes to the moon. But there is a danger now that our imaginations may be failing us. We have seen far, but not far enough. We still think too narrowly and too closely about ourselves as individuals and as a species and too little about the consequences of our actions. To make the best of our time together on this small and crowded planet, we have to develop—consciously and rigorously—our powers of imagination and creativity within a different framework of human purpose. Michelangelo once said, "The greatest danger for most of us is not that our aim is too high and we miss it, but that it is too low and we reach it." For all our futures, we need to aim high and be determined to succeed.

To do that each of us individually and all of us together need to discover the Element.

Notes

Chapter One: The Element

GILLIAN LYNNE: All material in this segment came from an original interview for this book.

MATT GROENING: All material in this segment came from an original interview for this book.

PAUL SAMUELSON: Paul Samuelson, "How I Became an Economist," http://nobelprize.org/nobel_prizes/economics/articles/samuelson-2/index.html.

Chapter Two: Think Differently

MICK FLEETWOOD: All material in this segment came from an original interview for this book.

SENSES: Kathryn Linn Geurts, *Culture and the Senses: Bodily Ways of Knowing in an African Community* (Berkeley and Los Angeles: University of California Press, 2003).

Andrew Cook, "Exploding the Five Senses," http://www.hummingbird-one.co.uk/humanbeing/five.html.

BART CONNER: All material in this segment came from an original interview for this book.

IQ, SAT, AND EUGENICS: Jan Strydom and Susan du Plessis, "IQ Test: Where Does It Come From and What Does It Measure?" http://www.audiblox2000.com/dyslexia_dyslexic/dyslexia014.htm.

"Timing of IQ Test Can Be a Life or Death Matter," *Science Daily Magazine*, December 6, 2003.

"The Future of the SAT," http://chronicle.com/colloquylive/2001/10/SAT/.

Alan Stoskepf, "The Forgotten History of Eugenics," http://www
.rethinkingschools.org/archive/13_03/eugenic.shtml.

ALEXIS LEMAIRE: http://www.news.com.au/story/0,23599,22768356
-13762,00.html.

GORDON PARKS: Andy Grundberg, "Gordon Parks, a Master of the Camera, Dies at 93," *New York Times*, March 8, 2006.

Corey Kilgannon, "By Gordon Parks, A View of Himself and, Yes, Pictures," *New York Times*, July 7, 2002.

http://www.pbs.org/newshour/bb/entertainment/jan-june98/gordon
_1-6.html.

http://www.aaa.si.edu/collections/oralhistories/transcripts/parks64
.htm.

R. BUCKMINSTER FULLER: http://www.designmuseum.org/design/
r-buckminster-fuller.

ALBERT EINSTEIN: Walter Isaacson, *Einstein: His Life and Universe* (New York: Simon & Schuster, 2007).

Chapter Three: Beyond Imagining

FAITH RINGGOLD: The majority of the material in this segment came from an interview conducted by the author. Additional details came from http://www.faithringgold.com/ringgold/bio.htm.

BERTRAND RUSSELL: *Bertrand Russell, A History of Western Philosophy, and Its Connection with Political and Social Circumstances from the Earliest Times to the Present Day* (New York: Simon & Schuster, 1945).

PLANETARY PHOTOS: Graphics by Pompei AD, New York.

THE TRAVELING WILBURYS: Original interview with John Beug, senior executive, Warner Music Group.

http://www.travelingwilburys.com/theband.html.

http://www.headbutler.com/music/traveling_wilburys.asp.

RICHARD FEYNMAN: Richard Phillips Feynman and Christopher Sykes, *No Ordinary Genius: The Illustrated Richard Feynman* (New York: W. W. Norton, 1994).

RIDLEY SCOTT: All material in this segment came from an original interview for this book.

PAUL MCCARTNEY: All material in this segment came from an original interview for this book.

Chapter Four: In the Zone

EWA LAURANCE: All material in this segment came from an original interview for this book.

AARON SORKIN: All material in this segment came from an original interview for this book.

ERIC CLAPTON: http://www.moretotheblues.com/lapton_sessions.shtml.

JOCHEN RINDT: http://www.evenflow.co.uk/mental.htm.

WILBUR WRIGHT: http://www.pilotpsy.com/flights/11.html.

MONICA SELES: M. Krug, personal interview of Monica Seles, 1999.

FLOW: Mihaly Csikszentmihalyi, *Flow: The Psychology of Optimal Experience* (New York: HarperCollins, 1990).

BLACK ICE: Simóne Banks, "Black Ice," *Scheme*, February 4, 2007.
http://www.musicremedy.com/b/Black_Ice/album/The_Death_of_Willie_Lynch-3238.html.

MIND MAPPING: http://www.imindmap.com/.

THE MYERS-BRIGGS TYPE INDICATOR: David J. Pittenger, "Measuring the MBTI . . . and Coming Up Short," Journal of Career Planning & Placement, Fall 1993.
http://www.juliand.com/psychological_type.html.
http://www.teamtechnology.co.uk/tt/t-articl/mb-simpl.htm.

HERMANN BRAIN DOMINANCE INSTRUMENT: http://www.juliand.com/thinking_style.html.

TERENCE TAO: http://blog.oup.com/2006/09/interview_with_/.
http://www.college.ucla.edu/news/05/terencetaomath.html.

Chapter Five: Finding Your Tribe

MEG RYAN: All material in this segment came from an original interview for this book.

DON LIPSKI: All material in this segment came from an original interview for this book.

HELEN PILCHER: Helen Pilcher, "A Funny Thing Happened on the Way to the Lab," *Science*, December 6, 2002.

BRIAN RAY: All material in this segment came from an original interview for this book.

DEBBIE ALLEN: All material in this segment came from an original interview for this book.

MICHAEL POLANYI: Michael Polanyi, "The Republic of Science: Its Political and Economic Theory," in *Knowing and Being* (Chicago: University of Chicago Press, 1969).

Bob Dylan: Bob Dylan, *Chronicles, Vol. 1* (New York: Simon & Schuster, 2004).

Randall Collins: Randall Collins, *The Sociology of Philosophies: A Global Theory of Intellectual Change* (Cambridge, Mass.: Belknap Press, 1998).

Dorothy Leonard and Walter Swap: Dorothy Leonard and Walter Swap, "Gurus in the Garage," *Harvard Business Review*, November–December 2000.

Great Groups: Warren G. Bennis and Patricia Ward Biederman, *Organizing Genius: The Secrets of Creative Collaboration* (New York: Perseus Books, 1997).

Kind of Blue: Bill Evans, liner notes to *Kind of Blue* by Miles Davis, Columbia Records, 1959.

Abraham Lincoln: Doris Kearns Goodwin, *Team of Rivals: The Political Genius of Abraham Lincoln* (New York: Simon & Schuster, 2005).

Robert Cialdini: Dr. Alan Eshleman, "BIRGing, CORFing and Blasting," *San Francisco Chronicle*, November 20, 2002.

Fan behavior: http://www.tcw.utwente.nl/theorieenoverzicht/Theory% 20clusters/Interpersonal%20Communication%20and%20Relations/ Social_Identity_Theory.doc/.
http://www.units.muohio.edu/psybersite/fans/sit.shtml.

Howard Cosell: Howard Cosell, *Cosell* (Chicago: Playboy Press, 1973). Howard Cosell, *I Never Played the Game* (New York: William Morrow, 1985).

Billy Connolly: Pamela Stephenson, *Billy* (New York: HarperCollins, 2001).

Chapter Six: What Will They Think?

Chuck Close: Jon Marmor, "Close Call," *Columns: The University of Washington Alumni Magazine*, June 1997.
http://www.aaa.si.edu/collections/oralhistories/transcripts/close87 .htm.

CandoCo Dance Company: Malcolm Tay, "In the Company of Able(D) Dancers," *Flying Inkpot*, October 2, 2000.

Paulo Coelho: Paulo Coelho, op-ed, *Indian Express*, February 7, 2006.

http://www.worldmind.com/Cannon/Culture/Interviews/coelho .html.

ARIANNA HUFFINGTON: All material in this segment came from an original interview for this book.

GROUPTHINK: Judith Rich Harris, *The Nurture Assumption: Why Children Turn Out the Way They Do* (New York: Free Press, 1998).

Vanessa Grigoriadis, "Smooth Operator," *New York,* January 17, 2005.

Solomon Asch, "Opinions and Social Pressure," *Scientific American,* 1955.

Jerry B. Harvey, *The Abilene Paradox and Other Meditations on Management* (Lexington, Mass.: Lexington Books, 1988).

ZAHA HADID: http://www.designmuseum.org/design/zaha-hadid.

Chapter Seven: Do You Feel Lucky?

JOHN WILSON: John Coles, *Blindness and the Visionary: The Life and Work of John Wilson* (London: Giles de la Mare, 2006).

Obituary, *Independent* (London), December 3, 1999.

Obituary, *New York Times*, December 7, 1999.

RICHARD WISEMAN: Richard Wiseman, *The Luck Factor* (New York: Miramax, 2003).

VIDAL SASSOON: All material in this segment came from an original interview for this book.

BRAD ZDANIVSKY: Pieta Woolley, "Hell on Wheels," Straight.com, July 7, 2005.

http://www.ctv.ca/servlet/ArticleNews/story/CTVNews/1123261552811 _118670752/?hub=Canada.

Chapter Eight: Somebody Help Me

WARREN BUFFETT: Roger Lowenstein, *Buffett: The Making of an American Capitalist* (New York: Random House, 1995).

RAY CHARLES: Harvard Mentoring Project, Harvard School of Public Health, http://www.whomentoredyou.org.

MARIAN WRIGHT EDELMAN: Matilda Raffa Cuomo, *The Person Who Changed My Life* (New York: Barnes & Noble, 2002).

PUBLIC/PRIVATE VENTURES: http://www.ppv.org/ppv/publications/assets/ 219_publication.pdf.

JACKIE ROBINSON: http://www.mentors.ca/Story13.pdf.

PAUL MCCARTNEY: All material in this segment came from an original interview for this book.

JAMES EARL JONES: Matilda Raffa Cuomo, *The Person Who Changed My Life* (New York: Barnes & Noble, 2002).

DAVID NEILS: http://www.telementor.org/aboutus.cfm.

Chapter Nine: Is It Too Late?

SUSAN JEFFERS: All material in this segment came from an original interview for this book.

HARRIET DOERR: Yvonne Daley, "Late Bloomer," *Stanford Magazine*, 1997.

PAUL POTTS: http://www.paulpottsuk.com.

JULIA CHILD AND MAGGIE KUHN: Lydia Bronte, "What Longevity Means to Your Career," *Five O'Clock Club News*, July 2001, http://www.fiveoclockclub.com/articles1_index.shtml#2001.

RIDLEY SCOTT: All material in this segment came from an original interview for this book.

DR. HENRY LODGE: Chris Crowley and Harry S. Lodge, M.D., *Younger Than Next Year: Live Strong, Fit, and Sexy—Until You're 80 and Beyond* (New York: Workman, 2005).

http://www.theupexperience.com/speakers.html.

DR. SUSAN GREENFIELD: Susan Greenfield, *The Human Brain: A Guided Tour* (London: Weidenfeld and Nicolson, 1997).

GRACE LIVING CENTER: Marti Attoun, "School of a Lifetime," American Profile.com, December 1, 2002.

SOPHIA LOREN: http://www.sophialoren.com/about/by.htm.

Chapter Ten: For Love or Money

GABRIEL TROP: All material in this segment came from an original interview for this book.

"THE PRO-AM REVOLUTION": Charles Leadbeater and Paul Miller, "The Pro-Am Revolution: How Enthusiasts are Changing Our Economy and Society," www.demos.co.uk, 2004.

ARTHUR C. CLARKE: http://www.pbs.org/wgbh/nova/orchid/amateurs.html#fea_top.

http://lakdiva.org/clarke/1945ww/.

SUSAN HENDRICKSON: http://www.geocities.com/stegob/susanhendrickson.html.

http://www.pbs.org/wgbh/nova/orchid/amateurs.html#fea_top.

"TIFF" WOOD: David Halberstam, *The Amateurs: The Story of Four Young Men and Their Quest for an Olympic Gold Medal* (New York: Ballantine Books, 1985).

A LEG TO STAND ON: Burt Helm, "Hedge Funders Band Together for Charity," *Business Week*, October 20, 2006.

KHALED HOSSEINI: http://www.bloomsbury.com/Authors/microsite.asp?id =480&section=1&aid=1873.

http://www.bookbrowse.com/biographies/index.cfm?author_number =900.

MILES WATERS: http://www.nature.com/bdj/journal/v201/n1/full/4813815a .html.

JOHN WOOD: Bob Cooper, "Rich in Books," *San Francisco Chronicle*, September 26, 2004.

http://www.roomtoread.org/media/press/2007_09_27_cgi.html.

SUZANNE PETERSON: All material in this segment came from an original interview for this book.

MICHAEL FORDYCE: http://gethappy.net/v202.htm.

Chapter Eleven: Making the Grade

RICHARD BRANSON: All material in this segment came from an original interview for this book.

PAUL MCCARTNEY: All material in this segment came from an original interview for this book.

"THIS LOOKED-DOWN-UPON THING": Courtesy of Takeshi Haoriguchi.

UNEMPLOYMENT RATES FOR COLLEGE GRADUATES: http://www.epi.org/ content.cfm/webfeatures_snapshots_archive_03172004.

COLLEGE-LEVEL JOB OPENINGS IN THE UK: http://newsvote.bbc.co .uk/mpapps/pagetools/print/news.bbc.co.uk/2/hi/business/ 3068443.stm.

EARNINGS OF COLLEGE GRADUATES: http://www.usatoday.com/news/ nation/census/2002-07-18-degree-dollars.htm.

GRADUATION RATES AROUND THE WORLD: http://www.economist.com/ PrinterFriendly.cfm?story_id=9823950.

CRAM SCHOOLS: Sheryl WuDunn, "In Japan, Even Toddlers Feel the Pressure to Excel," *New York Times*, January 23, 1996.

THE TESTING INDUSTRY: Barbara Miner, "Keeping Public Schools Public," *Rethinking Schools*, Winter 2004–5.

PAUL MCCARTNEY: All material in this segment came from an original interview for this book.

REGGIO SCHOOLS: Carolyn Edwards, Lella Gandini, and George Forman, *The Hundred Languages of Children: The Reggio Emilia Approach Advanced Reflections* (Greenwich, Conn.: Ablex, 1998).

LORIS MALAGUZZI: Loris Malaguzzi, "Invece il cento c'e," translated by Lella Gandini.
http://www.brainy-child.com/article/reggioemilia.html.
http://www.reggioalliance.org/schools/index.html.

GRANGETON: Portions of this segment came from an original interview for this book.
http://www.tes.co.uk/search/story/?story_id=2043774.
http://www.teachernet.gov.uk/casestudies/casestudy.cfm?id=344.

OKLAHOMA A+ SCHOOLS: Nicole Ashby, "Arts Integration at Oklahoma School Provides Multiple Paths for Learning," *Achiever*, June 1, 2007.
http://www.aplusok.org/.

Index